DRUGS and the
Limits of Liberalism

DRUGS
AND THE
⎯LIMITS OF
LIBERALISM
MORAL AND LEGAL ISSUES

EDITED BY **Pablo De Greiff**

CORNELL UNIVERSITY PRESS

ITHACA AND LONDON

First published 1999 by Cornell University Press.

Printed in the United States of America

Library of Congress Cataloging-in-Publication Data

Drugs and the limits of liberalism : moral and legal issues /
    edited by Pablo De Greiff.
        p.   cm.
    Includes bibliographical references and index.
    ISBN 0-8014-3561-7 (cloth : alk. paper)
        1. Drug abuse–United States–Prevention.   2. Drug abuse–Moral and
    ethical aspects.   3. Liberalism–Moral and ethical aspects.   4. Drug abuse–
    Government policy–United States.   I. De Greiff, Pablo.
    HV5825.D812   1998
    362.29′17′0973–dc21   98-48115

Cornell University Press strives to use environmentally responsible suppliers and
materials to the fullest extent possible in the publishing of its books.
Such materials include vegetable-based, low-VOC inks and acid-free
papers that are recycled, totally chlorine-free, or partly
composed of nonwood fibers.

Cloth printing   10   9   8   7   6   5   4   3   2   1

Contents

Acknowledgments

I had the good fortune of receiving assistance and support from many persons who offered generous advice at various stages of the planning and development of this project. William Connolly, Thomas McCarthy, and Thomas Pogge have been particularly helpful all along. Guyora Binder's insight and advice were crucial and much appreciated. I also thank Anita Allen, Robert Fullinwider, Douglas Husak, Jaime Malamud-Goti, Ethan Nadelmann, Jan Narveson, Jay and Richard Rorty, Henry Shue, John P. Walters, and Marcia Lyn Wicker.

My colleagues at SUNY Buffalo were supportive of this endeavor. My gratitude to all of them, but particularly to Newton Garver, Jorge Gracia, Peter Hare, John Kearns, David Nyberg, Jerome Slater, and Barry Smith.

Needless to say, the project would not have gotten off the ground without the financial support of various foundations and institutions. I am deeply grateful to the Bavaria Foundation, the Lindesmith Center, the Mitchell Lecture Fund, the Conversations in the Disciplines Program, SUNY, the Conferences in the Disciplines Program, SUNY, and the Baldy Law and Society Center.

Organizational support given by Laura Mangan, Eva Koepsell, Jason Adsit, and Shannon Kincaid made the project an enjoyable, and not only a productive, experience. My wife, Clara Eugenia, my sister Verónica, and her husband, Kumar, became experts on the content of this project. I express my gratitude for their willingness to think, talk, and hear about it.

I thank Carol Betsch and Roger Haydon at Cornell University Press and

Stephen Weldon not only for superb professional assistance but also for their grace and encouragement in the face of many interruptions.

Finally, I dedicate this book to Gustavo De Greiff, who in his role as father taught me, among many other things, to admire the rule of law, and in his role as general prosecutor of Colombia courageously lived up to his teachings. I also dedicate this book to my mother and my siblings, who, with equal courage, changed their lives forever.

P. De G.

DRUGS and the
Limits of Liberalism

Liberal Commitments and the Problem of Drugs

Pablo De Greiff

Liberal political and moral theory is frequently charged with being morally deficient in a variety of ways: its individualism, according to critics, erodes a robust sense of community and ultimately rests on indifference or callousness toward others; its emphasis on negative freedom undermines a sense of solidarity. The essays presented here, however, are a response to the charge of moral inadequacy.[1] The fact that they are largely critical of present-day drug prohibition makes them all the more of a challenge to the critics. If we can show that even when liberalism is critical of some forms of prohibition it is still morally richer than its critics allege, then the moral richness of liberalism will be easier to establish in less controversial cases.

This volume is an effort to do philosophy in a manner that engages social problems, and to do so in a self-reflective way, that is, one that is aware of the possibilities and limits of philosophical reflection concerning social issues that involve a large empirical component. The guiding idea is not that of the Platonic philosopher-king who aspires to produce a blueprint for a perfect society, but rather that of the philosopher-citizen who, while having no monopoly on the truth about social matters, still has something important to contribute to the public conversation about common public concerns.

The volume, therefore, is neither a book on drug policy, nor an instruction book for those who make drug policy. Nothing in the training of academic philosophers makes them particularly suited for writing either kind of book. On the other hand, the volume is not a collection of essays on ab-

1

stract moral or political theory. Rather its aim is to allow philosophers to carry on with the activities for which they are competent in the face of an urgent social issue. The result is a set of essays that share two goals. First, they examine whether some of the normative commitments that citizens make in living in liberal democracies—commitments to ideals such as rationality, equality, justice, and democratic forms of decision making—have implications concerning how these societies should address the problem of drugs. Second, they consider whether the problem of drugs itself provides theoreticians with reasons to rethink their usual ways of dealing with the familiar tools of their trade—that is, the same ideals of rationality, equality, justice, and democratic forms of decision making mentioned above. In other words, engaging a social problem seriously in this context means not only asking philosophers to turn their attention to one such problem, it also means asking them to think about the adequacy of the philosophical machinery itself for coming to grips with that problem, in this case, the issue of drugs.

The chapters in Part I are concerned with a thin concept of rationality that intends to leave most political and moral questions open; those in Parts II and III address ideals that find their place within liberal democratic societies.[2] Although the authors seem largely critical of the drug policy presently implemented in the United States, there is no agreement among them concerning what is the best understanding of liberal democratic commitments, nor about what the best drug policy choice would be. In a sense, they all defend what may be called "moderate" positions regarding the problem of drugs: although there are differences among them about where a liberal democracy can legitimately draw a prohibitionist line most of them concede that it *is* theoretically possible to draw such a line.[3] Moreover, none of the authors of these essays defends a position regarding the legal status of a particular drug by appealing to the real or presumed benefits of consuming such drug.[4] The authors are searching for the justification for policies that engage problems of consumption and social disintegration, policies that are at the same time compatible with the moral and political commitments that in their view citizens of liberal democratic societies already make.

Part I. Rationality and Drugs

In "Rationality and Addiction," Jon Elster examines in detail a multifactor conception of addiction. Elster reviews some of the most common criteria appealed to in definitions of addiction—tolerance, withdrawal symptoms, harm, craving, inability to quit, and desire to quit—concluding that only withdrawal symptoms and craving are essential to the phenomenon of addiction.[5] But the point of his argument is not merely definitional. Rather, it is to defend the view that addictive behavior is in most actual cases irrational. Instead of introducing a substantive or morally loaded notion of rationality, which would by definition establish that addiction is irrational, Elster uses a thin concept of rationality that not only puts aside all moral questions, but also that even bars the attempt to assess the rationality of desires from a point of view external to the subject himself. For Elster, rational choice involves three optimizations: "of action, given desires and beliefs; of beliefs, given the available information; [and] of information acquisition, given desires and beliefs." Given this understanding of rational choice, when Elster claims that addiction is irrational he does not mean that the addict is irrational because of her desires, but only because of her beliefs or her information acquisition. Although Elster's definition of rationality is a thin one, it does call for a complex sort of anticipatory reflexivity: for addictive behavior to be rational, it must be based on rational beliefs about the consequences of engaging in behavior that might lead to an addiction. This, in turn, requires having rational beliefs about the objective harms and benefits of engaging in such behavior as well as of the subjective impact of actually engaging in it. These latter beliefs further require having rational beliefs about that behavior's impact on one's own ability to maintain rational beliefs about the objective harms and benefits of engaging in addictive behavior. Elster suspects—on the basis of studies of belief formation in other forms of addiction such as smoking and alcoholism—that potential drug addicts are likely not to have rational prior beliefs about the objective consequences of addiction. Moreover, he suspects that even if at an early stage of their drug consumption careers, potential addicts have rational beliefs about the subjective impact that addictive behavior will have on them over time, it is questionable whether they have the ability to rationally update their beliefs. In other words, for Elster, the addict fails to accomplish one of the three optimizations on which the rationality of action depends, that is, the optimization of belief given available information.

But this is not the only way in which the addict fails, according to Elster: "A rational addict would not simply form beliefs on the basis of the evidence immediately available to him, but go on to look for more evidence up to the point where the expected value of more information equals the costs." Here there are important differences between the distinct forms of addiction. While some gamblers overinvest in information acquisition by, for example, reading the Monte Carlo *Revue Scientifique*, which logs successive outcomes of roulette, Elster "suspect[s] but cannot prove that most drug users invest too little" in forming rational beliefs about the objective and subjective impact of engaging in addictive behavior. If he is right, the addict then has failed to meet a second out of three optimizations required by rational action, the optimization of information acquisition, given desires and beliefs.

Thus, for Elster, even assuming a formal concept of rationality that does not prejudge questions about the rationality or desirability (moral or otherwise) of having different desires, one can argue that addictive behavior is irrational both from the standpoint of belief formation and from the standpoint of information acquisition.

Thomas Pogge, in his essay "The Irrationality of Addiction—And Does It Matter?" is not so sanguine as Elster either about the possibility of coming to such a determinate judgment about the (ir)rational nature of addiction or about the usefulness for policy purposes of doing so. After raising questions about Elster's characterization of addiction in terms of withdrawal symptoms and cravings, Pogge argues that, even for one who accepts Elster's thin notion of rationality, determining whether addiction is rational is more difficult than Elster suggests. Part of the difficulty stems from the fact that Elster's understanding of a rational act as an optimal response to the agent's beliefs and desires presupposes that we can know what these beliefs and desires are. Ordinarily, these beliefs and desires are inferred from observable behavior, but in the context of drug addiction doing so would beg the question, for the inference from conduct to beliefs and desires already presupposes that the conduct in question is a plausible attempt to fulfill the agent's desires. This is to say that the inference already presupposes what is at stake, namely the rationality of behavior.

The alternative to inferring beliefs and desires, then, is to ask the agent what beliefs and desires he is trying to satisfy in acting as he does. But deciding whether an agent's conduct is an optimal response to his beliefs and desires requires more than merely knowing what he believes and wants in a general way. It requires, more specifically, knowing the relative strength of his various desires in relation to one another, and even in our own case— let alone someone else's—it is not clear that there are reliable ways of gaining this sort of insight into our own belief and motivation structure.

This difficulty has far-reaching consequences: if we cannot know with any degree of exactness whether our own conduct is rational, then we cannot shape our conduct in order to try to guarantee its rationality either. This means, for Pogge, that probably most of people's own conduct is affected by some degree of irrationality. While this may give some indirect support to Elster's contention that most addiction is irrational, it does so only at a high price: "if conduct irrationality is involved in almost everything we do, then it is not big news that it is involved in addiction as well." In light of this conclusion, Pogge suggests that we are better off thinking of rationality as a matter of degree.

If the first optimization constitutive of rational behavior (that is, the optimization of action, given desires and beliefs) is problematic, the remaining two optimizations—that of beliefs, given available information, and that of information acquisition, given desires and beliefs—are not any less puzzling. Elster's defense of the irrationality of addiction was motivated by the desire to come to a better understanding of the causes of addiction, an understanding that might sustain the hope of designing better social policies. But Pogge's argument suggests that that hope might be ungrounded. The same skeptical argument raises doubts concerning whether the other use of Elster's conclusion—as a justification for the regulation of the behavior of putatively irrational addicts, akin to the justification for the regulation of behavior of people who are not fully competent—rests on sufficiently solid ground to legitimate public policy in a liberal society.

If there are questions concerning whether a thin notion of rationality sheds enough light on how we should proceed with respect to the problem of drugs, then we have to turn to the normative commitments involved in living in liberal democracies.

Part II. Liberal Political Morality and Drugs

One of the aims of the second section of this volume is to inquire whether some of our basic moral-political concepts provide any guidance regarding the legal status of drugs in a liberal society. Both Michael Moore and Samuel Freeman focus their investigation on what is perhaps the cornerstone of liberalism, that is, the notion of liberty.

Before even attempting to address the specific question of the legal status of drugs, Moore defines the scope of liberty by clarifying three different rights to liberty. In the first place, Moore defends the unpopular position that there is such a thing as a general right to liberty, defined simply as a right to the absence of coercive legislation without regard to the moral quality of the actions protected by such general right. Given that this broad-ranging right threatens the basis of morality and of civil society, he acknowledges that it is better thought of in terms of a "presumption" rather than a "right" to liberty. This defeasible presumption against coercive legislation can be defended, on his account, by attending to four values that ·are served by this negative conception of liberty:

(a) Coercive legislation limits the possibilities of choice. All things being equal it is better for individuals to have a broad range of alternatives because the broader the range, the more likely it will be that a person will succeed in a particular endeavor.

(b) Morality cares not only about people doing right actions, but also about their doing those actions for the right reasons. Coercive legislation gives people an incentive to act prudently, thereby decreasing the possibility that they will act out of the right reasons. Coercive legislation, then, diminishes Kantian autonomy.

(c) Individuals normally prefer to make decisions on their own, rather than having their behavior dictated by others. Coercive legislation, then, fails to maximize people's satisfaction of preferences.

(d) Negative freedom helps us save the costs that accompany coercive legislation. Criminal prohibitions consume scarce resources, both directly and indirectly.

In conclusion, in support of a general notion of liberty, Moore argues that these four values give content to our interest in negative freedom, even if that freedom is used to perform morally objectionable actions.

The breadth of this presumption, however—the fact that it protects morally reprehensible actions—means at least that, at the limits, no moral or feasible civil order can endure if constructed solely on the basis of a general notion of liberty. Nevertheless, the acknowledgement that negative freedom protects values that we ought to care about creates a presumption of freedom that limits coercive legislation only to those acts that are seriously immoral and which criminal legislation has a reasonable chance of preventing.

This presumption of liberty, though, does not exhaust the interest citizens of a liberal society have in freedom. According to Moore, we also have a "derived right to liberty," derived because it is a correlate of a duty on the part of legislators. This right entitles citizens not to have their behavior regulated for the wrong reasons. The specification of the reasons that are admissible for the purposes of legislation gets us close to one of the central debates in liberalism. J. S. Mill argued that harm to others is the only reason which authorizes governmental regulation of behavior.[6] Departing from tradition again, Moore argues instead for a legal-moralist position, according to which the only legitimate aim of criminal legislation is the punishment of moral wrongs. Agreeing with conservative critics of Mill, Moore argues that the reason why we are disposed to use harm as a criterion of criminality is that causing harm to others is morally wrong. But not only is harm insufficiently foundational: harm also fails to explain why we punish omissions, why we punish harmless wrongdoings, and why we refuse to prohibit harmful acts which are not morally wrong. According to Moore's alternative, we punish omissions because morality sometimes obligates us to help; we punish harmless wrongdoings because although no one is harmed, the act is still morally wrong; and we refuse to prohibit harmful acts that are not morally wrong precisely because the target of legitimate legislation is moral wrongdoing, not harms.

Given the relation between morality and law postulated by Moore's legal moralism, it is imperative for him to define our moral obligations. His approach is a modified consequentialism that seeks to avoid the two usual objections to consequence-based approaches to morality. Consequentialism has been charged with limiting the scope of individual liberty to a vanishing point because it obligates us to maximize good consequences.[7] Second, consequentialism has been brought to task because it supposedly justifies sacrificing the interests of some persons if the consequences of doing so increase the good by whatever metric might be in use. Moore addresses these charges by introducing agent-relative permissions and obligations. His revised consequentialism, then, allows us to divide all actions into three categories: (1) Actions we are not obligated to do or not to do because they fall under an agent-relative permission and do not fall under any agent-relative obligation. (2) Actions which we are either obligated to do or not to do by the consequentialist principle itself. (3) Actions we are obligated not to do by an agent-relative prohibition. If the legal moralist will only punish moral wrongdoings, then citizens have a derived right to liberty protecting them against the criminalization of actions in the first category, for these actions either fall under a permission or do not fall under any obligation. Only behaviors under categories (2) and (3) are legitimate objects of regulation. Even here, though, the presumption of liberty tempers the inclination to use criminal law for the regulation of actions falling under the second category to only those instances where the good of criminalization outweighs the goods served by the presumption of liberty.

In summary, Moore insists that his legal moralism succeeds where the standard harm-based liberal account fails, that is, with respect to the difficult cases in our penal practices: cases of omission, harmless wrongdoing, and the causing of harm which is not morally wrong. Additionally, he claims that his legal moralism coheres with our well-settled liberal intuitions in prohibiting the use of criminal legislation in cases of moral and nonmoral paternalism, of supererogatory acts, and of offense to others. As long as one accepts the view that morality regards much of our conduct as beyond the bounds of obligation, Moore's legal moralism, which limits the permissible aims of state coercion to the punishment of moral wrongs, does not lead to an overactive, super-regulatory state. Indeed, it is intended to clarify the duty of legislators to be parsimonious in their use of criminal legislation.

Despite the fact that Moore has attempted to give content and force to the two preceding interests in freedom, they still fail to capture the strength of the rights that we associate with freedom of speech and with the performance of actions such as abortion, which might be morally objectionable but which nevertheless are immunized from state regulation save for the most compelling of reasons. After reviewing previous attempts to account for a sphere of behavior immune from state intervention (Mill's self-regarding choices, indirect utilitarianism, the libertarian's sphere of omissions), Moore argues that the U.S. Supreme Court since the *Griswold* decision has been trying to define a "basic right to liberty" which covers choices that are "fundamental" in the sense that they define the sort of person one will become. What makes these attempts worthwhile, according to Moore, is that this basic right protects and promotes the values of coherency of character and integrity, that is, the authorship of one's own character.

Having spelled out the different reasons and values that explain why we ought to be interested in individual freedom, Moore turns to the specific question of whether any of the rights to liberty he endorses protect the recreational use of drugs. Different questions follow from each of the different interests in liberty. In order to decide whether the presumption of liberty protects recreational drug use, one must find out whether such use is immoral and, furthermore, whether it is sufficiently immoral that the good of punishing it outweighs the costs such punishment imposes (in terms of positive liberty, Kantian autonomy, preference satisfaction, and other indices of social welfare). Whether recreational drug use is protected by the derived right to liberty depends on whether such use is immoral in the sense of breaking our obligations, because, according to Moore's legal moralism, this is the only justification for using criminal law. Finally, whether recreational drug use is protected by the basic right to liberty depends on whether such use can count as a self-defining choice and on the state lacking sufficient reason to override this right because of the greater harms caused by drug use.

After conceding to the prohibitionist the factual claims about the dangers of drugs—and consequently stating plainly his own opposition to frequent drug use—Moore expresses doubts about a blanket prohibition on *recreational* drug use. He argues that although a life of addiction and intoxication would be immoral because it would conflict with an agent-relative obligation not to destroy that which is valuable about ourselves, namely, our rationality and our autonomy, he at the same time finds the absolute prohibitionist argument unsatisfactory. Recreational drug use, for Moore, in contrast to a life of total addiction and intoxication, is not immoral as such, and therefore it is protected by both the presumption of liberty and the derived right to liberty. Finally, Moore argues that although a life of drug consumption "is usually an unjustified, wrongful and even pathetic choice," it is still a self-defining choice and, as such, is protected by the basic right to liberty. Needless to say, such protection does not immunize users from being punished if they commit wrongs. But their punishment will be for wrongs committed, not for their self-defining choice. Although Moore is ready to use the criminal law for the defense of morality (indeed, on his view, this is the only aim that criminal law can legitimately serve), even if we assume (as he does) that a life of drug use constitutes a failure of *virtue*, this is still not a failure of *moral obligation*. Criminalizing failures of virtue, entails then, punishing people who have committed no wrongs—a position that no respectable theory of punishment can defend.

Freeman, like Moore, is interested in finding the limits of liberty and, only then, asking whether the boundaries of that freedom include the liberty to use drugs recreationally. Ultimately, he argues that liberals have overstated the argument that as long as drug use is voluntary and informed, and does not cause harm to the rights and interests of others, individuals have a right to indulge in drugs whatever the adverse consequences for themselves. Freeman's aim is to dispute the thesis that voluntariness and the absence of harm to others are sufficient conditions for immunity from state regulation. In his view, a liberal state can legitimately restrict self-destructive conduct even if it is voluntary and "rational," so long as the purpose of the restriction is to maintain the moral and rational integrity of the person.

In making his argument in defense of restrictions Freeman attacks an influential strain of the liberal tradition running from J. S. Mill to Joel Feinberg.[8] Feinberg views Mill's harm principle as central to liberalism and takes it to imply an underived right to self-determination or to autonomy, which is a right to act on one's own voluntary choices. But since voluntary choices are not necessarily rational, if we have a right to autonomy then, according to Feinberg we have "a right to make unreasonable decisions even to the point of acting self-destructively."

This discussion about the sufficiency of voluntariness brings Freeman to examine another basic feature of traditional liberalism, its separation of the right and the good, which I will examine in some detail in the last part of this introduction. Freeman takes Feinberg's assertion that the right to autonomy is underived to mean (1) that autonomy takes precedence over the person's good in decisions about what we ought to do in actions that affect her, and, more important, (2) that in the order of justification, the right to autonomy is not grounded in any conception about the agent's good. The right and the good, on Feinberg's account are completely independent of one another; indeed, for him it should be possible to specify a person's liberal rights without appealing to a particular conception of the good, for if autonomy were simply instrumental to the good, liberal rights would be made contingent upon changing circumstances, and the equality of those rights would be difficult to guarantee.

Freeman's liberalism is quite different. It is rather Kantian and Rawlsian in spirit. For Freeman, rights to autonomy are not underived, as they are for Feinberg, nor are they merely instrumental to a conception of the good, as they are for communitarians and other critics of liberalism. Rights to autonomy are grounded in a normative ideal of the person; this ideal portrays human beings as free—that is, "self-governing agents who are responsible for their actions and their ends"—and equal—that is, as having roughly comparable degrees of the minimum necessary competencies to be free. The ideal is normative in two senses: It is not a *metaphysical* conception of the person as free from causal determination but a *moral* ideal of persons as free by right and as possessing equal moral and civic status. It is, also, a normative ideal in the sense that we cannot define what this ideal is without appealing to moral principles of right and justice.

The articulation of these principles of right and justice, in turn, involves asking what qualities persons must have in order to be self-governing moral agents? Freeman's Kantian answer is that in order for persons to be free and equal they must be thought of as having certain developed competencies that allow them to select their ends, and to order their behavior so as to attain those ends. That is, persons must be seen as having "rational powers of agency." Additionally, they must be thought of as having "other powers of reasoning [that] equip persons to understand, apply, and abide by those moral rules that are a condition of social life. . . . These capacities, when fully developed, enable people to comprehend and justify their actions in terms of moral principles that are publicly acceptable to reasonable moral agents." These are the "moral powers of agency."

On this understanding of liberalism, the role played by the rights to autonomy secures the conditions under which persons can maintain and develop their rational and moral capacities, as well as express their individuality through the exercise of those capacities. The argument is important not only because it provides an interesting perspective on the question of the foundations of rights, but also, and again from a theoretical perspective, because it establishes a link between the right and the good which is pregnant with consequences for the issue of the legal status of rights. On Freeman's Kantian/Rawlsian liberalism, if it is true that rights to autonomy are basic precisely because they protect the conditions under which persons can consider themselves as rational and moral agents, these rights will protect from intervention by others and by the state a large range of conceptions of the good but not an infinite range of possibilities—in particular, not those which result in the destruction of one's capacities for agency.

It would be mistaken, according to Freeman, to arrive at the conclusion that the preceding argument authorizes a liberal state to prohibit any action that does not lead to the optimization of the capacities for rational and moral agency. In this he agrees with Moore, who limits the reach of his consequentialism by means of agent-centered permissions. Rather than seeing these capacities as incremental goods that persons stand under the obligation to maximize, Freeman argues that they are the essential conditions for citizenship in a liberal society where persons can both pursue their own conception of the good and at the same time comply with the conception of justice shared in their society. The correct conclusion to draw, according to Freeman is that if there are "intrinsically debilitating activities" (as opposed to the normal risk-taking that is involved in the pursuit of activities we value), a liberal state is authorized to regulate those activities, because doing so protects the necessary conditions of agency in a liberal society. Whether any of the available psychoactive drugs is "intrinsically debilitating" in the required sense—in other words, in the sense that its consumption is not merely addictive or *temporarily* incapacitating, but rather that it *permanently* impairs one's capacities for agency—is an empirical question. If there are such drugs, Freeman argues that a liberal state is entitled to regulate their consumption.

There is plenty of disagreement between Moore and Freeman about the proper aims of legislation, about the usefulness of discussions over paternalism, and about the scope of liberty itself. Nevertheless, they agree on the centrality of individual freedom, and despite their disagreement regarding the proper legal status of self-destructive drugs in a liberal society (protected by the basic right to liberty according to Moore, regulatable according to Freeman), they agree that the state has the burden of conclusively establishing that there are drugs which have the effects that prohibitionists have loosely claimed for all psychoactive drugs.

Part III. Democracy, Politics, and Drugs

The essays in Part II are intended both to answer whether the basic concepts of liberal political morality provide any guidance with respect to the problem of drugs and to search for greater clarity about the nature of liberalism by confronting the drug issue. The papers in Part III share this double intention, except that the object of investigation is not liberalism but democracy and democratic politics.

In "Democracy and Drugs," J. Donald Moon argues against the present prohibitionist regime on the basis of two sorts of considerations. The first one is that the current antidrug legislation violates the principle of democratic legitimacy. Following John Rawls and T. M. Scanlon,[9] Moon argues that in a democratic society legitimacy is a function of acting in ways that can be justified to others because one acts on the basis of principles they could not reasonably reject. It is the requirement that citizens should be able to endorse the grounds of the implementation of authority that makes them self-governing.

According to Moon, such a broad consensus regarding the proper ambit of governmental authority is attainable in a morally pluralistic society (where different conceptions of the end of human life compete against one another) only if political power is limited. No perfectionist norm (one that promotes a particular conception of the good life) will satisfy the requirements of democratic legitimacy under conditions of pluralism. Hence, Moon supports the demand of impartiality, long seen by many as a necessary part of liberalism, except that in his case, this demand does not flow from a pragmatic "strategy of avoidance" motivated by the desire to reach agreement with others, but rather, from a "moral obligation rooted in a deep commitment to moral action as action that can be justified to others."[10]

Moon's first qualm over drug prohibition concerns its acceptability to all those who persist in using drugs, and especially, to the more than "300,000 people in state and federal prisons (not counting those in local jails) serving time for drug offenses." Freeman's earlier essay offers what seems to be a counterargument to Moon's position. According to Freeman's justification of liberal rights, if these rights are meant to protect and promote the capacities of rational and moral agency that are necessary for life in a liberal-democratic society, then when deciding which activities ought to be protected by means of rights, people's desires need not be taken as given. Instead, a liberal regime might appeal to the normative ideal of the person as free and equal (on which liberalism itself stands) in order to decide which activities deserve protection. On Freeman's account, antidrug legislation does not necessarily conflict with liberal neutrality, for prohibition is not intended to promote a particular conception of the good life: prohibition, for Freeman, seeks to regulate not goals but activities, leaving open a wide range of views about the purpose of life. The aim of antidrug legislation is to preserve the competencies that are the necessary conditions of liberal citizenship.

Moon acknowledges that "the commitment to democratic legitimacy entails a commitment to providing those rights and powers necessary to exercise the capacities of agency" (and that this commitment to agency implies not merely negative rights but also certain welfare rights and, importantly, some duties). He acknowledges, in short, that "because of the centrality of agency, there is a kind of residual perfectionism implicit in the conception of democracy I have defended." The question for Moon—as for Freeman—is whether recreational drug use constitutes a sufficient threat to the capacity for agency to justify its prohibition solely on this basis. Freeman is content with pointing out that the degree to which a given drug threatens the capacity for agency is largely an empirical issue; his point is that *if* there is a drug which permanently undermines agency, *then* a liberal state is authorized in prohibiting its consumption.

Moon goes further, following this conclusion with an analysis of the concept of addiction. Addiction, according to him, would justify prohibition only on the condition that "addiction renders drug use nonvoluntary." His skepticism that most drugs have this alleged power is supported by empirical studies about controlled use and about how the majority of users eventually give up consumption. Moon then proceeds to examine the role that the vocabulary of addiction has come to play in discussions about drug policy. He points out how the metaphor of illness which accompanies the discourse of addiction is functional for drug users, since it allows them to deflect social disapproval "by attributing their behavior to addiction, thereby discharging them from responsibility for their actions by removing [these actions] from the realm of choice." Similarly, the use of the metaphor of illness serves the interests of social service providers, for once the problem is seen in this light, its solution calls for "a medical response, in which "experts" provide treatment programs designed to enable the victims of addiction to overcome their disability." Indeed, following John Booth Davies, Moon ultimately wants to argue that the notion of addiction plays into the hands not just of drug users and service providers, but of society at large, for in our cultural-political context it is only the metaphor of illness that "gives us permission to help people we [would otherwise] see as bad."[11] The point of this analysis, which aims at clarifying the complex functional roles the notion of addiction plays in our culture, is to raise doubts about whether, on its own, the notion of addiction can be used to determine the impact of drug use on our rational and moral capacities for agency without, thereby, smuggling in particular conceptions of the good life. These doubts are sufficiently significant in Moon's mind, and thus he concludes that drug prohibition violates neutrality, and therefore the principle of democratic legitimacy as well.

According to Moon, however, the injustice of the current prohibitionist regime is not limited only to undercutting the principle of democracy. Current prohibitionism is unjust in two additional senses: it treats drug users as instruments for the well-being of others (which I will not review here), and it distributes the costs of enforcement unfairly, most of these costs being borne by the least-advantaged members of society. As for this latter argument, Moon's point is that the large profits associated with black markets, and the political under-representation of the lower classes, have led to poor neighborhoods carrying a disproportionate burden of the problem of drugs. The profit margins of the drug business make people with dismally low employment alternatives more likely to participate in the commerce of drugs. At the same time these people lack political clout. This makes it easy for the affluent middle class to maintain drug policies that further the status quo and that contain the violence associated with the drug trade a safe distance from suburban residential areas.

In my article I am also concerned with questions of justice and democracy, except that I take a perspective that is conspicuously absent from discussions about drug policy in the United States. American drug policy is designed with little regard for its external consequences. First, I review some of the objections that have been raised in Latin America against the fairness of U.S. drug policy. Like most discussions about drugs, the discussion in Latin America has suffered from being normatively weak. Needless to say, pragmatic objections of different kinds have been raised there, as they have in discussions within the United States. The practical shortcomings of criminalization are particularly easy to see in countries where drug-related violence has become endemic.[12] Whenever the discussion turns from pragmatic to moral issues, though, Latin American commentators and politicians appeal to an ordinary conception of justice defined in terms of an equitable distribution of benefits and burdens. From that standpoint, they argue, U.S. antidrug policy is unfair, for it disproportionately burdens drug-producing countries. I am sympathetic to this argument, for however one measures these burdens—be it economically, in terms of GDP spent fighting drugs, or in terms related to social welfare—it is arguably true that producing countries have shouldered a larger share than the United States. However, when the international discussion has been conducted in these terms, it has never led to any changes in American policy, and progress has ultimately stalemated.

Rather than carry on this debate, I approach the question of the transnational fairness of antidrug legislation from a different perspective. The international drug problem raises an important question about the meaning of democratic legitimacy and national sovereignty in an increasingly integrated world. The general assumption behind debates about drug policy seems to be that the *internal* legitimacy of laws that criminalize drugs exhausts the question of legitimacy. But given the size of the American market for drugs, the economic incentives to participate in this business created by the American market, and the impact of U.S. policy in producing countries, any political system committed to the idea of equality will have difficulties insisting that the legitimacy of these laws is a purely internal matter. While it is true that the U.S. government can hardly be held accountable for the consumption decisions of its citizens, the country is, of course, responsible for its own legislation. Given that antidrug laws play a constitutive role in forming the present international market for narcotics—obviously not by creating demand for drugs, but by shaping the economic incentives of the market via the "risk mark up" that characterize illegal trade—it can be argued that the question of legal legitimacy is one that requires the transnational extension of present convictions about legitimacy.

In the current international system, which was born after the treaty of Westphalia (1648), the issue of legitimacy is a purely internal matter.[13] The rise of democracy in the eighteenth and nineteenth centuries did not change this, only the procedures of legitimation. Legitimacy is now gained by allowing those who are affected by a norm a voice in the articulation and enactment of the norm. This territorial closure of the concept of legitimacy made sense in a world of relatively isolated nation-states, but it is questionable whether it still makes sense in a world in which the legislative actions of one county may have deep and, in the case of drug legislation, devastating consequences beyond the country's own borders. As long as one is willing to acknowledge that there is a relationship between morality and law and that morality has a universalistic core, then there are reasons to think that democratic legitimacy necessitates granting to those who are affected by norms some voice in the articulation of the norms, *even if those affected live beyond the borders of the nation.*

The case of drugs serves as a good example in reference to which different proposals concerning cosmopolitan democracy might be thought through. The unfairness of U.S. drug policy might be framed, then, in normatively weightier, and at the same time more familiar terms than before: U.S. legislation, in the articulation of which Latin Americans have absolutely no representation, dramatically shapes life in most producing countries, even if there were no attempts at "diplomatic" interference. Even if the United States did not coerce other countries to adopt a particular drug policy, the sheer size of the market and the magnitude of its economic incentives has such an enormous impact on other countries that politically, economically, and morally speaking, antidrug laws cannot be simply a question of national sovereignty to be decided solely by U.S. citizens. The sense of injustice that U.S. antidrug policy awakens, I am arguing, stems from the intuition that there is a moral obligation, which legislators in particular bear, an obligation which requires them to assess the impact of their law-making in terms that go beyond considerations of national expediency. In order to spell out, and to defend this intuition, I make use of Jürgen Habermas's reconstruction of the relationship between morality and law, extending his argument to the realm of transnational democracy.[14]

Finally, William Connolly demonstrates in his essay, yet again, that there is more than one way of doing political philosophy, and that there are important insights to be gained from doing the sort of political and institutional microanalysis that interested Michel Foucault so much.[15] The object of Connolly's interest is the rhetoric of the war on drugs, and specifically, the way in which William Bennett, former Drug Czar (Director of the Office of National Drug Control Policy), speaks about the war on drugs. But Connolly's intentions are not merely textual. His paper is a response to the charge that drug policy reform is "culturally unrealistic and politically utopian."[16] Part of the strategic point of Connolly's paper is that Bennett has been far more successful than reformers at defining the terms of the discussion.

According to Connolly, Bennett sees the war on drugs as merely one battle in a wider cultural fight "between the traditional culture of working, religious, responsible individuals and a variety of elites in the media, the academy and a few churches who have corrupted the culture." The fight, in Connolly's words, is for the "renationalization of America," a term he uses to refer to Bennett's intention to re-create a society based on a particular definition of "the regular individual." Such an individual is one characterized by the following convictions: "individual responsibility for your own fate, faith in the capitalist market, belief in a moral god, commitment to the opportunity society, opposition to the welfare state, support for family values, identification with the military as guarantor of the nation in the last resort, and commitment to normal sexuality." The renationalization of America, then, consists in the broad application of the following formula by individuals themselves, as well as by governmental officials: "to be generically skeptical toward the state, fervently committed to a nation of regular individuals, and selectively disposed to the state whenever it wages cultural war against deviants from this enigmatic nation."

That for Bennett the war on drugs is little more than a battle in this more ambitious cultural war Connolly concludes not only from the expense, inefficiency and intrusiveness of antidrug policy, but from Bennett's own account of some of the skirmishes he initiated as drug czar. Bennett himself tells that he was "freelancing" when he advocated during a TV interview the use of American troops in drug producing countries—with or without their consent. He was also "freelancing" when under similar circumstances, he advocated the imposition of capital punishment for drug sellers. Rather than advocating these measures for their virtues as instruments in bringing the drug problem under control, he offered them to the public as means of drawing a new line in the mud, of redefining the terms of the debate so as to consolidate a constituency that stands behind the vision of a lost nation of regular individuals that we must re-create. The rhetoric of the war on drugs, according to Connolly, "clarifies and concentrates a series of vague, shifting anxieties and resentments in everyday life. It brings within the apparent reach of political agency threats that otherwise seem to be beyond reach. . . . They might involve, for some, the threat of black violence in the city; or the loss of good working-class jobs . . . ; or the shifting ethnic and racial composition of the country . . . ; or the reduced capacity of the state to control its fate in a globalized economy; or the unsettling diversification of religious and irreligious creeds; or the porosity of territorial boundaries; or the feeling that taxes are high while their positive effects on the quality of life are low."

Connolly advocates a sort of drug policy which aims at reducing the self-destruction and social violence that accompanies addiction to some drugs by implementing programs to provide jobs, housing, education, and safety to those in need; decriminalizing some drugs and using the proceeds for imparting drug education, prevention, and treatment; and preserving the illegal status of some drugs, and replacing random drug tests by task-specific performance tests (as a way of guaranteeing the bite of this reduced prohibitionist regime without sacrificing other important rights in the process). But if this proposal is to overcome the utopian ring that accompanies it in the present political context, Connolly argues that intellectuals need to become more attuned to the anxieties that move different constituencies and more sensitive to the ways in which Bennett's discourse against drugs has succeeded in discrediting academic work on drugs precisely by aligning people in academia with social deviants who fail the standard of the "regular individual"—much as drug users themselves do. Additionally, intellectuals need to clarify to themselves and others the ramifications of Bennett's vision of society: such a society that has been re-nationalized around the idea of the regular individual multiplies its enemies and makes a pluralistic society unworkable. Worse, this vision might "mobilize antistatism. . . . But it cannot nourish a positive, democratic state capable of acting in support of the institutional, ethical, and spiritual conditions of a pluralistic democracy." The task, for Connolly, then, becomes one of showing how pluralism is promoted through the supportive denationalization of the state.

Liberalism and Morality

It should be clear from the summary above, that the kind of liberalism that is supported by the authors in this collection is very different from the defensive liberalism that has sought to justify itself on the basis of moral skepticism or relativism—and which therefore has made itself an easy target for the charge that its interest in freedom was really the expression of, or ultimately led to, moral indifference. Even when the present authors argue in favor of constraining the reach of prohibitionist legislation, they do so on the basis of *moral* reasons. Thus, Moore defends the three interests in freedom that he identifies not by appeal to the sophomoric cry, Who is the government to tell us what we should do? but rather, by appeal to moral considerations. The presumption of freedom is defended at least in part because it allows people to act for moral rather than prudential reasons; the derived right to liberty is in fact part of a legal-moralist account, and the basic right to liberty finds its point precisely as a defense of the values of character coherence and integrity.

Similarly, Freeman's defense of autonomy and Moon's defense of the principle of democracy rest on explicitly moral considerations. Both make use of Rawls's attempt to provide a justification for a type of liberalism that, while falling short of a comprehensive doctrine, is still a morally grounded political theory that contrasts with mere modus vivendi liberalism. Hence, Freeman's stance in favor of autonomy rests upon a normative ideal of citizens as free and equal, and Moon's defense of pluralistic democracy is not predicated upon either relativistic premises or a merely pragmatic desire for stability, but rather, upon a conception of moral action as action that can be justified to others.

In my view, the extension of the democratic principle transnationally does not settle the question of the legal status of drugs but leaves it open to democratic participation in a cross-national "electoral district." My argument takes its point of departure in the close relationship between morality, understood in universalistic terms, and legal legitimacy, understood in procedural, democratic terms. Finally, Connolly's critique of recent attempts to renationalize the country is grounded on a moral appreciation (not merely a factual observation) of pluralism and of the conditions under which it can be sustained. I am afraid, though, that simply pointing out that liberalism is being defended on the basis of values will not quell the critics. For, as Nancy Rosenblum puts it,

> those who accuse liberalism of moral failing often acknowledge that it rests on and promotes some moral vision for public and private life, but judge its values deficient, even depraved. Liberal virtues are really vices (greed, uncontrolled selfishness generally, intellectual hubris). Or signs of pathology (impartiality is a weird and abnormal sort of self-distancing). Or, critics charge that the inevitable consequence of liberal values is viciousness; for example, tolerance of a plurality of views of the good life weakens the duties and consolations of religion and invites abominable license. (Nancy Rosenblum, "Introduction," in Rosenblum, ed. *Liberalism and the Moral Life*, p. 7.)

Thus, one additional step needs to be taken in order to deflect the charge that liberal attempts at drug-policy reform are a form of callousness cloaked in deceitful rhetoric about respect for autonomy or other values—especially when the reform is defended by those who otherwise see nothing particularly virtuous in drug consumption. This additional step is a simple one: it can take the form of a reminder. Although the authors of these essays agree with present policymakers about regulating the consumption of some drugs, most of them are reluctant to address the problem mainly in terms of the criminal law apparatus of the state. But one moves from this reluctance to the conclusion that liberal positions on drugs are callous only by assuming that power is defined entirely in terms of the capacity to punish. This assumption is unjustified. Defenders of the current prohibitionist regime sometimes speak of all liberal drug policy reform as if it constituted a capitulation of the rule of law. Supporters of such reform can remind their critics that in reality their proposals exhibit a much deeper trust in the rule of law than they receive credit for. At the heart of liberal proposals lies the fundamental trust in the ability of legitimate laws to regulate social interaction by means that are not primarily punitive, but that appeal to the rational and moral capacities of citizens who are guaranteed a decent chance of living a successful life.[17]

Part of the point behind some attempts at drug-policy reform consists precisely in shifting the responsibility for dealing with the problem of drug abuse from the penal system to other state institutions, not simply because pragmatically the former has not shown much success in addressing the problem, but because morally the present policy is deemed unfair in the different ways discussed in these essays. Furthermore, it is thought that self-destructive and socially fragmenting behavior correlates with structural aspects of social life for which responsibility ought to be more widely spread. In conclusion, liberal commitments can be deployed for the sake of redirecting drug policy for positive reasons, rather than as a mere sign of defeat in the war on drugs. Given the importance of prohibitionist legislation in generating a "risk mark up" which leads to the profits characteristic of the drug business, one can argue that it is unfair to sustain, *through state action*, rates of profits that no honest business can match. Among other consequences, this undermines the relationship between effort and success that lies at the basis of all viable and fair societies. That there is *some* relationship between drug consumption and this (eroding) link between effort and success can be seen in the socioeconomic distribution of consumption. The problem of narcotics opens up, yet again, the broader question about distributive fairness and gives reason to think that without sustained efforts to reestablish the links between effort and success across society, and between societies, laws, medical treatments, and educational programs are nothing more than coping mechanisms.

One of the conclusions that might be derived from the essays in this volume is that the vocabulary of the rule of law and of a public morality is also accessible to defenders of drug-policy reform. Confidence in the rule of law can be expressed in ways that differ from an insufficiently effective appeal to the criminal law apparatus of the state. Of course, the political climate in both the United States and in other countries is such that there are deep suspicions about the effectiveness of governmental programs in coping with broad social problems. But if there is suspicion about government initiatives in general, there is no blunter, less differentiated, less sophisticated program than the prison system, which is fast becoming the preferred behavior-altering tool of governments everywhere.[18]

PART I

RATIONALITY
AND DRUGS

CHAPTER ONE

Rationality and Addiction

Jon Elster

Addictive behavior appears to be a paradigm of irrationality. Not only do addicts seem to behave in an objectively harmful way, by ruining their bodies, their finances, and their social life. They also, more relevantly, seem to act against their own better judgment. They want to quit, but can't. They could make theirs the words of St. Paul, "I do not do the good I want, but the evil I do not want is what I do" (Romans 7:19). This kind of behavior is usually seen as a form of weakness of will, a paradigm of irrationality.[1]

In recent work, Gary Becker and his collaborators argue that addiction is, in fact, perfectly rational.[2] On the one hand, these writers construct theoretical models in which high-level consumption of addictive substances is optimal behavior for the consumer. On the other hand, they find that the implications of these models fit well with stylized or systematic data on the behavior of addicts.

Against this reinterpretation, I want to defend the traditional view. I do not believe that addiction is, in general, a form of rational behavior. There may be cases in which addiction is a form of "rational self-medication," but I do not believe they form a large proportion of the addictions we observe.[3] Instead, most addictive behavior can be traced back to irrationality in the choice, the belief formation, or the information acquisition of the agent. In arguing for this view, I shall not address myself directly to the Becker-Murphy model, partly because I have no competence to assess the econometric arguments and partly because I believe it is useful to take a more general approach to the question. In the final section, however, I consider an important aspect of the Becker-Murphy model in the light of the previous discussion.

The Nature of Addiction

In the final analysis, the question of the nature of addiction is inseparable from that of the explanation of addictive behavior. The relation between these two questions can be brought out by considering the homogeneity of the behaviors that are commonly classified as addictive. Alcoholism and compulsive gambling, for instance, may seem closely related in many ways, but are they really produced by similar causal mechanisms? In a discussion of the "psychomotor stimulant theory of addiction," Roy Wise and Michael Bozarth distinguish between homology and analogy as explanatory heuristics.[4] Whereas analogies do not necessarily extend beyond the superficial similarities that were originally noted, homologies, resulting from common causal mechanisms, do allow such predictive extensions. Consider the following diagram, figure 1:

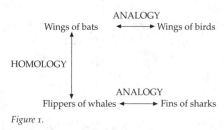

Figure 1.

A key problem in the study of putative addictions is whether they relate to each other merely by analogy, as bat wings to bird wings or whale flippers to shark fins, or whether they are unified by a common causal mechanism. Although there may be some purposes for which the concepts "creatures that fly" (including flying fish!) or "creatures that live in the sea" are useful, the concepts of mammals, birds, and fish are indispensable for scientific purposes. Similarly, it is not very useful to define addiction phenomenologically as, say, "irresistible craving" if different cravings arise in different ways and are overcome or prevented by different means.

Let me give an example of how one may be led astray in thinking about addiction by considering phenomenological similarities rather than causal commonalities:

The more alcoholics drink, the more shame they feel; the more shame they feel, the more they drink to forget the shame, or at least make it bearable. The more compulsive overeaters eat, the fatter they grow; the fatter they grow, the more disgusting they find themselves to be, and the more they turn to food on search of comfort in the face of that self-disgust. The more compulsive gamblers gamble, the deeper into debt they go, and the more they gamble to pay off those debts. (Francis Seeburger, *Addiction and Responsibility* [New York: Crossroad, 1993], pp. 20–21.)

Drinking and overeating may indeed be self-sustaining activities, in the sense that people may drink or eat to escape from the awareness that they are alcoholic or obese. It has also been argued that people may gamble to forget the shame associated with their gambling.[5] The mechanism mentioned in the last sentence of the quoted paragraph, however, is entirely different. At a superficial level, it may appear similar to the two other phenomena that are identified. As with drinking and overeating, gambling "both creates the problem and is a way of resolving that problem."[6] But in alcoholism or overeating, there is no causal mechanism that is even remotely similar to the need to gamble in order to earn money to pay off gambling debts. The latter mechanism is more similar to what happens when an embezzler steals money from one account in order to put money back into another. Presumably nobody would refer to that phenomenon as a form of addiction.

The distinction between analogy and homology must be kept in mind in the following discussion of the main properties usually ascribed to addictions. Even if a given behavioral pattern exhibits, say, the properties of tolerance and withdrawal, we should not immediately conclude that it is usefully classified under the same heading as dependence on opioids. To tell homology from analogy, we need the full causal story. With regard to chemical addictions, recent advances in neuropharmacology allow us to piece together many parts of that story.[7] Much less is known about behavioral addictions such as overeating, gambling, or excessive sexual behavior. Moreover, what is known often points in a quite different direction.

Attempts to define addiction tend to emphasize one of two clusters of criteria. On the one hand there are proposals to define addiction in terms of more or less objective factors, notably tolerance, withdrawal, and objective harm. On the other hand, there are more subjectively oriented proposals, which define addiction in terms of craving, a desire to quit, and an inability to quit. Most authors tend in fact to give some weight to all six criteria, but, as I said, emphasis tends to differ.

Tolerance

In common parlance, tolerance is the phenomenon that as time passes the agent needs more of a given substance (or activity) to obtain the same "thrill" or "high." This effect is very marked for the opiates and alcohol, much less so for cannabis and cocaine. It may be caused either by neuro-adaptation in the brain reward system or by an increased rate of metabolism. Tolerance can also obtain for other effects of drugs, notably their lethality. The regular heroin dose of a heavy user would be lethal to the novice or to a previously heavy user who has abstained for some time.

With regard to behavioral addictions, the question of tolerance is less well understood. Again, gambling will provide a useful illustration. There is an observed tendency for heavy gamblers to raise the stakes and/or the odds. It is not clear, however, that this phenomenon reflects tolerance with regard to the thrills of gambling. The escalation might also be due to the need to make larger and riskier gambles in order to repay old debts. But suppose that Henry R. Lesieur is right in that the nature of "action" in gambling has "an uncanny similarity to 'tolerance' among alcohol, barbiturate, and narcotics addicts. Once the 'high' of a five-hundred-dollar event has been reached, the two-dollar bet no longer achieves the desired effect."[8] We still cannot conclude to the existence of tolerance: the escalation might originally be caused by the need to repay debts and then be sustained by a "contrast effect."[9] Before you've experienced the best, you're happy with the second-best; but once you've been exposed to the best, perhaps by accident, there is little thrill to be got from the second-best. Although the contrast effect and the phenomenon of tolerance are superficially similar, the underlying causal mechanisms are quite different.

Withdrawal

In its most general form, withdrawal means that upon the cessation of consumptive behavior or other activity, an unpleasant consequence occurs. That concept, however, is much too broad to be useful. For one thing, we need to define the baseline with respect to which the consequence is said to be unpleasant. For another, we need to understand the nature of the unpleasant consequence and the mechanism by which it is brought about.

To aid our understanding of this problem, consider figure 2 below. The normal state of the organism is state A, the addictive one is state B, and the immediate postaddictive one is state C. These relate to each other as follows in the figure (with time measured on the horizontal axis and welfare on the vertical axis):

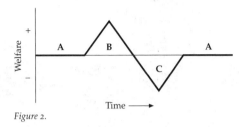

Figure 2.

I stipulate that the baseline for assessing the withdrawal symptoms in state C should be state A rather than state B. If one chose B as the baseline, one would certainly risk confusing sharks and whales. Insulin and aspirin, for instance, would then be said to produce withdrawal symptoms. When people engage in activities such as TV-watching or reading to escape from the misery of everyday life, the return of the misery upon cessation of the activity does not, on this more restricted definition, count as a withdrawal symptom. By contrast, when people drink or take heroin to escape from a drab life, the cessation causes their life to be even worse than the one they escaped from.

The reduction of welfare in stage C compared to stage A that characterizes addiction must be distinguished from the general tendency for welfare to drop momentarily upon the cessation of any pleasurable activity.[10] A sudden interruption of sexual experience, for instance, causes welfare to drop below the preintercourse level and to remain there for a while before the subject returns to the baseline level. In George Ainslie's phrase, this mechanism is part of "the natural history of consumption."[11] It does not—pace Tibor Scitovsky—suffice to define a behavior as addictive.[12] To distinguish between this tendency and the more specific phenomenon of withdrawal, one can note that the temporal profile of addiction is very different. Addiction takes time to build. The withdrawal symptoms are not caused by single episodes, but by a cumulative history of consumption. The symptoms persist for days or weeks, occasionally for months, rather than minutes or hours. Also, in addiction, repeated episodes of consumption and abstention have a pattern not found in the consumption of ordinary goods, as shown in figure 3:

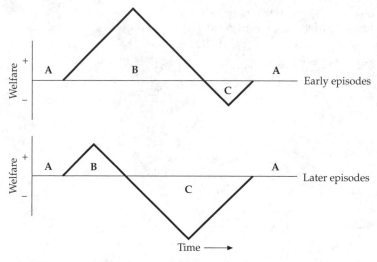

Figure 3.

The reduction of welfare in stage C compared to stage A may be caused by the recollection of stage B. There are several ways in which memory may be involved in such welfare losses. Consider first the person who looks back at a wonderful experience with LSD. The memory, together with the knowledge that LSD is currently unavailable, makes him more unhappy than before he had the experience. Loss of a sexual partner can have the same effect: it may be *worse* to have loved and lost than never to have loved at all. (One is also reminded of Donne's " 'Tis better to be foul than to have been fair.") This negative "contrast effect" usually coexists, however, with a positive "endowment effect," caused by the fact that the memory of a pleasurable experience is a pleasurable memory.[13] In general, the net effect of these two mechanisms is indeterminate.

Consider next the alcoholic who drinks to escape the awareness of the fact that he is an alcoholic. Here the welfare loss experienced upon cessation takes the form of an acutely unpleasant recollection of the way he has been ruining his life and that of others by drinking. This mechanism obviously cannot explain why people get hooked on addictive uses and behaviors. The alcoholism which the alcoholic is trying to forget by drinking cannot itself have been caused by such escapism. Such *secondary withdrawal symptoms*, as I shall call them, can help explain the persistence of addiction, but hardly its emergence in the first place. Moreover, they do not seem equally important for all addictions. They may play a role in sustaining alcoholism, overeating, and compulsive gambling, but not in maintaining smoking behavior or cocaine abuse.

These memory-mediated withdrawal symptoms do not (I assume) play any role in animal addiction. The physiological or *primary withdrawal symptoms*, common to both animals and humans, fall in two categories: somatic symptoms such as tremors, sweating, and the like; and feelings of dysphoria and anhedonia. Some addictive drugs, such as cocaine, do not produce somatic withdrawal symptoms. All addictive drugs, however, produce dysphoria upon cessation. These symptoms are produced by the brain reward system and are indissociable, therefore, from the euphoric effects. Little is known about primary withdrawal symptoms in behavioral addictions.

Harm

Addiction can ravage lives and communities. For an outside observer, this is perhaps the most striking aspect of the phenomenon. There are good reasons, however, for considering the harm caused by addiction as a frequently occurring effect of the behavior rather than as a constitutive and invariable component. Caffeine is uncontroversially addictive, yet the damage to body, mind, or purse caused by coffee drinking is minimal or nil. Methadone users are addicted but otherwise as normal and healthy as nonaddicts. A compulsive gambler with a large fortune to draw on need not suffer any harm—unless the thrill from gambling depends on there being a real possibility of losing everything.

Craving

The varieties of craving can be classified along two dimensions, as shown in figure 4:

	Positive (Supplying pleasure)	Negative (Relieving pain)
Primary effect	(1)	(2)
Secondary effect	(3)	(4)

Figure 4.

(1) Craving may refer to the intensely pleasant experience caused by release of dopamine in the brain-reward system. This is a common element in all chemical addictions. The specific mechanisms by which drugs increase the amount of dopamine differ from drug to drug, but the final result is the same. Nothing is known about similar mechanisms for behavioral addictions. In many cases, however, what is craved is not a positive experience of euphoria but rather an escape from a miserable existence. Alcohol and heroin are often sought for their numbness-inducing effect, not for any euphoric qualities.[14]

(2) Craving may also derive from the desire to get rid of primary withdrawal symptoms, whether these are somatic or psychological (dysphoria). Earlier writers on addiction tended to overestimate the desire for relief from somatic withdrawal as a component of craving. Animals will self-administer drugs directly to the reward centers of the brain even when there are no somatic withdrawal symptoms. By contrast, the desire for relief from dysphoria is probably an important component of craving in most cases.

(3) Craving may derive from what I shall call *secondary reinforcers*. As a former heavy smoker, who quit twenty-five years ago when my consumption reached forty cigarettes a day, I remember vividly what it was like to organize my whole life around smoking. When things went well, I reached for a cigarette. When things went badly, I did the same. I smoked before breakfast, after a meal, and when I had a drink. I lit up before doing something difficult, and I did so afterward. I always had an excuse for smoking. In addition, smoking became a ritual that served to highlight salient aspects of experience and to impose structure on what would otherwise have been a confusing morass of events. Smoking provided the commas, semi-colons, question marks, exclamation points, and periods of experience. It helped me to achieve a feeling of mastery, the feeling that I was in charge of events rather than submitting to them.[15] This craving for cigarettes amounted to a desire for order and control, not for nicotine.

(4) Finally, craving may derive from secondary withdrawal symptoms. The awareness that one is ruining one's life, and perhaps that of others, may be so intensely unpleasant that one craves for relief.

These different forms of craving will appear at different stages. The desire to achieve euphoria or to escape dysphoria are prior to the fear of primary withdrawal symptoms, which in turn will tend to appear before the fear of secondary withdrawal and secondary rewards. Their place in the etiology of addiction will differ correspondingly. I hypothesize that the cue-elicited cravings that are responsible for many cases of relapse may belong to any of the four categories.

Inability to Quit

This feature of addiction plausibly may be supposed to be fully explained by the various forms of craving. To be addicted *is* to be subject to craving of such a strength that it is or would be difficult to quit. (Note that this criterion may be satisfied even if there is no desire to quit.) The inability to quit has an important time dimension, in that it may be either a "within-episode" phenomenon or a "between-episode" phenomenon. Elvin M. Jellinek draws a distinction between "gamma alcoholism," characterized by "loss of control," and "delta alcoholism," characterized by "inability to abstain." With the latter, he writes, "there is no ability to 'go on the water wagon' for even a day without the manifestation of withdrawal symptoms; the ability to control the amount of intake on any given occasion, however, remains intact."[16] Similar distinctions apply to overeating, cocaine addiction, and gambling, but not to smoking or opiates. (There are no out-of-control binge smokers.)

Desire to Quit

Many writers use the desire to quit as an important indication of addiction. For some writers, this desire must be an actual subjective fact. Thus Stanton Peele argues that it is absurd to say that people "can depend on what they can't detect and don't care about."[17] I disagree. Consider the nineteenth-century heavy smoker who lived (and died) in happy ignorance that he was destroying his body by nicotine. I would still claim he was addicted if it were true that, had he known the facts about smoking, he would have wanted to quit but been unable to. Although, as we have seen, the causal process of addiction may be speeded up by the addict's knowledge that he is addicted (by the production of secondary withdrawal symptoms), this is far from being a necessary feature.

The Theory of Rational Choice

The theory of rational choice is first and foremost a normative or prescriptive theory. It tells people how to choose and act in order to achieve their aims as well as possible. It offers also, but only secondarily, an explanatory account of human behavior. In this perspective, the hypothesis is that one can explain how people act by assuming that they follow the prescriptions of the normative theory. In what follows, I adopt the latter perspective.

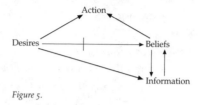

Figure 5.

The standard version of the rational-choice explanation of behavior is set out in figure 5.[18] It involves three distinct conditions. First, for an action to be rational, it has to be the best means of satisfying the desires of the agent, given his beliefs. An agent is irrational if, in considering how to act, he opts for an action that *according to his own judgment* is inferior to another action he could have chosen. This kind of irrationality is an instance of weakness of will, briefly mentioned above and further discussed in the next section.

In itself, this first requirement is weak. If I want to kill a person, and I believe that the best way of doing so is to make a doll representing him and stick a pin through it, then according to this weak definition I act rationally if I make the doll and pierce it with a pin. We would hardly be satisfied with this conclusion, however, not because the homicidal desire is irrational (it may be immoral, but that is another matter), but because the beliefs are transparently ill-founded.

Second, therefore, we need to stipulate that the beliefs themselves are rational, in the sense of being grounded in the information that is available to the agent. These may be beliefs about factual matters or about general lawlike connections. In particular, they will include beliefs about the opportunities available to the agent. In fact, rational-choice theory is often stated in terms of desires and opportunities rather than desires and beliefs. In that "reduced" version, the theory says that a rational agent chooses the most-preferred element in his opportunity set. In some simple choice situations, this formulation is adequate enough. In general, however, we need to take account of the fact that the full set of objective opportunities available to the agent may not be known to him. Today, for instance, governments do not really know whether it is possible to develop commercially viable fusion power. Or, to take a more mundane example, an automobilist arriving in an unknown city without a map will not know the full set of paths that will take him through it.

In such cases, the agent must use whatever information he has to form some belief or subjective estimate of the alternatives. The fact that it is subjective does not in itself detract from its rationality. On the contrary, *the concept of rationality is subjective through and through.* To be rational does not mean that one is invariably successful in realizing one's aims: it means only that one has no reason, after the fact, to think that one should have acted differently. Nor does a rational belief have to be true: it must only be well-grounded in the available information. Beliefs are rational if they are formed by procedures that in the long run tend to produce more true beliefs than any alternative procedure, but on any particular occasion the belief thus formed may not correspond to the facts. This said, belief formation *is* vulnerable to distorting influences of various kinds. Some of these influences are in the nature of mistakes (cold irrationality), as when we get sums wrong in arithmetic. Others, however, belong to the category of hot or motivated irrationality, as when the errors in adding made by a salesman systematically (although non-intentionally) work out to his favor.

However, a belief is not made rational simply by being well-grounded in the available information. If the driver is in a hurry, he should perhaps buy a map to acquire more information about the feasible paths. The third condition for rational behavior, therefore, is that the agent should acquire an optimal amount of information, or more accurately, invest an optimal amount of time, energy, and money in gathering such information. Clearly, it will often be irrational not to invest any time in collecting information. If one is buying a house or a car, one should compare several options and in-vestigate each of them in some depth. Equally clearly, there are occasions when there is a danger of gathering too much information. If a doctor makes too many tests before deciding on treatment, the patient may die under his hands. A general who insists on accurate information about the enemy's movement before attacking can easily be taken by surprise. In between these extremes, there exists an optimal level of search, a "golden mean." (Whether this optimum can be known is, of course, another matter.)

As depicted in figure 5, there are several factors which determine the amount of information that a rational agent will gather. The agent's beliefs about the expected costs and expected value of gathering the information will obviously matter. His desires—that is, how important the decision is to him—will also enter into the calculus. Indirectly, therefore, the desires of the agents will affect the process of belief formation. However, the blocked arrow from desires to beliefs in figure 5 is intended to indicate that a direct influence, as in wishful thinking, is inadmissible in rational-choice behavior.

From inspection of figure 5 it is clear that the desires stand in a privileged position, as the unmoved mover of rational choice. This corresponds to a long-standing tradition in philosophy. As David Hume said, "Reason is, and ought only to be, the slave of the passions."[19] If one were to talk about rational desires, or about conditions under which a given desire might be said to be rational or irrational, one would elevate reason to the role of judge rather than slave. However, as indicated by the blocked arrow above, passion should not be allowed to set itself up as an arbitrary tyrant. Even a slave needs some independence to serve his master well; beliefs born of passion serve passion badly.

Another succinct expression of the supremacy of desires is the proverbial expression, "De gustibus non est disputandum." One cannot argue about ends, only about means. Any desire, or taste, is as good as any others. This argument applies not only to substantive preferences for one good over another, but also to what we may call "formal preferences" such as degrees of risk aversion or time discounting. Time discounting is just another preference. Some people like chocolate ice cream, whereas others have a taste for vanilla: this is just a brute fact, and it would be absurd to say that one preference is more rational than the other. Similarly, it is just a brute fact that some like the present, whereas others have a taste for the future. If a person heavily discounts the future, then consuming an addictive substance may, for him, be a form of rational behavior.

This argument may seem counterintuitive. I believe, however, that if we want to use rational-choice theory to explain behavior on the bare assumption that people make the most out of what they have, then the standard version is exactly right. If some individuals have the bad luck to be born with genes or to be exposed to external influences that make them discount the future heavily, myopic and perhaps self-destructive behavior may, for them, be their best option. We cannot expect them to reduce their rate of time discounting, because to want to be motivated by long-term concerns ipso facto *is* to be motivated by long-term concerns. If they do not have that motivation in the first place, they cannot be motivated to acquire it.

Rational choice, I have argued, involves three distinct optimizations: that of action, given desires and beliefs; that of beliefs, given available information; and that of information acquisition, given desires and beliefs. In this section, I discuss whether addictive behavior is optimal in these three respects. I begin, nevertheless, by considering an approach that might appear to deny the relevance of choice altogether. The neurophysiological study of chemical addictions seems to support a view of the addict as driven by irresistible cravings that leave no room for choice. On reflection, however, this view is untenable. The neurophysiological study of addiction is entirely compatible with a choice-oriented approach. In theory, it does not even exclude a rational-choice approach.

The central topic in the neurophysiological study of addiction is the reward system of the brain—the fine grain of the mechanisms by which consumption of drugs, and its interruption, can produce extremes of both euphoria and dysphoria. While tolerance, craving, withdrawal, conditioning, and similar phenomena change the parameters of choice, they need not undermine the possibility of choice. One might well view the addict as making optimal choices within the modified reward structure induced by the action of drugs.

Thus, one view of the pharmacological action of drugs is that they affect only the reward structure, while leaving the capacity for making rational choices unaffected. If drug use interferes with the time preferences of the agent, causing him to discount the future more heavily than he would in a nonaddicted state, that, too, affects the reward structure and not the capacity to make rational choices. An alternative view is that drugs also undermine the rational-choice capacity. Because the action of drugs is intimately connected with emotional and volitional centers in the brain, this might give rise to one or more of the known forms of irrationality, notably weakness of will or wishful thinking. Although at present neurophysiological science is unable to settle the question, the arguments made below suggest an answer that favors the second view.

Weakness of Will

It is hard to deny that many addicts desperately want to quit, yet are unable to do so. Many succeed for a while and then relapse time and again. For smokers, this is a particularly pervasive and well-documented tendency. As noted initially, such behavior might seem to be a paradigm of weakness of will. Yet as noted by Olav Gjelsvik, the weakness of will found in such cases may not be the one that qualifies as irrational behavior.[20] On the traditional conception, the weak-willed agent acts against the judgment he holds *at the moment of action*. Given the choice between x and y, his belief that x and y are incompatible, and his judgment that, all things considered, x is better, he nevertheless chooses y.[21]

Such behavior, if and when it occurs, is certainly irrational. It is hard to tell whether addicts behave in this way. It is plausible, as argued by George Loewenstein, that the "visceral" strength of addictive craving is capable of short-circuiting rational choice.[22] It may do so, however, by driving other options out of consciousness rather than by inducing the agent to act against his own conscious judgment. This was Aristotle's conception of weakness of will, which he explained by "the possibility of having knowledge in a sense and yet not having it, as in the instance of a man asleep, mad or drunk. But now this is just the condition of men under the influence of passions; for outbursts of anger and sexual appetites and some other such passions, it is evident, actually alter our bodily condition, and in some men even produce fits of madness. It is plain, then, that incontinent men must be in a similar condition to these."[23]

A third conception of weakness of will, proposed by George Ainslie, rests on the premise that animals, including humans, tend to discount the future hyperbolically, as illustrated in figure 6.[24]

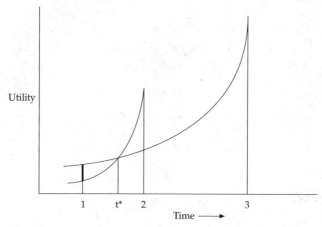

Figure 6.

In figure 6, the agent has a choice between a small reward that will be made available at time 2 and a larger reward that will be made available at time 3. The curves show how these future rewards are discounted to a present value at earlier times. Before t*, when the present value of the larger reward is above that of the smaller reward, the agent intends to choose the larger reward. After t*, however, the present value of the smaller reward dominates. At time 2, he therefore chooses the smaller reward. There is no point in time at which the agent both prefers the larger reward and chooses the smaller. The agent is subject to a preference reversal and never acts against his preference.

Whether or not one thinks of this behavior as a form of weakness of will, it is not at all clear that it is irrational. One might argue, perhaps, that an agent is irrational if he knows himself to be subject to preference reversals and yet fails to take proper precautions against them by precommitment or other techniques.[25] But even that claim may not go through. Precommitment, typically, is costly. Suppose that the agent, at time 1, contemplates precommitting himself to choosing the larger, delayed reward. He may rationally choose not to do so, if the costs of precommitment are larger than the difference (the thick line in figure 6) between the present values of the two rewards. Alternatively he may, as Ainslie argues, overcome the problem by "bunching." If he can bring himself to see a choice of the small reward on this occasion as a predictor of the same choice on later occasions, he may be rationally motivated to choose the large reward now. But is there really a rational basis for seeing present choices as predictive of future choices? Although I cannot go into the question here, I tend to think that there isn't.

Ainslie's view may simplify too much in one respect. Human beings, unlike animals, remember their previous intentions. When the smoker who tries to quit arrives at a party and somebody offers him a cigarette, he will typically remember his resolution to quit. Moreover, he will not think of his current preference as resulting from a straightforward change of mind. There will be an unpleasant tension between the current preference for smoking and the recollection of his former preference for abstaining. To act on the current preference and to override the earlier one is not exactly weakness of will in the sense of Davidson, but nor is it simply a case of preference reversal. I do not know how to develop this idea, but it seems to capture an important aspect of many instances of weakness of will.

Belief Rationality

For addiction to be rational, it must be based on rational beliefs about the consequences of engaging in it. Specifically, addicts must be able to form rational assessments of the following effects of addiction:

(i) The objective dangers and benefits entailed by addiction

(ii) The subjective impact on the addicts themselves of these contingencies when they arise, including notably the following:

(iia) The visceral-emotional impact of the experience itself and the possibility that it might lead the addicts to neglect future consequences of present behavior

(iib) The devastating subjective experience of somatic, financial, or social ruin

(iic) The impact of addiction on the addicts' abilities to maintain rational beliefs about (i)

Even if addicts at the outset of their career have rational beliefs about some consequences of addiction, they may not have rational beliefs about its impact on their future belief formation. Because of failure to anticipate (iia) and (iic), addicts may not be able to "stop in time." Even in the absence of these mechanisms, however, the failure to fully and vividly visualize (iib)— how bad the worst-case scenario actually is—may be sufficient to undermine rational choice.[26] In the following discussion, I focus on (i) and (iic).

Kip Viscusi presents data on perceptions of the risks associated with cigarette smoking and finds that all categories of individuals tend to have exaggerated beliefs about the risk of getting lung cancer from smoking but that the beliefs held by people who smoke are closer to the correct values. He notes that if smokers have lower estimates the cause may be either "the self-selection of people with low risk assessments into smoking" or "cognitive dissonance."[27] The former explanation fits well into a rational-choice model of addiction: namely, people who smoke do so because they have, on average, a better understanding of the risks of smoking. The latter explanation relies on the mechanism of wishful thinking: that is, because I smoke, smoking can't be so dangerous.[28] On this hypothesis, there would be two biases working in opposite directions. On the one hand, smokers as well as nonsmokers are subject to misleading information about the dangers of smoking that induce exaggerated perceptions. On the other hand, smokers are subject to a self-serving bias that induces them to discount the risks. Although the latter bias does not fully cancel the former, it does make the beliefs of smokers more nearly accurate than those of nonsmokers. It does not, however, make the beliefs more *rational*. From the point of view of rationality, being subject to two biases is worse than being subject to only one of them.

As long as we cannot decide between the two explanations, the belief rationality of smokers is an open question. Within the range of behaviors that may plausibly be seen as addictive, gambling provides the clearest case of belief irrationality. The occasional gambler may well have an accurate perception of the chances of winning. He gambles for the fun of it, not because he expects to win. Whether he chooses to lose his money at the roulette table or on the race track, he knows that the odds are rigged against him and that skill is either irrelevant or marginal. With more heavy involvement, however, rationality suffers; in fact it suffers doubly. There is evidence not only that "as frequency of betting increases so does the belief that one's selection involves more skill," but also that "the observed behaviour actually becomes less skillful, with escalating stakes, hurried bet-selection and last minute changes in selection."[29] Alcohol notoriously has a similar dual effect of enhancing confidence in one's skill while reducing the actual skillfulness.

The most striking form of belief irrationality in gambling comes from games of pure chance.[30] Some gamblers believe that if red has come up five times in a row, it is more likely to come up next time as well. Others believe that if red has come up five times in a row, black is more likely to come up next time. And some gamblers take near-misses at roulette as evidence that they were onto something. Although these beliefs may appear to be forms of "cold irrationality" that are based on erroneous statistical reasoning or on the use of misleading heuristics, I believe that they are endogenous to the gambling situation and are motivated by the need to believe in the possibility of a large win. "In order for a person to continue gambling at a regular pace, the losses *must* be rationalized in some fashion or other."[31] Rather than being self-selected into gambling because they have a proneness to such reasoning, people commit these fallacies when and because they get deeply involved in gambling. In other words, the relevant breakdown of rationality occurs with regard to (iic) rather than (i).

Orphanides and Zervos propose a model of rational addiction with learning, in which individuals who are initially uncertain about how an addictive drug will affect them resolve the uncertainty by experimenting with it.[32] Some will find that they can consume safely. Others will discover that they are at risk early enough to back out. And still others will make the discovery only when it is too late. *Ex post*, they will regret that they ever started, yet *ex ante*, the decision to experiment may have been an optimal one. As with any decision, however, the decision to start consuming a potentially addictive drug is no more rational than the weakest link in the chain. Do potential addicts form rational prior beliefs about the likelihood of suffering harmful consequences from addiction? Do they have rational beliefs about their specific vulnerability to getting lung cancer from smoking or liver cirrhosis from drinking?

The data presented by Viscusi do not allow us to answer this question, as they concern only the perception of individuals of the average risk of smoking, not of the risk to them.[33] Nor do I know of any other studies that throw light on this question. Casual observation and introspection suggest that such priors may be subject to various cold and hot biases. Some individuals may refrain from smoking marijuana because irrational use of the representativeness heuristic leads them to think that if they did, they would go on to become heroin users.[34] Individuals who are subject to strong peer pressure may willfully ignore the risks ("it can't happen to me"). Note that these issues belong to subcategory (i) above. The ability of individuals to form rational priors about (iia), (iib), and (iic) is even more questionable. As Orphanides and Zervos rely heavily on rational updating of the priors, this is another respect in which their model seems unrealistic.

Gathering Information

A rational addict would not simply form rational beliefs on the basis of the evidence immediately available to him, but go on to look for more evidence up to the point where the expected value of more information equals the costs. To form a rational prior about one's vulnerability to addictive drugs, one should have a medical checkup and look into one's family history for evidence of inheritable risk. To update the priors, people who suspect they drink too much should take regular liver tests. Racetrack gamblers ought to gather information about the prior performance of the horses and their riders.

Irrationality can take the form of investing either too little or too much in gathering new evidence. I suspect but cannot prove that most drug users invest too little, both with regard to (i) and (ii). By contrast, some forms of gambling are characterized by an overinvestment in information. The very existence of the Monte Carlo *Revue Scientifique*, which logs successive outcomes at roulette, is proof that gamblers are willing to spend money gathering worthless information.[35] In games of pure chance, *any* investment in information is by definition excessive. In games of mixed skill and chance, gathering and processing of information can improve the odds. On the racetrack, for instance, "professional gambling is typified by a rational and controlled approach sustained by hours of information collection, detailed accounting and the like."[36] What distinguishes the professional gambler from the compulsive gambler (and steady loser) is probably not that the former more closely approximates the optimal investment in information, but that he has superior processing skills and is better able to resist impulses to deviate from his plans.

Overall Assessment

There are many addictive behaviors and, for each of them, many patterns and degrees of being addicted. It is hard, therefore, to generalize about the rationality of addicts. At one extreme, the habitual coffee drinker who keeps track of the state of medical research on the effects of coffee may conform to all the canons of rational behavior. At the other extreme, gamblers caught up in a self-destructive frenzy of betting are massively subject to weakness of will and wishful thinking. I find it impossible to believe that such behavior was a calculated risk—that they anticipated from the beginning that this might happen to them. Between these extremes, there are many nuances. As a rough qualitative assessment, however, I believe that, in the behavior of addicts, irrationality dominates.

Becker on Discounting

My concluding comments draw on the previous discussion of the role of time discounting in the Becker-Murphy theory of rational addiction (BM). The BM model relies "on a weak concept of rationality that does not rule out strong discounts of future events."[37] In itself, this stipulation is unobjectionable as I have pointed out above. One may take issue, however, with the assumption that time discounting is exponential or time-consistent. Becker, Grossman, and Murphy contrast the BM model with a "myopic" model in which consumers of addictive goods "fail to consider the impact of current consumption on future utility and future consumption."[38] Not surprisingly, perhaps, the BM model outperforms the myopic model in econometric testing. Yet a more plausible alternative to their theory would seem to be an Ainslie-like theory of hyperbolic discounting rather than the extreme theory of total discounting.

A strong if impressionistic argument in favor of the hyperbolic assumption is the fact that addicts regularly use precommitment strategies to control their behavior. Alcoholics use Antabuse; former cocaine addicts write self-incriminating letters to prevent themselves from relapsing;[39] and smokers who want to quit tell their friends so as to raise the costs of relapse. If addicts discounted the future exponentially, we would not observe this behavior. Both in the case of strategic behavior and in the presently considered case of parametric choice, use of precommitment strategies is a good indicator of time-inconsistency.[40]

Harder (but more indirect) evidence comes from a study that "examined the effects of an experimental Saturday closing of liquor retail stores in Sweden. [It] found a decline in the number of arrests for drunkenness by about 10% and also a decline in the number of domestic disturbances, as well as in outdoor and indoor assaults. On the other hand, the evaluation did not demonstrate any effect on total consumption of alcohol."[41] A Norwegian study yielded similar findings. This effect would be predicted by hyperbolic discounting. In terms of figure 6, the individual at time 1 who decides not to drink at time 2 and then changes his mind will nevertheless abstain if the liquor store is closed at time 2. By contrast, exponential discounting cannot account for this effect. The heavy drinkers who are responsible for public drunkenness and alcohol-related violence are presumably those who form an intention to abstain from weekend drinking yet fail to carry it out when the time comes. If the impact of shorter opening hours on their drinking was mediated only by the higher transaction costs of purchasing liquor, it would show up in the behavior of other consumers as well.

Becker writes that "A habit may be raised into an addiction by exposure to the habit itself. Certain habits, like drug use and heavy drinking, may reduce the attention to future consequences—there is no reason to assume discount rates on the future are just given and fixed."[42] Here, Becker tacitly assumes that the addicts' awareness of the future consequences is not impaired—simply that the consequences are given less weight in the utility function. But how can he tell the difference? To be sure, by stipulating that the drug works on the discounting and not on the beliefs, he can still claim that the addiction is rational, given the rational-choice premise that desires and preferences cannot be assessed as more or less rational. This cannot, however, be a sufficient reason for making the stipulation. What we observe is simply that the addict is less swayed by future consequences than he was before he took up the drug. In the "visceral theory of addiction" this effect is due to the Aristotelian form of weakness of will discussed above rather than to a change in discounting.[43]

Even if Becker is right on this point, I find his view hard to square with his idea of rational addicts. Earlier, I said that addiction may be rational for individuals who suffer the bad luck of genes or external influences that make them discount the future heavily. If the heavy discounting is due to their own behavior, however, matters are entirely different. In the BM model, individuals have perfect foresight. They ought to be able to predict, therefore, not only what addiction might do to their health (i), but also what it might to do their discount rate (iia). It might seem, therefore, as if Becker himself implicitly admits the irrationality of his rational addicts.

CHAPTER TWO

The Irrationality of Addiction – And Does It Matter?

Thomas Pogge

In a number of important and influential articles, Gary Becker and his collaborators have argued in recent years that addiction is perfectly rational.[1] In his contribution to the present volume, Jon Elster sets out to dispute this claim. My task here will be twofold. In the first part of this essay, I will critically examine the way Elster constructs the disagreement between the traditional view (defended by himself) and the revisionist view (defended by Becker et al.) as well as the arguments he adduces in favor of the former. In the second part, I will then explore whether this whole debate about the rationality of addiction has any practical importance for the social problems arising from addictive behaviors which we face in modern societies.

The Main Issue

As Elster reconstructs the debate, the traditional view and the revisionist view disagree about an empirical issue—about whether the actual social phenomenon of addiction, as it occurs in contemporary Western societies, arises from persons responding rationally to their situations. The traditional view, as defended by Elster, concedes that addiction *can* be rational—that the notion of a rational addict is neither incoherent nor empirically unrealizable among human agents. This view differs from the revisionist one in claiming that most actual cases of addiction involve irrationality. Seeing that what is in question here is both the rationality of becoming addicted and the rationality of remaining addicted, we can characterize the traditional view by two central claims: (1) most of those who risk addiction are irrational in taking this risk; and (2) most of those already addicted are irrational when servicing their habit. In order to understand the meaning of these two claims, we need to define the two key terms they employ: addiction and rationality.

What Is Addiction?

Taking for granted that a person can be addicted only to something that she has been exposed to, what are the criteria for deciding whether she is addicted or not? Elster discusses six factors that might be used to define addiction and, in the end, settles on two of these as being jointly constitutive of the phenomenon: A person is addicted to X if and only if he is both subject to *withdrawal* and liable to experience *cravings* for X and for the cessation of withdrawal.

Let me begin with the first of these two constitutive features. As Elster realizes, it is not necessary for a person to be addicted in order for her to actually undergo withdrawal. An alcoholic is no less an addict for managing to avoid even a single sober day. What is necessary for a person to be addicted is merely that she should be subject to withdrawal, or (more precisely) that, if she were unexposed to X for a significant period of time, she would undergo withdrawal. Since withdrawal involves displeasure, we can say that the statement "A person is subject to withdrawal" means at least that if that person were unexposed to X for a significant period of time, then she would experience displeasure—or, as Elster says more specifically, then her welfare would drop below her baseline welfare level. Elster has some difficulty in defining the relevant baseline, but I think what he has in mind is, intuitively speaking, the normal welfare level the person had before she became addicted (or the normal welfare level she would have, if she had not become addicted). Of course, we must not put things this way because it leads us to circular definitions (defining addiction in terms of withdrawal and then defining withdrawal in terms of addiction). But putting things correctly is complicated because different formulations may be required depending on the object of the addiction. One might say that the statement "A person is subject to heroin withdrawal" means that a week without heroin would be much worse for her now than a heroin-free week was for her before she ever tried heroin (or than a heroin-free week would be for her now, had she never tried heroin). For cases of food addiction (overeating), sex addiction, and coffee addiction one would need to find different formulations in the same spirit because here the normal baseline is presumably predicated on a life with modest amounts of food, coffee, or sex. But even the apparently simpler cases seem daunting enough. Consider a person who has been a regular user of heroin for four years. We can find out how badly she feels without regular heroin by depriving her of the drug for a week. But comparing her welfare level at the end of this week with her normal welfare level five years ago, or with the welfare level she would now have if she had never started on heroin, seems both difficult and somewhat irrelevant. Perhaps she was extremely depressed five years ago. And perhaps, had she not started on heroin, she and her husband would have stayed together in a singularly dull and unhappy marriage. It is tempting to throw in a quick "other things being equal" here, but this leads into even more remote subjunctives. How badly would her present week without heroin feel if she were still as depressed as she was five years ago or if she and her husband had stayed together despite her heroin consumption? How would she have felt five years ago if she had been as free of depression as she is now? How would she now feel if she had never started on heroin but she and her husband had split up anyway? It is silly to think that we must have answers to such questions in order to decide whether someone is addicted. So perhaps the best thing to say in the end is something like this: Being subject to heroin withdrawal means at least that, if one had no heroin for a week, then one would feel quite bad—much worse than how almost all people feel almost all of the time.

But if this is the best we can say, we face the difficulty that our notion of withdrawal becomes overly broad. Some persons are miserable if they are deprived for a week of seeing their spouse or of getting the news. Is that withdrawal? At this point, another condition discussed by Elster proves helpful. One is subject to withdrawal, he states, only if the pain from being unexposed for a given period becomes greater as the person's exposure increases. This is typically the case with users of heroin. The more heroin encounters they have had, the more unbearable they find it to be without heroin for a week. But this is hardly ever the case with persons who miss their spouses or the news. Their pain of deprivation remains constant or perhaps even declines.

But are there not cases where the love of another (perhaps of one's child) builds over time, so that a week without him does become progressively worse the longer one has loved him? Here a final condition mentioned by

Elster may be helpful. In cases of withdrawal, nonexposure becomes progressively worse even while exposure also becomes less pleasurable. As love builds over time, it may become harder and harder to be apart for a week—but this happens only in conjunction with it also becoming more and more delightful to be together. By contrast, a week without heroin becomes worse and worse the more often one has been exposed even while exposure to heroin becomes less pleasurable.

Taking all three elements together, we might then formulate Elster's definition of withdrawal as follows: The statement "A person is subject to withdrawal" means that, if he were unexposed to X for a significant period of time, (1) his welfare would drop below his baseline welfare level, (2) it would do so to an extent that increases with the number of past exposures, and this would happen even while (3) the pleasure derived from each exposure diminishes. Any person who is not subject to withdrawal in this sense does not count as being addicted to X.

Cravings are extremely powerful desires that are very difficult to resist. As in the case of withdrawal, what seems necessary for addiction is not that the addict should experience cravings, but merely that she be liable to experience cravings. A well-supplied addict need never experience any cravings at all. In the absence of renewed exposure, however, all addicts experience cravings. Such cravings are presumably of two kinds, which we can classify with Elster's useful terminology as *positive cravings* for X and *negative cravings* for the cessation of the pains of withdrawal. Cravings of both kinds create the desire for reexposure to X, so that the addict finds it difficult to resist acting in ways that promise renewed exposure. Any person who is not liable to experience cravings of these kinds should not be considered to be addicted. Conversely, someone does count as being addicted if she is subject to withdrawal and also liable to experience positive and negative cravings.[2]

What Is Rationality?

Elster works with a thin notion of rationality, pursuant to which a person is rational just in case her desires, beliefs, evidence, and conduct fit appropriately with one another. This thin conception of rationality is, as Elster says, "subjective through and through," in that it does not allow any external criticism of an agent's desires, beliefs, or conduct—no matter how outlandish these may be. Desires, beliefs, and conduct can be criticized as irrational only from the inside, that is, by appeal to the agent's own desires and beliefs. An agent is irrational, by the lights of the thin conception, only insofar as her desires, beliefs, or conduct in a particular situation do not fit with the totality of her own desires, beliefs, and evidence.

This thin notion of rationality contrasts with thicker notions which impose external constraints and desiderata on a rational agent's beliefs and desires, which require, for example, that rational agents hold mostly true beliefs, strive for a rich diversity of experiences (so that the desire to spend one's whole life at a slot machine is irrational), and/or seek to live in accordance with the categorical imperative (so that the desire to deceive others is irrational).[3] By invoking a thin notion of rationality, which supports no such external criticisms, Elster makes it harder for himself to show that addiction is irrational, and in this sense his choice is fair and appropriate. He suggests another reason for relying on the thin notion, which I will discuss below. Because thick notions of rationality hold conduct up to an external standard, their verdict may not reveal anything about the causal mechanism through which this conduct is brought about. Honest conduct may not be causally different from deceitful conduct (both, for example, may be motivated by a desire to succeed) just as shots that hit their target may not differ with respect to their causation from shots that miss.

Elster suggests that matters are different with the thin notion of rationality. Here the distinction between rationality and irrationality marks an empirical distinction between causal mechanisms. If he is correct, then the answer to the question of whether or not the conduct of addicts is, for the most part, rational has implications for how such conduct is caused. And such information about the causal mechanisms underlying addiction could be quite important for the question of how we as a society should best respond to the conduct of addicts. To the contrary, I will argue below that the distinction between rationality and irrationality (in the thin sense) does not mark a distinction between causal mechanisms and is therefore of no use in guiding our responses to phenomena such as addiction.

Elster claims, on the basis of such a thin notion of rationality, that no desires can be criticized as irrational. However, this claim is false for derivative desires, such as a stranded sailor's desire to catch and eat a particular beetle, a behavior which is wholly based on his desire to survive. If the sailor believes that the beetle is poisonous and that its consumption would kill him, then his (derivative) desire to eat the beetle (for the sake of surviving) is irrational.

Is it then true, at least of fundamental (nonderivative) desires, that these desires cannot be irrational? I think not. One may be irrational in develop-

ing or maintaining a certain fundamental desire if, according to one's beliefs, this desire will bring only frustration by, for example, forcing one to
forgo its fulfillment or else by forcing one to fulfill it at massive cost to the
fulfillment of one's other desires. A fundamental desire to walk around
naked may be an example. Given what we know about the world, having
this desire is irrational for almost anyone. It would be irrational to develop
it and irrational not to get rid of it to the extent that one can. Ironically,
David Hume, whom Elster adduces as a main proponent of the thin notion
of rationality, is quite clear about this point and advises his reader that, to
the extent that the reader has any "power of modelling his own dispositions," he should seek to cultivate the virtues praised in his society and
thus to become someone who truly desires to treat others with honesty
and kindness.[4] Other examples of fundamental desires that would (at least
for most persons under normal circumstances) be irrational even according to the thin conception of rationality are a desire for a low welfare level
or a desire for poverty. To be sure, a person is irrational only if he cultivates
a desire for poverty in conjunction with other desires whose fulfillment requires money. But this suffices to make the point that a fundamental desire
to be poor can be irrational by the thin conception.[5] Though contrary to
Elster, this point is helpful to his main objective (to vindicate the traditional view that addiction is irrational) because it opens a route to showing that, even on the thin conception of rationality, it is irrational for most
persons to have desires whose fulfillment involves the risk of addiction and
desires that are the result of addiction.

We have identified two ways in which a person may be irrational by the
thin conception in virtue of her desires. She may have derivative desires
that do not fit with her beliefs and fundamental desires (the desire to eat a
beetle she believes to be poisonous in order to survive), and she may have
disharmonious fundamental desires that, in the world as she believes it to
be, are bound to lead to severe frustration. What other forms of irrationality are there? How can a person be irrational even while her desires cannot
be criticized on the basis of the thin conception of rationality? There are
two possibilities, both recognized and discussed by Elster. First, an agent
may be irrational by holding beliefs that jar with the evidence he has.[6] For
example, knowing that most of those who have tried heroin have become
addicted, I nevertheless believe that if I try heroin, I will not become addicted. Such belief irrationality may involve a mere error in reasoning
("cold bias") or it may be inspired by desire ("hot bias") as in wishful
thinking, where the agent forms an unsupported belief simply because she

would like it to be true. Second, an agent's conduct may not be an optimal response to his beliefs and desires. Thus, it is irrational not to set out to go to the kitchen when one desires only food and also believes that the only accessible food is in the kitchen and that one is able to go there. There is a special case of the second kind of irrationality, which Elster treats separately: when the agent's evidence-gathering conduct is not an optimal response to her beliefs and desires. You are irrational in this way, for example, when you do not ask for directions even though you desire only to arrive quickly and you believe that asking would cost less time than it saves.

The thin notion of rationality thus can support charges of desire irrationality (which may be aimed both at derivative and at fundamental desires), charges of belief irrationality, and charges of conduct irrationality (including charges of nonoptimal evidence gathering).

Is Addiction Irrational?

Recall that the issue is supposed to be an empirical one. The question is whether most of those who actually risk addiction are irrational in taking this risk and whether most actual addicts are irrational when servicing their habit. Elster clearly recognizes that it can be rational to risk addiction and also rational not to quit. One example he gives is that of a coffee addiction in the context of a secure supply. Another example—which it may be interesting to add in light of Elster's previous work[7]—is that of deliberately addicting oneself in an effort to "tie oneself to the mast." Some people in the 1960s sought to addict themselves to drugs so as to prevent their future selves from being co-opted into "the Establishment." Elster asserts that most actual cases of risking addiction and most actual cases of not quitting involve irrationality. Becker, by contrast, holds that in most of these cases the agent is acting rationally or at least behaving as if she were rational. What empirical evidence might decide this dispute?

For reasons Elster gives, among others, it is extremely hard to diagnose conduct irrationality.[8] In order to find out whether an agent's conduct at time t is or is not an optimal response to her beliefs and desires at time t, we need to find out what her beliefs and desires are at time t. Ordinarily we infer these from her conduct. But using this procedure in the present context would beg our question. Such inferences would have to assume that her conduct is a plausible attempt to fulfill her desires, given her beliefs; but this is tantamount to assuming rationality, which is here at issue.

Since any given conduct can be explained as a rational response to some belief-desire sets and also as an irrational response to others, conduct alone will not disambiguate. You may think that we can just ask the agent what her beliefs and desires were at t, thus relying on her remembered introspection. This will surely work up to a point. But not very far. For whether what I did at t was rational depends not merely on what desires I had but also on how strong they were relative to one another. And this information is not easily available even to introspection. Let me give an example. I am among those typical males who, when in unfamiliar territory, often waste a lot of time seeking their destination in situations where most women would just ask for directions and find their way more quickly. Am I being irrational? I honestly do not know. To be sure, I do desire to get to my destination quickly. But I also desire to get there on my own and therefore have some aversion to asking. I can think of no way of ascertaining the strengths of these two desires for purposes of calculating whether my "strategy" of not asking is optimal for me.

The last example shows that it may be difficult to tell whether or not a person displays conduct irrationality—and this not just for analyzing the behavior of others (from the outside), but even for the person himself. But if we cannot assess even our own present conduct rationality, because we do not know the relative strengths of our own desires with any exactness, then we also cannot shape our own conduct so as to ensure its conduct rationality—at least not in most actual situations (as opposed to sparse laboratory conditions), where the choice among several available conduct options will affect the degree of fulfillment of several desires. And if we cannot so shape our own conduct, then most such conduct will probably display conduct irrationality to some degree. This will affect not merely trivial choices concerning travel arrangements, comparison shopping, and the like. It is likely that almost all of us have made suboptimal decisions about whom to marry, how many offspring to produce, which profession to choose, and where to live. Also almost all of us probably have made these decisions with too much research or too little research or suboptimal kinds of research—and also with a suboptimal kind and amount of metaresearch into how much and what kinds of research we should do. These points favor the traditional view. It is unlikely that those risking addiction have done exactly the optimal kinds and amounts of research in advance. But the point also tends severely to deflate the thrust of the traditional view. "So what?" one can respond, "The same is true of those who get married, those who have children, those who accept jobs, those who buy homes, and all the rest." If conduct irrationality is involved in almost everything we do, then it is not big news that it is involved in addiction as well.

This discussion shows, I believe, that we should think of conduct irrationality (and perhaps of other forms of irrationality as well) as a matter of degree—and this possibly in two dimensions. We should ask not merely whether a person's conduct is rational or irrational, but also (1) how (cognitively) accessible a more rational course of conduct is to the agent and (2) how much more rational his alternative options are. Both of these issues concern matters of degree. The first question asks how certain the agent could have been at the time of choice that some alternative option was superior (a better response to his beliefs and desires). The second question asks how much better this alternative option could have been estimated to be by the agent at the time. Only with such a more nuanced account of conduct irrationality can we hope to reach significant conclusions. We might hope to show, for example, that addicts and those risking addiction tend to be more irrational than the rest of us, more reckless and negligent—that they do, modulo their beliefs and desires, far too little or far too much research and research of quite the wrong kind. But such a finding would require a lot more evidence, and of a more sophisticated kind, than seems to be available thus far.

Elster's defense of the traditional view is more convincing when he discusses belief irrationality. But even here his argument is less than compelling. Yes, gambling addicts often believe that, even in what we call "games of pure chance," the past holds clues to predicting the future (the "gambler's fallacy"). And this belief is, of course, false. But this is beside the point—the relevant question is whether the agent's belief is irrational, that is, jars with the agent's own evidence. We all have a great deal of evidence that induction works in a wide range of domains. Thus, there is at least some reason to surmise—by an induction upon successful inductions—that it also works with games. Persons believing this will, of course, think of these not as games of pure chance, but as games of fortune in something like Machiavelli's sense. (Fortune, in this view, is like that dated, sexist conception of woman: "Damn hard to figure out, but if you manage to treat her right, Boy! will she make you happy!") This being the case, their belief that the past holds clues to the future can then be perfectly rational.[9]

The claim that addiction tends to involve belief irrationality runs into similar problems in the case of drugs. People taking drugs may indeed greatly underestimate the risks, but they may do so without irrationality.

They may simply not trust the information put out by the Establishment, having repeatedly found such information to be untrustworthy in the past. ("They lied to us about Marijuana and the Contras, why should we trust what they say about cocaine?").

Ironically, the most promising defense of the traditional view may be the one that Elster does not explore: the argument that, in most cases, addiction involves desire irrationality. In the world as we know it, strong desires for cigarettes, gambling, and drugs tend to lead to massive frustration, either of these desires themselves, if one chooses not to fulfill them, or of other, important and irrepressible desires otherwise. It is therefore irrational for most persons to develop such desires or not to weaken and erase them to the extent that they can. In contrast to the charge of conduct irrationality, this charge really hits home, because it is not true of most or even many human desires that they involve desire irrationality—certainly not to anything like the same extent.

Why Should It Matter?

What is the point of speculating about the rationality or irrationality of addiction? Elster does not say. But he suggests that the rational/irrational distinction, as it is drawn by the thin conception of rationality, marks an empirical distinction of causal mechanism and that learning whether addiction is rational or not might therefore help us in designing social policies to deal with it. This suggestion is implied in Elster's extended methodological remarks about appropriate concept formation (which are, however, primarily addressed to the concept of addiction). Elster's general point there is that, "for scientific purposes" we should seek to develop concepts that group items together on the basis of "causal commonalities" (or homologies) rather than "phenomenological similarities" (or analogies). He concludes therefore that "it is not very useful to define addiction phenomenologically as, say, 'irresistible craving,' if different cravings arise in different ways and are overcome or prevented by different means." I am assuming that Elster takes himself to be honoring the same methodological principle when he specifies the concept of rationality. I may be wrong in assuming this, and I may then be wrong to believe that Elster's interest in the irrationality of addiction is connected to the hope of coming to a better understanding of the causes of addiction and thereby to aid the search for better social policies in response to addictive behaviors. This hope is worth discussing nevertheless, because it is one plausible reason for taking an interest in that topic.

If the general thrust of my remarks in the first section of this essay is on track, the hope may be too optimistic. There may be specific irrationalities, such as wishful thinking, which display a genuine causal commonality and are open to attack by a single strategy. But nothing like this can be said of the broader notion of irrationality. Recall my point that much of our ordinary life is pervaded by conduct irrationality resulting quite simply from the fact that we do not have anything like exact information about the relative strengths of even our own desires. If this is right, then whether we make the rational decision (that is, whether we aim correctly) is to a significant extent subject to luck, just as whether we end up doing the right thing (that is, hit the target). There is no more reason to believe there to be any causal commonality among conduct that happens to be rational than there is reason to believe there to be a causal commonality among conduct that happens to meet some external constraints or desiderata.

The thin conception of rationality thus runs into the same sort of problem as thicker conceptions. One way to solve this problem might be to retreat to an even thinner conception of rationality. This conception would not require that conduct be an optimal response to the agent's beliefs and desires, but rather that conduct be an optimal response to the agent's beliefs including his beliefs about his desires (and, in particular, about their relative strengths). Similarly, this conception would not require that derivative desires be an optimal response to the agent's beliefs and fundamental desires, but rather that they be an optimal response to the agent's beliefs including his beliefs about his fundamental desires. But, if we go down this road, where is the thinning supposed to end? Do I display belief irrationality only when the beliefs I take myself to have do not fit with the evidence I take myself to have, or perhaps only when I *believe* that my beliefs do not to fit with my evidence? And instead of saying that the agent's conduct and derivative desires must be an optimal response to . . . , should we not really be saying that the agent's believed conduct and believed derivative desires must be believed by her to be an optimal response to . . . ? I cannot explore these fascinating possibilities further here, but will merely reiterate my worry that even the thin conception of rationality employed by Elster is too thick to identify causal commonalities.

Another daunting problem on the road to a successful causal analysis of rational and irrational agents is the empirical testing of appropriate hypotheses. In order to diagnose any form of rationality or irrationality, according to the thin conception, we must be able to ascertain what the agent's beliefs and desires are.[10] (In order to diagnose belief [ir]rationality, we must also be able to ascertain what the agent's evidence is; and in order to diagnose conduct [ir]rationality, we must also be able to ascertain what the agent's conduct is, that is, under what description she is choosing to do what she is doing. The same action may be an instance of "buying something from Karl to help him out" and "buying lottery tickets to build wealth." Whether the action is rational or not may depend on the description under which the agent chooses it.) Moreover, we must find out not merely whether a person desires X and believes Y, but also how strongly she desires X (relative to her other desires) and how firmly she believes Y. Obtaining such detailed information about an agent's beliefs and desires (as well as about her evidence and conduct) is, however, extremely difficult— at least in anything other than very sparse laboratory settings, where it may be possible to create situations in which most of the agent's beliefs and desires are rendered irrelevant. Thus, I see no credible evidence from behavioral science at present either for or against the empirical claims that most people who risk addiction are irrational in taking this risk and that most addicts are irrational when servicing their habit. I would like to see a credible analysis of a single addict, who, in a testable and justifiable way, would ascertain all her relevant beliefs and the strengths with which she holds them, all her relevant desires and their relative strengths, and all her relevant evidence, and who would then relate all this information to the decision that made her risk addiction or made her remain addicted. If someone could do this, we could test the hypothesis that the decision was irrational. I am convinced that no attempt at such an analysis would survive peer review. Without success along these lines, however, I also see no credible evidence for or against the claim that beliefs and desires play a central causal role in the development of human lives, or for or against the claim that the distinction between rationality and irrationality (as drawn by the thin conception of rationality or by even thinner ones) marks an empirical distinction of causal mechanisms.

If the distinction between rational and irrational conduct did indeed give us some insight into the causal mechanism underlying human living, then one would like to learn something about the practical value of such insight. Do rational and irrational persons differ in how, or how easily, they can be influenced? Can the Elster/Becker dispute be connected, for example, to differential predictions about the effects of various strategies for curbing the demand for hard drugs: driving up prices, providing empirical information, supplying methadone, increasing criminal penalties, rewarding abstention, offering group therapy, and so forth? Again, I see little promise in this direction.

There is quite a different significance one might attach to the question of whether addiction is irrational. One may think that criminalizing addictive behaviors is morally more acceptable if most persons who become and remain addicted are irrational in doing so. To be sure, there are other justifications for the war on drugs—justifications stressing the burdens that addictive behaviors impose on others. But these justifications are vulnerable in two ways. First, it is often claimed that these burdens are for the most part not the result of the behavior as such but the result of its criminalization. Second, it can also be claimed that most addictive behaviors do not impose greater burdens on others than many other enjoyable activities which are not criminalized (jet skiing, say). The claim that addiction is irrational might provide welcome relief. It could support the idea that drug taking, even when done on the agent's own initiative, may in most cases be bad for the agent himself. (With most other activities, by contrast, we accept the presumption that a person is the best judge of her own good. We generally consider what persons do voluntarily as being good for them.) The claim of irrationality could also support the further idea that, because drug takers are not fully competent, regulating them for their own good is more acceptable than it would be in the case of presumably mentally more competent skydivers, whose liberty must not be restricted for their own sake.

This line of argument (of which there is no hint in Elster's essay) squarely runs afoul of my skeptical conclusion in this chapter. So far, we lack a precise and operational conception of rationality which would allow us to measure in a reliable way whether addicts are, by and large, more irrational than the rest of us.

PART II

LIBERAL
POLITICAL
MORALITY
AND DRUGS

CHAPTER THREE

Liberty and Drugs

MICHAEL MOORE

I approach the topic of liberty in part by analyzing one perennial question facing legislators, namely, the question of whether to criminalize the recreational use of drugs. Although much of the essay works through the analysis in the abstract, the last section deals concretely with drugs and illuminates the general points made during the more abstract analysis.

My approach to the topic of the liberty presupposes much that I do not argue for here. First, I assume that the only proper end of punishment is the achievement of retributive justice. We should punish individuals because, and only because, they morally deserve punishment for what they have done, intended, or risked. Second, I by and large assume that a retributive theory of punishment demands a legal-moralist theory of legislation. On legislative issues, a legal moralist believes that all and only morally wrongful actions and morally culpable states of mind should be criminally punishable. A retributivist should be a legal moralist because, without moral wrongdoing or moral culpability, what is one to pay for by one's suffering of punishment?

Despite these retributivist/legal-moralist assumptions, I urge that legislators may nonetheless be quite liberal in the restrictions they place on what should be made criminal. Whether this is so in part depends on two substantive moral judgments: (1) How extensive are our moral obligations? and (2) Is there some value of liberty such that some of those actions that we are plainly obligated not to perform should not be criminalized? This essay approaches both questions under the guise of a right to liberty.

Anything that could be called a general right to liberty has proved elusive to the considerable number of philosophers who have pursued it. The nature of such a general right is elusive for two sorts of reasons. The first is conceptual: it is not clear that one coherent conception of liberty exists. To many people, the word "liberty" is both ambiguous and vague. It is ambiguous insofar as it refers to quite different sorts of things, such as political liberty versus the metaphysical liberty of free will, or negative liberty conceived of as absence of restraint versus positive liberty seen as the power to achieve something. "Liberty" is vague insofar as the kinds and degrees of restraint that deny liberty are underspecified. For example, do private threats, internal cravings, criminal sanctions, and tempting offers, all equally erode the recipient's liberty?

The second reason for the elusiveness of any general right to liberty is normative: even if some one thing is specified by "liberty" with enough precision to be worth talking about, it is not clear that there is anything intelligibly good about liberty as such. The liberty to be a murderer seems of little or no value, and thus liberty as such—without specifying the acts one is at liberty to do—seems to have little or no value. The liberty of speaking freely may have great value, for example, but that might be because of the existence of a particular right of free speech, not because there is a general right of liberty.

Attempting to make the general right to liberty less elusive is one of the tasks undertaken in this chapter. Such an undertaking is perhaps particularly useful in the context of the question of drug policy, for even amongst those theorists sympathetic to a rights-based approach to drugs, the analysis tends to be long on application of the concept of liberty but short on its explication.[1]

Political philosophy maximizes its chances of arriving at better answers when its questions are well framed, so I shall spend a moment framing my questions. In the first place, the right to liberty whose nature interests me is a moral right, not a legal (or more specifically, an American Constitutional) right. Although the badly misnamed "privacy" decisions of the U.S. Supreme Court for the last 30 years are the best known locus for any general right to liberty, such a legal right is not my concern. True enough, those who share my theory of constitutional interpretation will take the constitutional right to follow closely the underlying moral right.[2] But the nature of the latter is my concern, leaving it to another day to argue for the constitutional enforcement of such a moral right. This means that it is out of place to argue from U.S. Supreme Court precedents as if they gave an authoritative exposition of liberty. In this ethical enquiry such decisions have only the weight of the persuasiveness of the reasons offered within them, nothing more.

I thus focus this essay on a theory of legislation. Such a theory has as its audience legislators and those who would advise legislators, not courts. Part of the legislative role such a theory defines includes the protection of the moral rights of those citizens who are subject to the legislation in question, even if one's theory of adjudication is (like my own) one that also assigns to courts this duty to respect moral rights.

Second, I do not argue that people have moral rights. Rather, I assume that there are such moral entities as rights and frame my enquiry by asking whether a general right to liberty is among them. Since the very idea of a right (which the right holder may waive or choose to exercise) already involves the idea of liberty, this may seem like assuming an answer to my question before I start.[3] Yet one could easily assume that people have rights but still deny that any general right to liberty exists. On this view, there are only liberties, each of which has to be argued for individually because they are not part of some general right of liberty.[4]

This latter issue is worth pausing over because it is an important one. If there are only distinct liberties, each protecting distinct interests or goals, then liberty does not exist in the sense I care about. For on the latter view, "liberty" would be strictly abbreviatory of the rights persons possess, but those rights themselves would have nothing in common save that they are rights. For liberty to be a distinct right, it has to be more than the freedom involved whenever we have a right.

Third, I shall not engage in any lengthy conceptual analysis as to the primary or focal concept of liberty. Rather, I shall cut through this Gordian knot with a simple stipulative definition that adopts the traditional, negative definition of liberty: liberty is the absence of constraint, and political liberty is the absence of coercive legal sanctions. Unlike lexical definitions, stipulative definitions are not hostage to others' usage of the term being defined. To judge a stipulative definition is, thus, not to judge its accuracy as a report of any linguistic fact. Rather, my stipulation must be judged by how well it captures some salient moral facts. If liberty in the traditional sense that I intend captures a value or values usefully clustered together, that will justify my stipulation in the only way it can be justified.

Such "Alexandrian" solutions may seem inadequate with knotty problems such as that of negative versus positive liberty. Yet stipulations like mine do not solve such problems; rather, they begin an approach to such problems. My hypothesis is that absence of legal coercion may have unitary value. If so, my stipulation serves its purposes in forcing us to focus on that value. The enquiries temporarily put aside are then left open: is there a relationship between such values as are protected by negative political liberty and some larger value (such as the overall ability to choose) captured by the notion of positive liberty? And is the power to choose dependent on the absence of private threats and the presence of economic opportunities, as much as it is dependent upon the absence of legal coercion? And does the power to choose ultimately involve some kind of "libertarian" metaphysics? I haven't resolved any of these questions with my stipulative definition; only deferred them on the hypothesis (yet to be vindicated) that we are dealing with a problem that, like a pair of trousers, requires us to put one leg on at a time.

The fourth and last clarification of my enterprise in this chapter is to see that there is an alternative way of framing my enquiry that is revealing. Often the enquiry about a general *right* to liberty of citizens is framed as an enquiry about the general *duty* of legislators to respect certain principled limits in the use of state coercion. When the enquiry is put in the latter way, it is often put as a matter of finding the "limits of state action," the "limits of the criminal sanction," or the "limits of legislation."[5] These two questions— of citizen right and legislative duty—are highly related but not quite the same. They are related because here (although not generally)[6] it is plausible to suppose the correlativity thesis to be true: for any citizen right to liberty there is a correlative legislative duty, and vice versa. Even so, there is a difference between a right to liberty that is basic (from which the legislative duty is the mere correlative) and a right to liberty that is derived from the more basic legislative duty. Despite this difference, I intend the phrase "right to liberty" to encompass both such sorts of rights, if they exist.

Some Problems with Any General Right to Liberty

If political liberty is conceived of in the traditional way as the absence of governmental coercion, then a general right to such liberty would be a right generally to be free of coercive laws. It would approximate Louis Brandeis's famous definition of the general right of privacy: it is "the most comprehensive of rights and the right most valued by civilized men, the right to be let alone."[7]

Save for perhaps some extreme anarchists, everyone recognizes immediately the problem with such a right: it would abrogate those restraints at the heart of morality and civil society. As Robert Bork puts it: "A general right of freedom . . . is a manifest impossibility. Such a right would posit a state of nature, and its law would be that of the jungle."[8] Any theory that implies that we each have a right to murder, steal, and the like, at will, is a nonstarter.

There are only two strategies open to the defender of a general right to liberty (when that right is conceived as the right to be free of governmental coercion). One is to circumscribe the kinds of actions protected by the right so that acts of violence and such are outside the circle of liberty. The other is to weaken the right so that it can be overridden by other legitimate interests such as the interest of citizens in their bodily integrity.

The time-honored maxim for libertarians pursuing the first strategy is that the circle of liberty includes only those actions that are compatible with a like liberty for others.[9] The idea here is that liberty (of others) limits liberty (for each), so that no other value is needed to trump liberty—for if there were some such other value, then the right to liberty would apply to all actions but would be overridden in some cases, which is the second strategy. To pursue this first strategy is thus to hold that "only liberty can limit liberty," another time-honored maxim of libertarian philosophy.

Despite its distinguished lineage, the only reason that these maxims (and the strategy they instantiate) are not plainly false is that they are fuzzy enough to lack any clear truth value. Ask yourself this question: Why is not a Hobbesian society of war of all against all compatible with these maxims? Is not the liberty of one person to rob, murder, and pillage compatible with a like liberty for everyone else? The libertarian has to say no, that to harm others in these ways takes away their liberty and therefore such actions are not compatible with a like liberty for all.

This libertarian rejoinder makes very little sense, because there is a shift in the meaning of liberty when one equates being killed or being robbed with a loss of *liberty*. These are not losses of negative liberty, for the dead and the poor are just as free of governmental restraint after they are killed or robbed as they were before. When libertarians use the phrase "a like liberty for all," therefore, they must mean positive liberty, the power or opportunity to choose to do a variety of things, a power that death and poverty do diminish. Yet with this play on the meaning of "liberty," what sense are we to make of the maxim? In what sense are the powers or opportunities of others similar to the freedom from governmental restraint that we are to test under the maxim?

Perhaps we are to compare the amount of opportunity a given absence of governmental coercion will engender for one person with the amount of opportunity it will engender for everyone else. Since the amount of opportunities each of us has depends on many things besides the absence of legal coercion, this comparison cannot be between the total opportunity sets of all of us without failing completely as a test of negative liberty. Yet if we ask only about the *increment* of opportunity that the absence of legal coercion provides for each of us, then we find that the increment is the same—laws forbidding sleeping under the bridges of Paris equally affect the incremental opportunities of the rich and the poor to find shelter, so long as we ignore the obvious differences in the total opportunities of each of them with respect to housing.

The upshot is that we gain no clear sense that harming others diminishes their liberty. Moreover, even if one could give some sense to the equation, isn't the equation disingenuous in any event? After all, the equation suggests that what is wrong with murder is that it deprives the victim of his liberty. If we take liberty in the positive sense, then we mean that what is wrong with causing another to die is that death ends our choosing opportunities. And isn't this a bit of overintellectualization, the giving of one reason too many?[10] What's wrong with murder is that you end someone's life. Their life surely has a value beyond simply the opportunity to choose. Yet if life has value independent of its opportunities for choice, so that murder is wrong independently of its affect on positive liberty, then it is not liberty that is limiting liberty when we justify laws forbidding murder. Rather, it is another value, the value of life, that is trumping liberty, and to say this is to abandon the first strategy for the second.

The second strategy concedes that the circle of liberty extends to all actions, murderous ones as much as any others. Yet this second kind of defense of a general right to liberty argues that the right is justifiably overridden in cases of violence to others. This concession, too, leads to problems.

There are a variety of problems with any such fully general but easily overridable right. One is that which concerns Samuel Freeman: "surely there is nothing intrinsically valuable about the natural liberty to do wrong. . . . To assign intrinsic value to natural liberty as such would imply that legal restrictions per se diminish this intrinsic value and that there is ethical loss with the imposition of any legal restriction. But what could that loss be in the case of legal restrictions on clearly unjust or evil conduct?"[11]

A slightly different concern is Ronald Dworkin's: "we can maintain that idea only by so watering down the idea of a right that the right to liberty is something hardly worth having at all. . . . I can have a political right to liberty . . . only in such a weak sense of right that the so called right to liberty is not competitive with strong rights. . . . In any strong sense of right . . . there exists no general right to liberty at all."[12] Another concern is that of Joseph Raz: "We feel intuitively that some liberties are more important than others. The restriction of the more important liberties is a greater restriction of liberty than that of the less important ones."[13]

This chorus of criticisms concedes conceptually that we can isolate an element common to the freedoms to murder, to drive on a certain street, to choose with whom we will be sexually intimate—namely, the absence of state coercion. Still, what could be intelligibly thought good about this common element? Moreover, how could the possession of this goodness explain why we override the liberty to do some actions so much more easily than others? What common measure of liberty would find there to be little of it in the freedom to murder, and a lot of it in the freedom to choose sexual intimates? One needs to find a good common to all unfettered actions, no matter what their moral quality, and yet that good must be elastic enough to yield to other goods when we legally prohibit morally bad actions and not yield when the state purports to regulate morally good actions. Moreover, even if we find such a marvelously elastic, yet intelligible and common intrinsic good, how do we base a *right* on such a good when it loses so often and so easily to other goods?

The Presumption of Liberty

Despite these worries, there is an intelligible set of values served by negative liberty as such, values which apply equally to all actions no matter what their moral quality. One of these values we can get at in the following way. The touchstone of our culpability assessments of persons lies in the choices they make. Although such choices need not be contra-causally free, and although such choices need not proceed from the chooser's character, choice whose object is a moral wrong makes us blamable. Moreover, the conditions of excuse reveal that it is only when we have a fair opportunity to avoid choosing to do wrong that our choices make us fully and actually culpable. A threshold of fair opportunity, in other words, is a precondition of moral culpability.

None of this strictly requires that we find opportunities (above the baseline required for responsibility) to be intrinsically good. Nonetheless, such does seem to me to be the case. Having more opportunities is good because it allows us to have a large and more diverse set of projects with some realistic hope of success. As Rawls once put it in describing such liberty as a "primary good," the having of more opportunities is good because it allows you to get what you want, whatever it may be that you want.[14] If this is so, then positive liberty, conceived of in terms of size of the opportunity set, is one of the intrinsic goods to which freedom from legal coercion is a means.

This of course reduces negative liberty to an instrumental good, not an intrinsic good, but as an interest that applies to all actions, that is the most that can be said for negative liberty. Three other sets of values exist, however, to which negative liberty is the means, and these add somewhat to its strength.

One of these is what I shall call Kantian autonomy. According to Kant, morality cares at least as much about the reasons for which people act as about the actions they perform.[15] Specifically, the highest moral value attaches to good actions chosen by the agent because they are good, not to good actions alone. Accordingly, legal coercion always diminishes the possibility of attaining morality's highest value because the law's coercive sanctions induce many to act for those merely prudential reasons (fear of punishment) that have no moral worth.

Kantian autonomy operates rather differently than does positive liberty in giving weight to the instrumental value of negative liberty. Unlike the case of positive liberty, there is no value to be found in autonomous wrongful action as there is value in increased opportunities even when such opportunities are used to choose badly. Indeed, in Kant's sense the idea of autonomous *wrongful* action makes no sense. Autonomous action in this sense is doing right for the right reasons. Such autonomous decision—in the sense of acting out of a concern for morality and not merely out of prudence—is an important moral desideratum, and state coercion always renders such decision making less likely. Therefore, against the good of punishing and preventing any given wrongful behavior by criminal prohibition must be balanced the bad of preventing some autonomously chosen *rightful* behavior. It is the lost possibility of autonomously chosen rightful behavior that is the autonomy-related cost of criminal prohibition. Negative liberty is thus always good in that it serves to preserve this possibility of autonomously chosen rightful behavior.

The last two goods to which negative liberty is instrumental are utilitarian in character. One stems from a nearly universal preference of persons to make their own decisions free of the interference of others, including the state. One might even think that at some formative periods of their lives, persons must be free of such coercive influences in order to have preferences worth summing in a utilitarian calculus.

Another set of utilitarian considerations are to be found in the familiar factors mentioned in the "overcriminalization" debate of the 1960s and 1970s in America. Criminal prohibitions spend scarce social resources. If they are enforced, that taps those resources directly; if they are not enforced, that has less direct costs in terms of loss of respect for law and the like.

These four sets of values all combine to justify caution in the use of the criminal sanction. They thus all respond to Samuel Freeman's earlier expressed worry that nothing intelligibly good can be found in freedom from state coercion about morally odious actions. Negative liberty is a common means to these four items, each of which is good, even when the act one is free to do is morally odious. Moreover, this list of goods served by negative liberty also answer's Joseph Raz's worry. Each of these four goods is generally served, across the board, by negative liberty attaching to all actions. A general liberty interest that was common to all actions but elastic enough to have great strength for some actions and very little strength for others would be a puzzle. The negative liberty justified by its service of these four values is not elastic in this way; it uniformly applies to all actions.[16] Loss of such negative liberty is a constant cost to criminal prohibitions, to those that prohibit murder as well as to those that prohibit jaywalking.

With respect to Ronald Dworkin's criticism, it *is* a misnomer to speak of there being a general *right* to be free of legal coercion, for a right that loses so often is best not thought of as a right at all. It is better to conceptualize the instrumental goodness of negative liberty as a "presumption of liberty."[17] Contrary to what the critics of this way of conceptualizing it have thought,[18] "presumption" accurately captures the idea that there is always some reason not to legally coerce behavior, namely, that to do so diminishes the opportunities of those coerced, diminishes the likelihood of autonomously chosen rightful behavior, and so forth. It is the constancy and the relative weakness of this liberty interest that the phrase "presumption of liberty," is designed to capture.

The presumption of liberty should not be confused with two other demands that we might reasonably impose on criminal legislation. One of these is the demand of rationality in legislation. One might well think that simple rationality demands that legislation be reasoned. Actions done without reasons are done without reason, that is, are arational if not irrational. Yet rationality does not generate the strength of restriction on coercive legislation that is generated by the presumption of liberty. Rationality requires that legislators not enact legislation as they might write poetry in their spare time, for no reason save its own pleasure. But rationality (in the sense of having *some* reason) does not generate any kind of requirement that the reasons produced in favor of a piece of legislation have any amount of weight or force to them. Rather, legislation is reasoned (and rational in this sense) whenever some intelligibly good end is plausibly served by the legislation in question, irrespective of how compelling the end is.

Another distinct demand is that placed by the conservative principle, which holds that, other things being equal, the status quo is to be preserved. Such a principle is backed by the ideas that change always involves effort, that institutional change always disrupts expectations, and that the past has a presumption of wisdom in its favor; accordingly, the principle further holds, unless there is some off-setting benefit, change in law is to be avoided.[19] Yet what this principle demands is that legislation *changing the status quo* have some moderately compelling reason behind it. There is no demand from this source that *coercive* legislation be justified. After all, repealing legislation that removes coercive sanctions for some behavior would also have to have good reasons to justify it, by this Burkean kind of conservative principle.[20]

The presumption of liberty is not only distinct from the principles of rationality and Burkean conservatism, it is also stronger in the demands it places on a legislator to justify any use of coercive legal sanctions. The strong preference that most people have for liberty, the need of it to have preferences worth caring about, the desirability of maximal opportunities for choice, the goodness of rightly motivated choice, and the direct and indirect social costs of legal coercion, all combine to create a demand that legislators have quite good reasons to criminalize behavior.

With seriously immoral behavior that demand is easily satisfied. But for minor immoralities like breaking most promises, breaking confidentialities, and committing infidelities of various kinds, the presumption of liberty should stay the legislative hand. Punishing such immoralities is a good, but it is not so good that it outweighs the instrumental good of the liberty to be sacrificed for it.

Despite this not insignificant bite to the presumption of liberty, it remains true that it does not satisfy most libertarians' ambitions for a right to liberty. In the first place, it is sufficiently undemanding that it should not be thought of as a *right* at all. In the second place, it does not conceive of negative liberty as an intrinsic good, and this merely instrumental status does not match the hopes of a more ambitious libertarianism. I accordingly turn to two stronger rights to liberty, which I distinguish as a derived right and a basic right.

The Derived Right to Liberty

The derived right attaches to all actions, no matter what their moral status. This is not a right to do any action, nor is it a right to have any action unfettered by governmental restraint. Rather, the right is that of every citizen not to have his or her behavior regulated by the government *for the wrong reasons*. For example, one does not have a right to murder. Nor does one have the right that the government not prohibit and punish murder. Rather, one has a right that the government not prohibit murder because, say, of a view that murder is bad for the murderer's chances of salvation.

The right against improperly motivated legislation owes its content to the fact that the right is not basic but is the correlative of a more basic *duty* on the part of legislators to enact legislation for certain reasons but not others. Every legislator requires a theory of the legislative role, just as every judge requires a theory of the judicial role. A crucial part of such a theory for a legislator is a theory of the permissible aims of coercive legislation. The derived right to liberty is no more than a right that legislators hew to their duties in this respect.

Such a right does nothing to further the libertarian ambition that there be a sphere of action immune to governmental regulation. (This ambition I will explore further in the next section.) Nor does the derived right have anything to do with the presumption of liberty. In thinking of the derived right to liberty we need to put aside any general liberty weakly protecting all actions in favor of a more absolute right of a different content. This is the right to properly motivated use of state coercion, the right I call the derived right to liberty.

The content of the derived right to liberty is given in terms of the reasons that are improper to motivate coercive legislation. The most famous description of those improper reasons has been that given by John Stuart

Mill: that the behavior being prohibited would cause harm to someone other than the actor (and any consensual partners) sufficiently justifies legal prohibition, and no other reason is permissible.[21] On the latter part of Mill's thought specifically: neither the immorality of the targeted conduct, nor harm to the actor from such behavior, nor the offense such behavior might offer others, constitute reasons permissibly motivating coercive legislation.[22]

The most famous objection to Mill's scheme has been J. F. Stephen's conceptual one, to the effect that Mill could not separate actions affecting only the actor (which are not the state's business) from those affecting others (which can be the state's business). As Stephen put it: "The truth is that the principle about self-protection and self-regarding acts . . . is radically vicious. It assumes that some acts regard the agent only, and that some regard other people. In fact, by far the most important part of our conduct regards both ourselves and others."[23]

Insofar as "self-regarding acts" are defined by Mill as acts that affect no one but the actor, Stephen observed that "every act that we do either does or may affect both ourselves and others" and that therefore Mill's "distinction . . . is altogether fallacious and unfounded."[24] For example, riding a motorcycle without wearing a helmet may most obviously affect the rider, yet his injury also affects others because they see his bloody mishap and are made sick; or he is insufficiently insured and requires public medical assistance; or his injury causes suffering to his loved ones.

We shall have occasion in the next section to examine this familiar objection of Stephen's in light of Mill's anticipatory responses to it. For now, however, it is sufficient to see that Stephen's objection is wide of the mark insofar as Mill is talking about proper legislative ends. As such, Mill faces no need to isolate a sphere of action that is immune to state regulation and thus Mill has no need to isolate actions that affect no one save the actor. As a theory of proper legislative aims, Mill's injunction is to legislators to not aim at the good of the actor himself, the offense his behavior causes to others, and such. Motorcycle riders have no derived right to be free of coercive requirements of helmets; they only have the derived right that the state not coerce them into wearing helmets for their own protection, or because it offends others to see helmetless motorcycle accidents, or for some other illegitimate reason. Even if no action is without its harmful effects on others, those effects are not an inevitable part of the reasons for which the legislature prohibits the action. Thus a legislator can meaningfully be enjoined by Mill not to aim at preventing certain effects of certain kinds of actions.

The real worry about Mill's fleshing out of the legislature's duty, and of the correlative, derived right to liberty, is a normative worry, not a conceptual one. The normative worry is often encountered by Millian liberals when conservatives press the following four sorts of questions: (1) What makes harm to others a good reason to prohibit actions? Is it not the fact that causing most forms of harm to others is *morally wrong* that licenses state coercion? Indeed, isn't any morally useful concept of harm tied to the notion of a state of affairs that it is morally wrong to bring about?[25] So are not the limits of moral obligation (and thus of wrongness) the only true boundary to our liberty of action, to which limits the harm principle is but an imperfect proxy? (2) Further, how can we punish any omissions (which cause no harms although they may constitute failures to prevent harms) except on the ground that in some cases we are morally obligated not to omit to help? Indeed, does not Mill himself distinguish punishable omissions from the bulk of omissions precisely on the grounds of moral obligation and thus moral wrongness?[26] (3) Further, if there are harmless wrongdoings—to use Joel Feinberg's well-chosen phrase to name moral wrongs which harm no one—do not we properly punish some of them, such as cruelty to animals, defamation of the dead, distortion of history, extinction of beauty, and so forth?[27] If one admits that these are proper prohibitions, and one admits that they should apply across the board even when no person would be harmed by the prohibited behavior, must not one admit that the aim is to prohibit simply because these behaviors are morally odious? (4) Finally, if there are causings of harm that are not morally wrong such as knowingly bankrupting an economic competitor, do we not properly refuse to prohibit them? And does this not show again that the proper concern of a legislator is moral wrongdoing, not harmful effects on others?

I find this fourfold conservative fusillade difficult to duck. Indeed, most of it I have come to accept, distant as it is from the Millian liberalism with which I began political philosophy. The theory of proper legislative aim to which these suggestions point states that legislators should prohibit morally wrong actions and that they should do so precisely because those actions are morally wrongful. This is often called the legal-moralist theory of legislation, since it aims to legislate morality into law.

Perhaps Mill's most basic mistake here was to attempt to derive a theory of proper legislative aim from a defective theory of punishment based in utilitarianism. I refer not to Mill's well-known difficulty in moving logically from the utilitarian principle—with its well-known tendency to produce uncertain calculations of utility—to the resolute and crisp injunctions of his harm principle.[28] Rather, I refer to utilitarianism's inevitable dealing in harms rather than wrongs.

A properly retributive theory of punishment does not make this mistake. Retributivism, when combined both with the principle of legality and the insight that law as law does not even prima facie obligate citizen obedience, yields the legal-moralist theory of proper legislative aim: all and only moral wrongs should be prohibited by the criminal law, for the reason that such actions (or mental states) are wrongful (or culpable) and deserve punishment.

Liberal political theorists have often been tempted to think that one can justify principled limits to the reach of criminal legislation without taking a position on the proper theory of punishment. While this is true for the presumption of liberty and the basic right to liberty, both of which operate externally to constrain the attainment of the ends of punishment, it is not true for the derived right to liberty. Some theory of punishment has to be relied upon here because it is only in light of criminal law's general aims that one can derive what is permissible legislative motivation and, also, what is impermissible legislative motivation. For the derived right of liberty, there can be no shortcut that truncates this chain of inference.

If the legal-moralist theory of proper legislative aim is correct, then we quickly reach the question of substantive ethics: What are our moral obligations? On the legal-moralist theory of proper legislative aim (to which the derived right to liberty is the correlative), this central question of ethics is also determinative of the content of our derived right to liberty.

If one holds to a purely consequentialist theory about morality, then the content of any derived right to liberty contracts to the vanishing point. For one of the unsettling complications of a purely consequentialist ethics is that we are never free of the demands of moral obligation in our actions. Put another way, unbridled consequentialism always obligates us to maximize good consequences and minimize bad ones in everything we do. This is, as is commonly objected, only a morality for saints.

At the very least, such a morality has to be tempered with agent-relative permissions to do actions that predictably will not be optimal in their consequences.[29] Moreover, the consequentialist principle is (up to a certain threshold of horrendous consequences) preempted by agent-relative obligations, obligations that are imposed by morality on each of us not to do certain actions even when such actions would be productive of quite good consequences.

If this is correct so far, then all actions can be divided into three classes. (1) There are actions that we are not obligated to do or not do. Such actions are not the subject of any agent-relative prohibition or requirement, and they are the subject of an agent-relative permission allowing us not to optimize consequences. Much of our daily routine surely falls into this class of morally indifferent actions. (2) There are actions we are obligated to do, or to refrain from doing, but such obligation is only based on the consequentialist principle. These actions are not, that is, the subject of any agent-relative prohibition or requirement. Such consequentially based obligations are characteristically less stringent than are the obligations created by agent-relative prohibitions. (3) There are actions like the torturing of innocents, about which we have quite stringent obligations because such obligations are derived from an agent-relative prohibition or requirement.

The implications of this view of morality for the legal-moralist legislator should be obvious. Citizens have a derived right to liberty protecting them against the criminalization of actions in the first category. On my view of sex, for example, morality by and large does not concern itself with much of what passes for social mores in our society on the topic of sex. It trivializes morality to think that it obligates us about what organ we insert into what orifice of what gender of what species. Accordingly, retributivist/legal-moralist legislatures have no reason to criminalize the wide variety of sexual practices currently prohibited in many Anglo-American jurisdictions, and citizens have the moral right to have them not do so.

Only behaviors in the second two categories can be within the purview of a properly motivated legislator. Even here, however, it is worth noting that much of the behavior in the second category is not subject to moral obligations of sufficient stringency that the good of their punishment outweighs the goods protected by the presumption of liberty discussed in the last section. For example, our consequentially derived, positive obligations to render aid to strangers in distress are usually too weak to be used as the basis of justifying overriding the presumption of liberty. Our criminal law thus rightly draws back from criminalizing much of such positive obligations in the name of liberty.

If morality has the shape I suppose it to have in these ways, then a legal-moralist theory of legislation will be quite liberal in its content even if not in its form. Such a theory would not prohibit anything that is not immoral, and it would not prohibit much that is not so seriously immoral that the badness of not punishing it outweighed the good protected by the presumption of liberty.[30]

If morality has the shape that I think it to have, then the differences with Millian liberalism are less than first meets the eye. Although promoting morality is not excluded as an improper motive, as it is for classical liberals, nonetheless the limited view of what constitutes serious immoralities keeps much of our behavior unregulatable by the criminal law.

The difference between the legal-moralist liberal and the classical liberal thus lies not so much in the content of recommended restrictions on legislation, but in the form of the argument for those restrictions. Classical liberals refuse to challenge conservatives on first-order moral issues like the immorality of homosexuality, abortion, or drug usage; they prefer second-order arguments showing why the first-order arguments are inappropriate aims of legislation in a secular democracy. By contrast, legal-moralist liberals concede the appropriateness of legislating morality but have quite limited views in what they see that morality requiring.

Legal-moralist liberals thus do not exclude the aim of promoting morality through state coercion, as do classical liberals. What about paternalistically motivated legislation, the chief thing excluded by Mill's harm principle? Is the moral or other good of the actor whose behavior is being regulated permissible motivation for the regulation? Consider the moral good of the actor first and notice that there are two cases where the moral good of the actor seemingly could be enhanced by state coercion. One case is where the action coerced is morally obligatory, and the other is where the action coerced is supererogatory or otherwise virtuous but is not obligatory.

With respect to the prohibition and punishment of actions that are morally obligatory, some retributivists would not distinguish between the legislative motivation of punishing culpable wrongdoers through enacted law and the legislative motivation of promoting the moral good of offenders. Failing one's obligations is never good for an individual's moral ledger, and some retributivists have argued that only punishment can balance that individual's accounts. This is the familiar "restoration of the balance" metaphor of such retributivists. Such retributivists find the paternalistic concern with the moral welfare of offenders to be a part of the retributivist demand that moral wrong be punished, so that to aim for the one is to aim for the other.[31] For such retributivists there is no reason to deny this kind of moral paternalism a place among the permissible ends of criminal legislation.

It seems to me that such paternalistic versions of retributivism are motivated by a desire to put a nicer face on retributivism than it can in fact bear.

We rightly punish culpable wrongdoers because they deserve it, but I doubt that they deserve it because receipt of such punishment will make them better. At least, I doubt this if "better" means anything other than "to have received their just deserts." If "better" means that they come to feel guilty, see the error of their ways, accept morality's binding force, are no longer disposed to violate others rights, and so forth, then I doubt that punishment often achieves this, and I doubt that we really believe it does when we justify retributivism to ourselves. Furthermore, if making the offender better through punishment only means "he no longer deserves punishment because he has received his just deserts," then I would consign such paternalism to the scrap heap of discarded metaphors about retributivism.

The upshot is that legislators should not aim at the moral welfare of offenders in their framing of criminal prohibitions, even when that moral welfare involves an offender's breach of moral obligations. Still less should the legal-moralist legislator aim to promote the moral welfare of citizens when what is involved is in fact a moral virtue, not dereliction of moral duty.

Supererogatory but not obligatory actions are those actions which we have no moral duty to do but which would make us more virtuous if we were to do them. Camus' *The Fall* deals with this kind of action, for the protagonist in the novel fails to jump in to save a woman drowning in the Seine.[32] Given the risks involved in any rescue attempt, it is plausible to suppose that there is no duty to rescue in these circumstances. Still, attempting a rescue would be very much to the man's credit, morally speaking.

One might well think that the world would be a morally better place if people were more virtuous than they are, and that the promotion of that moral good could justify state coercion. One problem with coercing virtue lies in the difficulty of doing so, at least in the first instance. This is due to the fact that virtuous action depends heavily on the motivation of the actor. Gift giving is an extreme example, for to coerce the otherwise virtuous action of charitable giving is to make the action something else, something like paying a tax rather than giving a gift. It is perhaps true that long application of coercive sanctions to induce virtuous behavior might change the habits of the people coerced for the better, so that they eventually come to give gifts for their own sake and not for fear of punishment. Yet such educative by-products of punishment are rather incidental, difficult to effect, and haphazard.

In any event, suppose, at least *arguendo*, that some gain in virtue could be achieved in the long term by coercing virtuous behavior. Even so, it would be wrong for the state to punish people for failures of virtue. Fundamentally, such people do no wrong. Failing none of their moral obligations, such people do not deserve to be punished, and the right to be free of undeserved punishment trumps whatever gains of virtue could be induced by prohibiting less than virtuous, but nonobligatory, behavior.

Now suppose, alternatively, that virtue cannot be coercively induced, even in the long run. One might yet think that the world is better if virtuous actions are done (even if no virtue is achieved because such acts are done for the wrong reasons). It is somewhat better, for example, if people in peril are rescued by those who risk life or limb to rescue them, even if the rescuers exhibit no virtue in their actions because they did them only out of fear of legal sanctions. This would not be a more virtuous world, but only a better one because more innocent lives would be preserved than would be lost in failed rescue attempts. Yet notice how heavy would be the price of this somewhat better world. First, there is the cost *in virtue* because of the cost in autonomy attendant upon legal coercion: some who would have rescued for morally worthy reasons of beneficence now rescue for nonvirtuous, prudential reasons. Second, not all people will be induced by the law to undertake risky rescues, and those persons will be punished even though they do not deserve to be punished because they have not failed in any of their moral obligations. As before, each person's right to be free of undeserved punishment trumps whatever gains there might be in attempting to coerce virtuous behavior and thereby bringing about at least a better (if not a more virtuous) state of affairs.

Now let us consider nonmoral paternalism, where the state aims to enhance the welfare of a class of citizens even against that class's judgment of what that welfare is. Even if it is neither obligatory nor supererogatory to refrain from smoking, may the state aim at the happiness of smokers by banning it? Mill's answer was of course no, but for reasons that are hard to sustain in a post-Freudian world. Few today would unqualifiedly subscribe to Mill's view that each person is the best judge of what makes him happy or satisfied.[33] The fallibility of judgment of each of us on even fundamental matters like choice of marriage partners is too painfully obvious to reassert Mill's confident proclamation that we are each the supreme epistemic authority on what we truly desire.

The most that can be said for the epistemic argument is that the officials who make up the state too are fallible in their judgments of welfare, and that the relevant question is that of comparative epistemic positions. Certainly on many questions, some individuals are better situated epistemically to judge the conditions of their own happiness than is the state. Yet this is a topic-by-topic and individual-by-individual comparison that need not favor each individual's judgment. One might well think that cigarette smokers would be happier over the course of their lifetime if they did not smoke, even if that goes against their own judgments.

Despite this epistemic judgment, my own sense is that it would be wrong to criminalize smoking in private (where there is no secondary smoke harm to others, so that the aim of the prohibition would be the health of the smoker). It would be wrong because smoking in private is not morally wrong, nor is it even lacking in virtue. There is then no retributive justice to be achieved by punishing such behavior.[34]

It is easy to misapprehend the limits placed on the use of criminal sanctions by the retributive end of punishment. Critics of retributivism often charge that as an exclusive end of punishment retributivism would not allow prohibitions against traffic offenses or against a variety of other acts that solve coordination problems but are not moral wrongs. Yet the charge is groundless, because we each have a moral obligation to solve coordination problems to achieve important goods such as personal safety, so that the use of a criminal statute to set the salient conventions solving such problems may be appropriate on retributivist grounds.

Smoking in private, however, is not an act that requires that kind of coordination with the acts of others such that some public good is achieved that we all have an obligation to maintain. The only good in such a case is the welfare of the individual, and his failure to achieve that good is not morally wrong and therefore not punishable.

From the point of view of a thorough-going perfectionist/retributivist, any form of paternalistic motivation is thus out of bounds. What about the last of the Mill/Feinberg categories of possible legislative motivation, that of offense to others? May a legislature prohibit certain actions on the ground that such actions offend some number of citizens, either morally or otherwise? In one sense this question is easy to answer for a legal-moralist liberal, and in that sense of the question the answer is a resounding "No." If the view in question is that a majority's offense at certain behavior makes that behavior morally wrong[35]—because morality just is what the majority in society take offense at—then such a view must be rejected. What society believes is wrong is one thing, but what *is* wrong is something else entirely. Any meta-ethics that denies this basic distinction between mores versus morality, conventional versus critical morality, what is believed to be right and what is right, is hopelessly relativistic and is to be rejected out of hand.[36] The retributive theory of punishment, and its accompanying legal-moralist theory of legislation, enjoins legislators to prohibit actions that are morally wrong, no matter if such actions offend few citizens because they believe them to be wrong; conversely, these theories enjoin legislators not to prohibit actions that are not morally wrong, no matter how many citizens erroneously believe such actions to be morally wrong and take offense accordingly at such actions.

A second and more interesting view of offense as a reason for legislation emerges if we put aside relativistic ethics. It is plausible to suppose that the unnecessary causing of some forms of offense to other people is morally wrong; that is, it is really wrong and not just believed to be wrong by the society. Shocking the sensibilities or the senses of others for no good reason in some instances is wrong because unnecessary. The public changing of sanitary napkins on Feinberg's bus of offense is one well-known example, as are some cases of overloud music, public oral sex, and the like.[37] That the offense taken depends on cultural sensibilities that vary from place to place makes such impositions no less wrong, and there is no meta-ethical relativism in such judgments. The wrong is harming other people's sensibilities unnecessarily. Culture is relevant to the question of whether there are such sensibilities to be harmed, not to the question of whether it is right or wrong to harm them.

Despite this, a perfectionist liberal should be suspicious of offense as a justification of criminal legislation. For while it may be morally wrong to offend the sensibilities of others unnecessarily, it is not usually deeply immoral to do so. Usually, therefore, except for the grossest of behaviors, the good of punishing such minor immoralities is insufficient to overcome the presumption of liberty and the values it represents.

I conclude that the derived right to liberty is not as weak as it may have seemed when we began. True, it does not immunize any sphere of action from state coercion; it equally protects all potential actions from badly motivated state coercion. And it is true that the crisp limits on permissible legislative motivation that Mill defined with his harm principle cannot be defended. Yet for retributivists about punishment such as myself, the derived right of liberty has a good deal of life. By limiting the permissible aim of state coercion to the punishment of moral wrongs, paternalistically motivated prohibitions are impermissible, as are most prohibitions enacted to prevent moral offense to the majority in a society. By accepting the view that morality regards much of our conduct as beyond the bounds of obligation, much of the criminalization of sexual practices is also illegitimate even when those criminal prohibitions are aimed to prevent and punish these supposed immoralities.

The Basic Right to Liberty

Despite the robustness of both the presumption of liberty, and the derived right to liberty, there remains the sense that there is a stronger right to liberty, one that does immunize a sphere of action from all state regulation save for regulation justified by the most compelling of reasons. This stronger right to liberty is what the United States Supreme Court has been struggling to define since its *Griswold* decision in 1965, albeit often under the unhelpful rubric of "decisional privacy."[38]

Consider first a woman's right to have an abortion at issue in *Roe v. Wade*.[39] Concede for purposes of argument that a fetus is a full-blown person from the date of its conception. Such concession makes the killing of the fetus a quite serious wrong, not at all outweighed by the inconveniences of carrying the fetus to term if it is not aborted. Even so, at least in some cases such as rape, many people share Judy Thomson's intuition that the woman has the right to be free of state coercion that would force her not to do this great wrong.[40] Such a right trumps an admittedly legitimate reason for the use of state coercion, namely, the punishment of what (on the *arguendo* concession here assumed) would be morally wrong. Such a right thus cannot be a part of the presumption of liberty, for it is no minor immorality that is outweighed by the instrumental goodness of liberty. Nor is such a right derivative of some failure of legislative duty, because the legislature could be seeking to prohibit abortion because and only because it is morally wrong.

Notice that much the same can be said about suicide, mistakes in parenting, and certain seriously harmful speech. Suicide is often deeply hurtful to persons other than the actor, persons to whom the actor is bound by many ties and to whom the actor owes an obligation to stay alive. At the very least, we owe such duties to our children. We do a serious wrong to such people when we commit suicide, yet my firm sense is that no one (including the state) has the right to prevent someone from killing themselves.

Similarly, there are some people who clearly should never be parents because they are so lousy at it that they raise extraordinarily damaged and defective human beings. There are many kinds of parental abuse apart from physical and sexual abuse. Some parents make their favoritism between siblings apparent on a daily basis, causing the less favored to develop feelings of worthlessness and despair. Some parents, when they divorce, poison their children against the other parent. Some parents make servants out of their children, others spoil them rotten. Some parents dominate their children's ambition, telling them exactly what they will be in all aspects of life. Some imbue them with religious beliefs that can only be described as deranged; and some simply ignore their children emotionally, leaving them to find what warmth they can on their own. Given the dependence and blind trust of children on their parents, these are deeply immoral behaviors. Yet we tend to think that the state should not use the criminal law to punish such wrongs.

Lastly, consider free speech. As the early critics of Mill noted, often speech causes injuries to others. Revealing a damaging truth from the distant past of a now well-respected and virtuous citizen, so that the life he has so painstakingly reconstructed is destroyed, is an example of such harmful speech.[41] Imposing this harm on someone purely for motives of private gain is a plausible candidate for a serious moral wrong, and thus the punishment of such wrong is a legitimate state concern. Despite this, the right to be free of state coercion on the content of speech trumps this otherwise legitimate state concern.

It may seem that these examples need not betoken the existence of some right to liberty stronger than the presumption of liberty earlier delineated. After all, the goods that justify the presumption of liberty can also outweigh legitimate reasons prima facie justifying state coercion, and perhaps this explains why the state ought not to coerce citizens out of abortion, suicide, parental abuse, or harmful speech.

Yet there are two reasons to doubt that the presumption of liberty can explain our intuitions about such cases. One is the absoluteness we may feel about the liberty right that does not match the contingency of the balance of values being suggested to explain it. That balance is between the evil of wrongful actions going unpunished (if the acts are not prohibited) versus the evil of frustrating the goods behind the presumption of liberty (if the acts are prohibited). The delicacy and contingency of this balance does not match the certitude and absoluteness many feel about the liberty rights in question.

The second reason lies in the degree of moral wrongness that attaches to these actions, at least on the suppositions imagined. If fetuses are persons, then abortion is a form of active killing; if it is morally wrong, it is quite seriously so. Indeed, if such a wrong is performed by anyone other than the mother or by one who has her consent, the wrong done is so serious one may liken it to deliberate murder.[42] Likewise, to destroy the happiness of loved ones forever by suicide, to ruin a child forever, and to destroy someone's life by speaking about their distant past for profit or even mere pleasure, are serious moral wrongs. The goods to which negative liberty is instrumental and which give rise to the presumption of liberty seem too light a counterweight to outweigh the desirability of punishing moral wrongs of this degree of seriousness. Such goods plausibly outweigh the good of punishing the (usually) minor moral wrongs of lies, broken promises, breaches of confidence, most offensive behaviors, and even the breach of our comparatively weak, positive obligations to help strangers in peril.[43] But the goods behind the presumption of liberty lose hands down to the good of punishing murder, rape, theft, and other serious moral wrongs. If abortion and the like are more like the latter than the former, it takes something stronger than the presumption of liberty to trump the state's justification for use of coercion.

It may seem puzzling to think that morality could contain within it *both* the obligation on one person not to do some action and a liberty right of that person with respect to that very same action. It may even seem as though there is a formal contradiction in such examples. If these purported to be examples where it would be morally wrong of an actor to do some action A, yet the actor was morally permitted (had the right) to do A, then there would be a formal contradiction. Yet notice this is not what is being claimed about abortion rights, suicide rights, parental rights, or the right of free speech. If it is morally wrong of the actor to do A, then the actor is obligated not to do A; and if the actor is obligated not to do A, then it cannot be the case that the actor is permitted to do A. All this can be true, and yet it is consistent to think that it would be wrong of the state to coerce the actor to fulfill her obligation not to do A. The liberty right in question is no more than that the state not coerce the actor to fulfill her obligation. There is nothing formally contradictory about these two moral injunctions.

Still, even if there is no formal contradiction, one may think that it is a peculiar morality that makes wrong both an action, A, and another action, B, that would prevent A. If A is wrong, must not B be at least permissible, and perhaps even obligatory? Despite the apparent force of this query, any liberty worth having has to give us the right not to be interfered with as we do wrong. Notice that this is true of the presumption of liberty as much as it is of the basic right discussed in this section. If our liberty ends where our obligations begin, then, in an important sense, we have no liberty.[44]

The apparent oddness is perhaps due to confusion of the liberty right not to be interfered with in the doing of some wrong, with two other situations, both of which Heidi Hurd helpfully labels as violations of her "correspondence thesis."[45] Hurd rightly finds odd any morality that makes us "moral gladiators" against one another, so that one person's moral success can be attained only through some other person's moral failure. Such morality would be odd, not in the sense that it formally contradicted itself, but rather, in the sense that it would look like a cruel joke played on the human race by an unkindly god. Thus, if morality obligated one person to do some action, A, and also obligated another to prevent A; or if it permitted one person to do action, A, and also permitted or obligated another to prevent A, then Hurd's correspondence thesis would be violated.

Notice that the liberty right here in question is not odd in this way, for there is no gladiatorial aspect to such a right. One actor by hypothesis is obligated not to do some wrongful act, A, but no other actor is obligated or permitted to force the first actor not to do A. That would be gladiatorial and thus odd in this sense. On the contrary, if there is the liberty right I hypothesize, the second actor is obligated not to interfere with the first actor's choice, whether that is to do right or wrong. The second actor's moral success (in not interfering) is compatible with the first actor's moral success (in not doing A), for it is up to the latter whether he will succeed or fail. This is not a gladiatorial combat, but rather, the kind of restraint in allowing another to find his way, a restraint that is distinctive of liberty.

If such a basic right to liberty is both intuitive and not self-refuting, the next question is how we are to generalize from examples such as abortion so as to describe some *general* sphere of liberty of action that is immune from otherwise quite legitimate state coercion. Such a general sphere of liberty will be normatively plausible only if we can also find some value other than those behind the presumption of liberty to back up such a strong immunity from state coercion.

In seeking such a sphere and the value behind it, we should again start with John Stuart Mill. The motivational reading I earlier gave Mill's *On Liberty* is only one plausible reading. An equally plausible alternative interpretation is that Mill did intend to mark out a basic right to liberty with his harm principle, so that actions that harmfully affect no one other than the actor and his consensual partners cannot be prohibited by the state for any reason.

So construed, J. F. Stephen's old objection now comes into its own. The objection, it will be recalled, was that no action done in a society of persons is without its effects on others, and further, that no action that has a harmful effect on the actor will be without harmful effects on the others.

There have been two lines of defense of Mill against this familiar charge, both of which are suggested in Mill's essay *On Liberty*. The first I shall call the mechanical line of defense. Mill said that "there is a sphere of action in which society . . . has, if any, only an indirect interest." That sphere, he went on, included "all that portion of a person's life and conduct which affects only himself," with the qualification that "when I say only himself, I mean directly, and in the first instance: for whatever affects himself, may affect others *through* himself."[46] Mill's suggestion is that we limit ourselves to those proximate or direct effects when we ask whether an action affects only the actor. Those acts which injure those who care about the actor because they are acts which injure the actor are self-regarding acts, on this criterion, and may not be prohibited by the state. This limitation allows Mill to "fully admit that the mischief which a person does to himself, may seriously affect, both through their sympathies and their interests, those nearly connected with him" without conceding that such acts are anything but self-regarding.[47]

Mill also suggests a mechanical limitation distinct from the limitation to proximate effects. Some actions "primarily" concern the actor only, others "chiefly" concern society.[48] Mill's suggestion seems to be that we can sum all the effects of any action, and divide actions by whether their chief, primary, or major effects are on the actor himself or on others.

There are obvious difficulties with drawing a workable line with either of these suggestions, but the main difficulty with them lies elsewhere. However patched up, they seem unlikely to draw the line of permissible state coercion in an intuitive place. Surely the first and most direct effect of the self-mutilation of the draft dodger or the insurance defrauder is the injury to self; yet equally surely, those actions affect others enough (however indirectly) to justify state coercion against those actions. Conversely, the most direct effect of an abortion is to kill the fetus, yet the basic right to liberty may well immunize the woman's decision from state coercion despite this direct effect on another.

The second line of defense abandons a mechanical line for a moral one.

On this interpretation of Mill's distinction, it is not any effect on others that matters, but rather an effect injurious to a distinct *interest* of someone other than the actor. This was John Rees's well known interpretation of Mill's harm principle,[49] and it has been adopted by Joel Feinberg in his qualified defense of Mill insofar as Feinberg defines harms to others as set-backs to their interests.[50] Mill's actual language is important. Our liberty ends, he said when we injure "the interests of one another; or rather, certain interests, which either by express legal provision or by tacit understanding, ought to be considered as rights."[51] We leave our sphere of liberty, in other words, when our conduct causes that kind of harm to another's interests that he ought to have a legal right against suffering.

It should be apparent that this cannot serve as a way to define a basic right to liberty. If others ought to have a legal right to protection of a certain interest, then the actor ought to have a legal obligation not to do the action that unjustifiably injures that interest; that is, in such a situation the actor is outside his protected sphere of liberty. Yet what is the criterion for when injuries to the interests of others is of such kind or magnitude that they ought to have a legal right to protection? Without telling us this, Mill's criterion tells us nothing. Mill cannot mean that others ought to have a legal right to protection whenever the actor has a moral obligation not to so act, for then our liberty begins only where our obligations end, and we have no basic right to liberty. In cases such as abortion, suicide, free speech, or even good Samaritanism to strangers, our freedom from state coercion does not end where our obligations begin, for we ought to be free of state interference even when we are doing the wrong thing. It is the wrongness of such actions that gives the state good reason to legislate against them, which is why it takes liberty to trump this otherwise legitimate state interest.

Perhaps we should leave out Mill's rights qualification. Then the sphere of strongly protected liberty would be defined by actions that injure the interests of others (without regard to the unhelpful, further requirement that what is meant is only such injury to such interests as warrant legal protection). Yet this moral criterion will not work either. Surely fetuses, potential suicides, and those in peril have interests in continuing to live, just as children have interests in living a flourishing life, and just as people with a dark past have interests in continued secrecy. It is the insuring of such interests that grounds our moral obligation not to act in the requisite ways. If the basic right to liberty protects us in such cases anyway, it cannot be defined as a right that ends where other's interests begin.

We need thus some line other than Mill's harm principle, however construed, to demarcate the sphere of action in which we have the right to be free of state coercion even if we act wrongfully. One possibility is to revert to some kind of indirect utilitarianism so revived in our own time by Louis Schwartz, Sandy Kadish, Norval Morris, and Herbert Packer.[52] With this kind of utilitarianism in mind, we can isolate a class of morally wrongful behaviors that nonetheless should be immune from state prohibition because the costs of prohibition will usually outweigh any gains in punishing immoral behavior. Actions that are typically performed in private so that there are no nonparticipant witnesses, actions that have little direct effect on others besides the participants, so that they are "victimless crimes," and actions that are so strongly motivated that they will continue to take place even if legally prohibited, all are said to have a familiar litany of enforcement costs, which are typically higher for behaviors with these attributes than for behaviors without them. The conclusion is that the state should not criminalize such strongly motivated, private, consensual behaviors as prostitution, deviant sex, alcohol, tobacco, and (arguably) drugs, and citizens ought to have the correlative legal right to have them not do so.

As a rule of thumb, this seems roughly right, but I must make two points. First, it is only a rule of thumb about how the calculation of costs and benefits usually comes out. As such, it cannot match the certitude about liberty we may feel in cases like abortion or free speech. Second, even as a rule of thumb it is even roughly right only in those instances when the behavior in question is not seriously immoral. If one took the view that smoking, drinking, deviant sex, prostitution, or recreational drug use, for example, were all deeply immoral activities, then it is far from obvious that the enforcement costs would outweigh the punishment of such behavior made possible by legal prohibition.

The most that can be made of this utilitarian line is thus of a somewhat stronger presumption of liberty for behaviors with these four characteristics: where the immorality of a given behavior is small, yet the enforcement costs are high because of the private, strongly motivated, and consensual nature of the conduct, legislators ought to eschew prohibition, and citizens have the correlative right to have them do so. Like the presumption of liberty generally, however, this utility-based "right" is not capable of the bite demanded by a strong right to be free of state coercion even when doing seriously immoral actions.

A third tradition attempting to draw a line demarcating a sphere of strongly protected liberty uses the line between acts and omissions. Some libertarians would argue that at least part of the domain immune to state coercion is the domain of omissions.[53] The state can prohibit us from doing certain actions, but it may not require us to do certain actions through prohibiting the corresponding omissions.

There is plainly some appeal to this libertarian idea, but to define a basic right of liberty around it overstates it. To begin with, this could not be a complete definition of such a right because it would seriously *understate* the extent of our liberty. To say that the state may prohibit any action is far too expansive of state power. Abortion, suicide, many forms of parental abuse, and harmful speech are actions, yet any basic right to liberty should encompass them. Second, a complete freedom from positive legal requirements overstates the extent of our liberty. By my lights, we should not be free of state coercion with respect to rescuing our own child, for such rescue is neither a merely supererogatory act on our part nor is it only weakly obligatory. It is a strong moral obligation on the part of each of us, and I see no intuitively plausible restriction on the state's power to coerce us to conform to such strong obligations. Of course, often our positive moral obligations are weak enough that the costs of prohibition outweighs the good achieved by prohibition. But this much the presumption of liberty already protects, and in just these terms.

I come thus to the fourth and last way of defining the sphere of action protected by a basic right to liberty. The United States Supreme Court has been the most convenient expositor of this fourth way of defining the content of a basic right to liberty. This is so, even though the Court is ultimately concerned with the definition of American constitutional rights, not in the first instance moral rights. Yet the Court has sought to define a constitutional right in which " a certain private sphere of individual liberty will be kept largely beyond the reach of government,"[54] and the Court has recognized that such a constitutional right is based on an identical moral right that is "older than the Bill of Rights" in our Constitution.[55] Thus the Court has been engaged for thirty years in precisely the kind of political philosophy that is our concern here.

The Court has given various expressions to the "sphere of individual liberty" largely immune to governmental regulation. In *Roe* and *Griswold* themselves, the Court rather sparely noted that only those rights to make choices that are "fundamental" or "basic" are included in this protected sphere. In *Eisenstadt* this was fleshed out slightly: the sphere includes "matters so fundamentally affecting a person as the decision whether to bear or beget a child."[56] Only in the dissenting opinions of Justices Blackmun and

Stevens in *Bowers* v. *Hardwick* do we get any real attempt to articulate the boundaries of the sphere of protected liberty.

Justice Stevens continued to flesh out the idea of basic or fundamental decisions immune to state regulation in terms of the effect of such decisions on the decision maker's own life: the individual has the "right to make certain unusually important decisions that will affect his own, or his family's, destiny."[57] Thus, because the decisions over whether to conceive a child (*Griswold*), whether to carry it to term (*Roe*), and with whom and in what way one will be sexually intimate (*Bowers*), all have large effects on one's life, they are strongly protected decisions.

Perhaps Justice Blackmun had such a purely causal analysis in mind when he, too, described the sphere of strongly protected liberty in terms of decisions that "form so central a part of an individual's life," and when he partially defined centrality in terms of a decision that "contributes so powerfully to the happiness of individuals." Yet more likely, centrality to one's life is to be given a rather different reading. A decision is central, or important (or fundamental, or basic), not because it has major consequences for one's life, but because it determines the very sort of person one will become. In Blackmun's language, these are decisions that alter "dramatically an individual's self-definition";[58] protection of such decisions protects one's "ability independently to define one's identity";[59] these are decisions that are "central to . . . the development of human personality."[60]

What Blackmun was driving at was the idea that some decisions make us who we are and, in that sense, are self-defining. John Stuart Mill had the same idea insofar as he defended liberty on the grounds that we have to be allowed to make those choices about what we shall desire, feel, and believe, on pain of our having no character at all: "A person whose desires and impulses are his own . . . is said to have a character. One whose desires and impulses are not his own, has no character, no more than a steam-engine has a character."[61] Our desires, feelings, and beliefs are not our own, according to Mill, if they are merely the product of social coercion or mere conforming imitation of social convention: "He who lets the world . . . choose his plan of life for him has no need of any other faculty than the apelike one of imitation. . . . But what will be his comparative worth as a human being?"[62]

Both Blackmun and Mill are articulating a version of one of Aristotle's ideals, the ideal of the self-made individual in a distinctly noneconomic sense of the phrase. It is the ideal of each of us choosing our characters without undue influence of others (including the heavy-handed influence of state coercion). It is the ideal of the autonomous individual freely choosing the kind of person she will be, in a sense of autonomy that is considerably richer than the spare, Kantian notion (of acting for right reasons) that I employed as one of the goods justifying the presumption of negative liberty.

Aristotle thought that we choose our character as we choose all the many particular actions that cause us to be who we are. This is not the kind of choice I have in mind here, however. Being free of state coercion in making all the choices we make in daily life is a good, the good I explored in terms of positive liberty and its justification of the presumption of liberty. What is needed to make out a sphere of choices strongly immunized against state coercion is some line separating the choices meriting this extra protection from all the others. If we were to follow the suggestions of some members of the United States Supreme Court, we should draw this line in terms of choices so fundamental that they affect our identity, that is, in terms of what are called our "self-defining" choices.

There are two ways of conceptualizing the idea of self-defining choices. One is objective and harks back to the causal notions of Justice Stevens: some choices have more impact on our lives and, in that sense, such choices are more determinative of our character than others. Decisions about who we marry, whether to become a parent, what schools and courses of study to pursue, how to raise our children, what careers to pursue, when and how to die, have a lot more impact on our lives than decisions about where to take a vacation, or which route we take to work. The other conceptualization is subjective in that character is the object of our choice and not simply the product of it. That is, on this view, self-defining choices involve mental states (of desire, belief, and intention) whose objects are not actions but are further mental states or general traits of character.[63] On this view, our choices to become more considerate, to count material things less, to be more caring toward others, to believe the best about people, or to become more trustworthy, are self-defining choices. Correspondingly, choices to do some particular kind of action, to visit our parents tonight, to ignore evidence of a disreputable sort about a friend, and not to disclose a friend's secret to another, are not self-defining choices because the objects of such choices are particular actions.

There are problems with either of these views. A minor problem with the objective or purely causal conceptualization is its degree of vagueness. Except for those existentialists who believed that a few large choices determine the rest of our lives, most of us rightly sense that the degree of causal impact choices may have on a life varies along a smooth continuum. Still, this is minor problem in the sense that all line-drawing problems are minor. A whole great big bunch of stones plainly makes up a heap even if one cannot precisely say how many stones it takes to make a heap.

More serious is the seeming fortuity lurking in the fact that some choices have very large impacts upon our lives. Watching a particular movie, reading a particular book, deciding to switch airlines at the last moment from a plane that, as it turns out, crashes, deciding to pick up your Social Security check on a day when the Social Security office is bombed, all can change one's life forever. The fortuity of the degree of causal impact any choice may have does not match our intuitive sense that some choices are more worthy of protection than others.

One might think that this problem can be eliminated by saying that any particular choice that instantiates a type of choice that typically has a large impact on persons' lives is a character-forming choice, and therefore, is subject to the protections of the strong right to liberty. Yet without some restrictions on types of choices beyond simple causal judgments, any particular choice that has a large impact on the subject's life is an instance of this generalized type, making the category too broad. Take the choice of a person's route to work where the route chosen produces an accident and confinement to a wheelchair for life. This choice is not only an instance of the general type "choosing one's route to work," a type which typically does not include choices having a large impact on one's life, but also, in this case, an instance of the general type "choosing a route in the circumstance that one or more possible routes will result in disaster if chosen," a type which typically does include choices having a large impact.

One might reply that the actor did not choose to court disaster by her selection of route, but this is to leave the causal question—what effects does a choice produce—for the subjective question, what was the object of the choice? This takes us to the second and subjective conceptualization of a self-defining choice. It is only choices where the choosing subject knows of the relevant circumstances and of her power to alter her life, and chooses in light of that knowledge, that we have a self-defining choice protected by the basic right to liberty. One who chooses her route to work in ignorance of the life-changing potential of her choice does not make a self-defining choice, despite it being a choice that alters her life forever.

Unfortunately, the subjective conceptualization of self-defining choices seems to protect large numbers of trivial choices, too. If I choose to believe a friend on a given occasion, resolve not to think of some obsessionally re-curring melody, or choose to still my rage at a sudden remark, these are trivial choices even though their objects are mental states and not actions. Needed is some restriction in the objects of the choices beyond simply the restriction to mental states or character traits. Needed is a restriction to those choices that the choosing subject knows will have a broad impact over a long term on her life, or at least to those that she intends will have such an impact (recognizing the possibility of a weakness of will known to the subject herself).

If self-defining choices is the line we are to draw, then two interrelated questions spring to mind. One is whether, as a matter of psychology, such choices are really possible for us. The other is why unfettered ability to make such kinds of choices should have such value that it defines a moral *right* to liberty, and not just the normal presumption in favor of liberty.

Turning to the first of these two questions, elsewhere I have sought to put away one sense in which a person might say that we *cannot* choose our character. This was the incompatibilist's contra-causal sense of "can," where we can do something only if there are no causes of our doing it (other than our own choices, desires, or intentions to do it—in which event such mental states must themselves be uncaused). The relevant question is not whether our choices are caused by factors themselves unchosen—as a determinist, I assume that they are—rather, the question is whether our own characters are among the effects in the world that we can inten-tionally cause.

Our abilities here are plainly fragile. We have limited capacities to will individual mental states of belief, desire, or emotion into existence, although there are sometimes some indirect causal routes that we can employ to this end.[64] Our capacities to bring about long-term changes in our mental makeup, and in the actions that that makeup will cause, is surely at least as limited. That the best examples of weakness of will reside here evidence how often we fail at our various resolutions to change our character.

Our causal power over our characters is thus plainly limited. We have no meaningful power to cause ourselves to have a certain character initially, and we have limited power to change an already formed character that we do not like. Yet the value of being unfettered in the making of self-defining choices may not be wholly dependent on our causal powers in this regard.

To see whether this is so, let us interrupt this psychological investigation with the moral investigation I mentioned earlier: why would the power to choose one's character have value, assuming we have some of such power? One answer lies in terms of the value of having a character of integrity and coherence. Having one's actions, emotions, traits, and mental states possess some minimal threshold of coherence is necessary for a being to have any character, indeed, for it to be a person. Possessing such minimal coherence and integrity is of great value because being a person is of such great value. Yet above a minimal threshold of coherence, marked by our concept of mental illness, ever greater coherence of character is of ever greater value.

If this is so, then to the extent our sense of who we are and wish to be has coherence, and to the extent we have the causal power to change our character through choice made in light of an ego-ideal, then that power to choose will also have value. It has value because it is the means by which we bring greater integrity and coherence into our character, that is, into who we are (and not just who we think we are).

There is a second way in which our unfettered power to make self-defining choices has value other than the production of a character of integrity. This can be seen if we advert to a well-known thought experiment raised by T. H. Huxley. Suppose, Huxley said, we could have a virtuous character programmed into our hardware though no effort of our own. Should we not "instantly close with the offer," as Huxley thought?[65] What we would lose, of course, was the pride of authorship, the pride that we are the authors of our own virtues.

Such pride of authorship reveals who we think we are. The "we" who would be the author of our own character is the "we" of self-consciousness. Given the general importance of consciousness to our sense of self, it is not surprising that our strongest identifications are with the experiences of reflexive consciousness, where the objects of our musings are (the rest of) ourselves.

Given this locus of identification in self-consciousness, it becomes of great value to achieve congruence between our actual character and the sense possessed by self-awareness of who we are and wish to be. Yet the process of achieving such congruence is very much a two-way interaction. Sometimes, we change our character in response to what we choose. Perhaps more often, we change what we choose in light of the character we come to see ourselves as having. In either case, whether we "change for the better" or "come to like-ourselves better," we merge who we are with who we want to be. Such congruence is not only of great value, but in this way it demands less of the causal power to remake ourselves in our own image.[66]

The Liberty to Take Drugs

If we apply the foregoing analysis to the criminalization of recreational drug use, we should ask, first, whether the presumption of liberty is overcome by the desirability of punishing such drug use; second, whether such drug use is protected by the derived right to liberty because there is no immorality in such use to be aimed at by penal legislation; and third, whether such drug use is protected by the basic right to liberty because using drugs recreationally is a self-defining choice for users. With regard to the presumption of liberty, we need in turn to ask two basic questions: First, is it morally wrong to take drugs for recreational purposes? We need to ask this question in order to assess what retributive interest the state can have for prohibiting such drug usage. Even if it is morally wrong for anyone to use drugs recreationally, and even if the state were to prohibit such usage because of its moral wrongness, that only gives the state the possibility of justifying the prohibition. To actually justify the prohibition, we must answer a second question affirmatively: Is recreational drug use so wrong that the good achieved by punishment of such wrongs outweighs the costs (in positive liberty, Kantian autonomy, preference-satisfaction, and other indices of social welfare) such punishment imposes?

With regard to the derived right to liberty, the question of the immorality of drug use is also central. For if recreational drug use is not immoral in the sense of breaking our obligations, then there can be no moral wrongdoing for the penal legislation to aim at, and each citizen has the right not to have such prohibition enacted.

With regard to the basic right to liberty, two subquestions are implicated. The first is whether a choice to lead a life of regular drug use, with all the effects of intoxication and perhaps addiction, can qualify as a self-defining choice, or whether it is a choice to have no character, and as such, a choice precluded from being one of self-definition? Second, if it is a possible mode of self-definition to choose the life of intoxication, does the state nonetheless have sufficient reason to override this right because of the great harms caused by drug use?

The Morality of Recreational Drug Use

Central to all three interests in liberty is the question, Is there anything morally wrong with taking drugs for nonmedicinal reasons? Let me put aside momentarily the more fine-grained questions of whether it is morally obligatory on each of us not to use drugs for fun, or whether it would at least be more virtuous of us not to use drugs even though we are not obligated to refrain. My initial, coarse-grained question is this: Ought we to refrain from recreational drug use (where "ought" contains both the ought of obligation and the ought of supererogation and virtue)? I ask the coarse-grained question first because, if the answer to it were negative, one would not need to resolve the difficult issues lurking in the fine-grained questions.[67]

Some would deny that the coarse-grained question has any general answer applicable to all persons at all times. I am not primarily referring to those skeptics in meta-ethics who deny that any ethical question—be they about the good life or the good society—have answers. Rather, I refer to value pluralists like Joseph Raz who think that often two or more values conflict in their recommended action on a given occasion and that often (but not always) such values are incommensurable in the sense that there can be no correct weighing of one against the other.[68] One might think, for example, that recreational drug use gives pleasurable sensations and heightens certain forms of creative endeavors while at the same time lessening one's resolve not to harm others physically, and that there is no way to balance these values to arrive at an overall judgment on whether one ought to refrain from such drug use.

Mill was not a believer in the incommensurability of values. (Indeed, as a monistic utilitarian, how could he be?) Yet Mill, too, denied that there was likely a *general* answer to questions like those about recreational drug use. For Mill, there may well be an answer for each individual as to whether they ought to refrain; but what Mill denied was that there was any general answer, good for all persons. People's natures differ, and since for Mill the answer depends on one's nature, so must the answer depend on the individual.

I call these the three easy routes to liberalism, for notice how easy each of them can make belief in the restraint of state power. If one is muddle-headed enough to accept the skeptical proposition that no ethical questions have right answers and that therefore one right answer is that the state should not seek to enforce any purported right answers, then liberal toleration can "follow" from ethical skepticism. If one accepts the Razian theses that some values are incommensurable and that there are some cases where incommensurability prevents determinate answers, then in the latter cases the state must stay its hand because it has no moral ought to enforce with its legislation. If one accepts the Millian thesis that what we ought to do on issues like drugs varies from individual to individual, then the state may not prohibit generally such behavior, and if the carving out of individual cases is too difficult because of the near infinite variation of individual natures, then the state must not invoke a prohibition for anyone.

We should eschew all three of these easy routes to liberalism. The first, while common enough, is literally incoherent. The second I believe to be false, although that is no easy matter to show.[69] Our experience with hard moral choices tells us that there is no indeterminacy even in such cases, for we continue to agonize over what is the right choice long after we recognize the apparent difficulty of weighing different values. The third could be true, depending on what sort of moral norm makes drug use immoral. If, for example, the potential immorality of drug use were deemed to lie in the intoxicated drug user's propensity to do physical injury to others, and if such propensity varied enormously between persons, then Mill's thesis could be plausible. But as I explore below, I do not think that the immorality of drug use lies in such variables.

So—there is an answer here, and it is now legitimate to ask what that answer is. My own belief is that almost all people ought to refrain from sustained long-term recreational use of at least certain mind-altering drugs. I can think of five possible bases for reaching this judgment, and since it matters to the legal enforceability of this norm which is correct, I shall mention all five.

The first basis proceeds from an asceticism that is difficult to make even plausible today. Drug taking, like sex, can be quite pleasurable. To some temperaments, such pleasure, unjustified as it often is by loftier goals such as creativity or procreation, is sinful. I mention this basis mostly to put it aside, since asceticism is rarely avowed openly as an ideal by anyone these days, even outside of California.[70]

Still, it is important to raise this first consideration because I suspect that it explains why the liberty to take drugs has been so largely neglected, at least when compared to libertarian crusades on behalf of sexual orientation, abortion, free expression, and the like. Recreational drug use, like oral sex, is not typically motivated by some loftier goal that commands much respect. Its typically hedonic character thus tends to demotivate any impassioned crusades in its defense. This in no way is said to justify the laws we have prohibiting such drug use, only to explain the unconscious grip our own asceticism may have upon us. This asceticism has caused us to ignore what I ultimately argue is a rather clear violation of liberty by the widespread criminalization of drugs.

A second and more serious possibility of why drug use is morally wrong is to be found in the kind of wrongs to which drug taking may contribute. On this view, drug taking becomes morally wrong derivatively because it causes other things to occur, and these are clearly moral wrongs. The best variant of this form of argument is to point to the relaxed inhibitions, fuzzy judgment, or greater indifference produced by even moderate intoxication.[71] It might be thought that one ought to avoid recreational drug use because such use unnecessarily risks that the drug user will fail to support his children; will fail to prevent the conception of drug-damaged fetuses and babies; will engage in violent behavior, domestic abuse, reckless driving, and so forth.

Such risk taking can be morally culpable and thus properly punishable on retributive grounds. Even though one may succeed in doing no wrong, if such a wrong was the object of a desire, an intention, or a predictive belief—or if it should have been the object of a predictive belief, given what else we believed about the world—we are morally culpable and deserve to be punished for such culpability.[72]

Notice, however, that this is not to say that drug use as such is generally wrong or culpable. What is wrong are the further states of affairs that drug use is said to cause, and what is culpable is the having of the requisite mental state with those future wrongs as its object. That means that the person who is aware of a substantial and unjustifiable risk to others that his ingestion of a drug on a given occasion will cause, may be punished, as may the drug user who knows she is pregnant and should know the effect on fetal development of the drugs she is taking. But these cases are worlds removed from punishing drug use as such.

The deserved punishability of various forms of risk taking through the use of drugs goes no distance toward establishing the ought statement with which we began. We ought to support our children, we ought not run over people with our automobiles, and so forth, and we are morally culpable whenever we knowingly risk doing those wrongs for insufficient reason. The problem is that it is simply false to think that such culpability always, most of the time, or even typically accompanies drug usage.

Notice that one can say this and not deny that Anglo-American criminal law is correct in its punishment of most intoxicated defendants. The theory that makes such punishments correct, however, is not that drug taking is itself wrong or even that it is derivatively wrong because it risks other wrongs. Rather, what makes such punishments correct is that drug intoxicated persons culpably do wrong when they kill with their car, fail to support their children, and so on, so long as intoxication does not negate the mental states required for culpability (however much liberal "diminished capacity" theorists have thought so).[73] Likewise, by classifying drug taking as not wrong, we do not immunize such culpable individuals from punishment. But we should be clear what we rightly punish such people for. It is the wrongs culpably done under the influence of drugs, not for the taking of drugs with those influences.

Those who think that if we cannot punish intoxicated wrongdoers for becoming intoxicated we cannot punish them at all, usually make the following mistake. They think that because the act of taking drugs at a time, t_1, causes (in a but–for sense) the actor to do wrong at a time, t_2, that actor cannot be blameworthy for the act at t_2 because that act was not free. Suppose it is true that but for the ingestion of a certain drug one would not have had one's inhibitions lowered enough to punch someone else in the nose. This causal judgment in no way diminishes the blameworthiness of the batterer.[74] I can cause myself by one act to do a later act without in anyway diminishing my responsibility for the later act. For example, say that after having accidentally dropped a five dollar bill in an outhouse, I throw a fifty dollar bill in after it. Now I "have to" go in and retrieve the fiver. I have caused myself to do the later act, but it was still my freely chosen action.

We thus can punish the intoxicated driver, the intoxicated wife-beater, and so on, because of the culpable mental state in which they do such wrongs. We can even punish the intoxicated individual who knows that his act of intoxication substantially and unjustifiably risks the doing of such wrongs. When we punish in either case, we need not and should not be punishing someone simply because he is intoxicated, for that by itself is not the wrong.

It is true that in criminal law we sometimes use one morally innocuous act as a proxy for a morally wrongful act or mental state. Thus, many states criminalize the possession of certain sorts of tools useful exclusively for burglaries. The state can prove knowing possession of burglary tools more easily than it can prove an intent to burglarize, or attempted burglary, so such laws are argued for on this evidentiary ground. One might then argue that the prohibition of drug taking could serve this same kind of proxy function, which indeed it could, but the problem with the argument is its premise. Such "proxy crimes" are generally illegitimate.[75] For what is this "proxy function" but an evasion of our normal requirements of proof beyond a reasonable doubt? If when we punish drug taking we are really punishing culpable risk taking, then the "proxy function" allows us to prove the latter only in the Pickwickian sense that we are conclusively presuming it. If we think we should relax the burden of proof in criminal cases somewhat, why don't we be up front about it rather than hiding such relaxation of proof under the creation of proxy crimes? Of course, some defenders of proxy crimes say, "But possession of burglar's tools is *always* accompanied by the culpable intent to use them to burglarize." If this is so, then possession will be very good evidence of culpable intent; but the state should at least be forced to defend such alleged inevitable connections. *Mutatis mutandis* for prohibiting drug use as a proxy for wife beating, reckless driving, and other crimes.

Sometimes proxy crimes are defended on grounds other than short-circuiting proof problems for the prosecution. They are often defended on the preventative ground that they isolate a convenient point in time from which it is predictable that some moral wrongs will occur, and such wrongs can thus be efficiently prevented by preventing the earlier, nonwrongful act. It may be easier for the police to prevent burglaries by allowing them to arrest people for possession of burglary tools, for example, than it is to do so by waiting for the possessor to actually attempt a break-in with such tools. Likewise, it may be easier to prevent spousal abuse, child abuse, and other nonstranger violence of various kinds, if the police can arrest intoxicated individuals rather than having to wait for them to attempt these wrongs.

The problem with this defense of "wrongs by proxy" is that it gives liberty a strong kick in the teeth right at the start. Such an argument does not even pretend that there is any culpability or wrongdoing for which it would urge punishment; rather, punishment of a nonwrongful, nonculpable action is used for purely preventative ends. We rightfully eschew such preventative incapacitation generally in our punishment theories, and we should not allow such practices to enter unwittingly because they are disguised as supposedly independent crimes.

A third possible moral question about use of drugs stems from the observation that drug users "drop out" of socially useful occupations, at least during the period of their intoxication, and often over the longer period when they are not intoxicated but are so enamored of this one form of pleasure that they give up the attitudes of ambition and self-discipline inconsistent with a hedonistic outlook. The argument is that our talents are not ours to squander in this way, that we each hold our talents in trust for the betterment of society, that to abuse this trust is morally wrong. Benjamin Rush was a well-known expositor of this argument.[76] A clear example of such motivation at work is the mandatory closing hours for English pubs, justified on the grounds that abusers should not be allowed to squander their time and talents during working hours.[77]

One answer to Rush's argument is that given to the previous argument: when and if a person abuses drugs to the point that he is not contributing his share of the social product, then he should be punished. Prior to such breach of social obligation, punishment is premature and unjustified. A second and distinct answer should equally bar resort to this argument: morality does not obligate us to be good workers or, more generally, effective contributors to the social good. Whether and how we use our talents is up to us. There are better and worse ways of using our talents, and one good way is surely for social betterment in all its dimensions, but this is not the only good use of our talents. It is a peculiar blindness of those who have dedicated their talents to social reform to think this, but the sometimes magnificent (if ultimately selfish) achievement of artists and scientists belies any such narrow vision. Moreover, whether we use our talents in *any* good way is, as I shall argue shortly, not a matter of moral obligation. I certainly have many discrete obligations not to make the world worse; but my positive obligations to make it better are fewer and weaker, and do not include an obligation to be the most effective assembly line worker my (unintoxicated) talents might allow me to be.

One way in which drug usage may make people less willing to contribute their talents to the betterment of society is that they do not vote or otherwise participate in the political life of a democracy. And here, it might be said, we each have a duty to support just institutions, at least to the minimal extent of voting in public elections. If drug use leads people not to fulfill this obligation, then on that ground it may be prohibited.

Yet again, if voting is obligatory and not merely supererogatory, and if the act of not voting may be criminalized on just this ground, then why shouldn't we generally criminalize not voting for any reason? We do not criminalize nonvoting behavior because we realize the value of Kantian autonomy: the reason for which one votes matters. One whose voting is compelled, even if the content of his vote is not compelled, is one whose voice is not fully his own; the collective voice of a large group of nonvoters thus has less legitimating force. If this prevents us from criminalizing nonvoting itself, how could one possibly criminalize some other action, like taking drugs, on the ground that that action makes nonvoting more likely?[78] That would be like criminalizing dancing on the grounds that it leads to heterosexual intercourse while not criminalizing intercourse itself.

I come to the fourth sort of moral doubt one may have about recreational drug use. This stems from the belief that the haze of intoxication is not itself a form of human attainment and that in fact such intoxication inhibits genuine forms of human flourishing. Drug use may prevent students from doing well in school, artists from doing art, scientists from doing science, and social engineers from social engineering. Drugs in such a case undercut our perfectionist ambition to be the best we can be in any field of potential human excellence.

With these factual beliefs I am in agreement. I say this despite my exposure to the counterculture of the 1960s in America. Aldous Huxley told me when I was an undergraduate about the wonders of the Mexican mushroom, and Timothy Leary, that my generation should "tune in, turn on, and drop out" by tripping on LSD. David Richards, also of my vintage, echoes some of that overly optimistic attitude toward the "mind-expanding" potential of hallucinogenic drugs.[79] These echoes from the past are like the echoes one still hears occasionally from radical psychiatry on the topic of mental illness in contexts such as R. D. Laing's description of schizophrenia as an existential voyage of discovery for the few with the courage to take it.[80] Such grandiose descriptions of what in fact is a pretty pathetic condition are so false that it borders on cruelty to use them. The same is true for the 1960s euphoria about drugs. One has to be high on them already in order to be able to judge the states induced as any kind of path to profundity or "authenticity." Worthwhile human achievement is not so easily purchased.

Moreover, use of drugs can easily interfere with those creative endeavors of the best and the brightest of us. Here, one needs to keep a balanced view, for in some forms of artistic expression, drugs may enhance rather than retard one's abilities. In any case, suppose the effect of drugs for most forms of excellence is negative. That still leaves the moral conclusion to be drawn. Who has the right to demand that everyone achieve his highest potential? To whom are we obligated to be the best we can be? Was Mozart obligated to be Mozart, given the relative poverty, unhappiness, and ill health that the pursuit of his talents cost him? Was it our right to demand this of him?

There is surely something noble in the extremes of human achievement, and we rightly are stirred when we witness it or appreciate its fruits. But equally surely, no one owes us this. They do no wrong if they eschew the high and perilous road for the low and comfortable one. Criminalizing such failure of virtue, but not of obligation, seems out of the question. So, too, must be the criminalizing of behaviors that impede such creative quests. Not just Edward III's bowling, but bridge, television, action movies, excessive vacations, and all else that makes up the dulling narcotic of daily life should be criminalized or not on the same basis. Except in the amounts needed (like sleep) to keep questing, they all get in the way of our becoming more like a character in Ayn Rand's novels: immensely creative, heroically energetic, sucking in great draughts of life's essences with every breath. Nobody can be obligated to be this way, any more than they are obligated to be a moral saint in their dealings with others.

The fifth and last possible basis for regarding recreational use of drugs to be immoral stems as much from the allegedly addictive nature of regular drug use, as from the intoxicating effect of each such use. Both extreme intoxication and addiction are likened to a kind of suicide, a deadening of the capacities that make us moral agents. Unlike the last suspicion which we examined, where drug use was condemned for its disabling of us from our highest forms of flourishing, here the charge is that drug use drops us below the threshold of what makes us persons and moral agents. It is likened to voluntarily bringing on mental illness, where the capacities of rationality and autonomy are so eroded that we cease to count as a person—a kind of suicide

As before, we need to separate the factual claims here from the moral conclusions. The factual claims have to do with the degree to which our capacities for rational and autonomous action are eroded. Since these claims are different for intoxication than from addiction, let us consider each separately.

Intoxication erodes the cognitive capacities that constitute our practical rationality. When I speak of cognitive capacities, I am referring to the capacities that help us resolve conflicts between our desires so that we can perform a variety of functions: the formation of a stable preference order; the formation of rational beliefs in the sense of holding them only with that certainty proportionate to the probative force of the evidence available to us; the formation of intentions and plans that execute appropriately the background motivations formed by those preferences and beliefs; the execution of those plans and intentions with the appropriate physical movements; the retaining of our intentions consistent with our beliefs so that we do not attempt what we know to be impossible or even highly unlikely of success; and the restraint of those impulses and emotions whose satisfactions usually are not, on reflection, what we most want.[81] The difficult but highly relevant factual question is How much are these capacities degraded by intoxication?

The criminal law's armchair social science on this issue has long been in a mess. Our law has assumed that intoxication can often be so severe that the intoxicated actor is unable to form the intentions (or sometimes beliefs) required for conviction of various crimes. Yet intoxication, whether by alcohol or by other drugs, is almost never this severe. The intentions required for conviction of rape or murder, for example, are so simple that if an actor has not become so intoxicated that he has lost consciousness he almost certainly possesses the intention required for conviction if he does the acts in question.[82]

The erosion of our capacities of practical rationality is less severe, and subtler, than the law of diminished capacity often assumes. Nonetheless, such erosion does exist, and I assume that extreme states of intoxication approach the loss of reality testing that is often taken to be the mark of mental illness severe enough to be called legal insanity. When Kant likened such extremely intoxicated individuals to being "simply like a beast, not to be treated as a human being,"[83] he was echoing what his contemporaries thought of severe mental disease.[84]

About addiction, whether to alcohol or to other drugs, the evidence is also in conflict.[85] Despite this conflict, perhaps we can at least pinpoint what factual issues are of most relevance in asking whether addiction, as extreme intoxication, can be a kind of suicide of personhood (an insanity). Addiction, like intoxication, is not plausibly thought of as an across-the-board reduction in our capacities for practical rationality. Addiction is more like what Freud used to call his "obsessional neurotic" patients.[86] There is in addiction a kind of fixation of desire somewhat analogous to the frozen beliefs of the paranoid schizophrenic. This is the "craving" conception of addiction, where the desire for drugs of the unintoxicated addict has the following qualities: (1) it is experienced phenomenologically as a hunger, that is, as a datable sensation of need; (2) it is experienced as "ego-alien," that is, as an urge alien to one's sense of self and an intruder on that self's sense of control; (3) it is unamenable to correction, restraint, or even delay by other desires that the actor in quieter moments might say he values more; (4) it is accompanied by the belief that, if the desire is not satisfied, the threat of the unpleasant consequences of withdrawal will ensue; and (5) its need for drugs increases constantly.

Jon Elster in this volume quite properly urges that we look for (and expect to find) the physiological correlates of these psychological states. For present purposes it will not matter whether there are such physical states nor what their contours might be,[87] for we can establish the issue of "moral suicide" with the psychological variables alone. The claim would be that addiction is a kind of possession, not by demons, witches, spirits, or agents of any kind, but rather, by the imperious necessity of ego-alien desire. There is a driven-ness, and a lack of freedom, in both addiction and obsessional neurosis when pictured in this way.

There are a number of factual questions: To what extent is this picture true? How urgent are the experienced cravings of the addict or the obsessional neurotic? How divided is the consciousness of the addict and of the obsessional neurotic, so that such cravings are repressed into unconsciousness—projected, or otherwise defended against—to the point that when experienced they are experienced as impulses alien to one's self, as a kind of unwelcome intruder? How dominant are such desires behaviorally, so that in any contest with other (nonalien) desires, the craving always wins?[88] How often do addicts predict that they will suffer withdrawal symptoms if they cease taking drugs? How severe do they foresee such symptoms as being? How much do such predictive beliefs of addicts figure in the reasons that motivate their continued drug taking? Finally, to what extent do addicts actually develop a tolerance for their drugs (in the sense that it takes ever increasing amounts to generate the same psychological effects), and to what extent do their drug-taking behaviors reflect this?

Since I have no more than armchair hunches about the answers to these questions, I shall concede the drug prohibitionist his best factual case here. Assume there is a large degree of all five of these things, sufficiently so that when we assess the moral responsibility of addicts for their drug-seeking behaviors, we excuse them to the same extent that we excuse obsessional neurotics, "kleptomaniacs," and those who kill under the influence of a strong emotion aroused by the provoking acts of their victim. Such conditions do not amount to anything like insanity, but they might amount (under the generous factual assumptions here indulged) to a partial excuse of inner compulsion.[89]

We are now freed to ask the moral question about both intoxication and addiction: Is there anything morally troubling about voluntarily placing one's self in these states of intoxication and addiction? Surely, on these factual assumptions, the answer is yes. We are each of value as persons, and we plainly diminish what is valuable about us as persons when we erode our rationality and our autonomy in these ways. Addiction of course is mild in the degree of its erosion of personality compared to extreme intoxication; but because the obsessive desire (symptomatic of addiction) is to do actions producing such intoxication, addiction will be morally troublesome for precisely the same sort of degradation of personality as is intoxication.

Moreover, it is here, at last, that we reach a moral obligation not to take drugs. Just as we sometimes have a moral obligation not to commit literal suicide, so, too, we sometimes have a moral obligation not to commit the kind of metaphorical suicide that (on the factual assumptions here made) addiction represents. Certainly when we are responsible for young children, but also when there are others who love us or depend or us, we are obligated to stick around.

This moral obligation does not readily translate into a general obligation not to take drugs recreationally, which is what the legal-moralist legislator needs in order to justify a blanket prohibition on recreational drug use. In the first place, just as some kinds of actual suicides are not wrongful, so some kinds of mental/moral suicides are also not wrongful. One's health may be so deteriorated, one's grief or other pain may be so intense, or in any number of other circumstances the balance of life's prospects against its burdens may be so unfavorable, that one is justified in actually killing himself. One would in like circumstances also be justified in deadening the pain by deadening one's capacities through addiction and continuous intoxication. So there can be no across-the-board condemnation of suicide of either kind by the legislator whose criminal law would track moral obligation.[90]

Second, to say that addiction can be a kind of moral suicide is not to say anything about what sort of act it takes to become an addict. Only on the very strong assumption that addiction is caused by taking just one drink, just one puff, or just one shot, could one liken acts of drug use to acts like putting a gun to one's head. If becoming an addict is more a chosen way of life, as Herbert Fingarette urges that alcohol addiction is, then individual acts of drug taking are moral suicide only in the extended sense that individual acts of smoking or of overeating are a killing of oneself.[91]

Liberty with Respect to Drug Use

If the foregoing argument is correct, then with one possible exception every citizen has a derived right to liberty against criminalization of recreational drug use. For on a legal moralist theory of proper legislative motivation, a legislator may criminalize only that which he may condemn as morally wrong, and there is by-and-large no breach of moral obligation in taking drugs.

Theorists who wish to dispute this rather obvious conclusion, who are tempted to criminalize drug taking even if it is not morally wrong but so long as it is lacking in virtue, forget a basic fact about criminalization: we have to punish people who violate criminal laws. Such theorists tend to think of criminal laws as pure preventatives, so that if some act is morally undesirable—whether wrong or not, no matter—that is sufficient reason to criminalize it. Yet crime demands punishment, and on any morally respectable theory of punishment those who do no wrong cannot be punished. One cannot simply pass a law criminalizing drug taking and have that undesirable practice stop; one will have violators of such a law, and one has to be willing to punish them if one is willing to prohibit their behavior (on pain, among other things, of there being no prevention achieved by prohibition).

The one exception to this otherwise crisp conclusion is the obligation we sometimes have not to commit moral suicide, which may translate into an obligation not to take drugs regularly enough that we regularly lose our moral personality. Since there is such an obligation, when it is violated there is a moral wrong that could be the basis of justified legislation. To see whether this is so, we must examine the presumption of liberty and the basic right to liberty, which I now propose to do.[92]

About the basic right to liberty I can be relatively brief. For the very arguments that convince prohibitionists of the immorality of drug taking should also convince them that a chosen life of such drug taking is the kind of self-defining choice protected by the basic right to liberty. That is, grant the case outlined above—that addicted drug taking is a kind of suicide, and that that is what obligates us not to do it. By my lights, that same analogy also generates the conclusion that it would be wrong of the state to prohibit this form of suicide, as any other. How we end our life is a "defining moment" for us. It is our final way of saying to the future who we were. It is our final signature. The same is true for the "little death" the loss of ourselves in drugs is said to be. It can be a way of saying that we found so little of value in the normal life in our society that we "dropped out" of it, not just economically but mentally and morally.

One does not have to be a Timothy Leary to think this. Indeed, as I said before, I am not another Leary. Concede that such dropping out, like suicide itself, is usually an unjustified, wrongful, and even pathetic choice. Yet even on these assumptions it is a self-defining choice, in the morally neutral sense of that phrase. Although I don't like the self-definitions of many people and I find some people's styles of life morally wrong, nevertheless it is their right to so constitute themselves, at least, up to some threshold of moral awfulness.[93]

In truth, of course, the analogy of addiction-caused drug taking (whatever that might be) to suicide is only an analogy. For, in fact, addiction only degrades aspects of our moral personhood; it doesn't end them. Some might therefore urge that the more proper analogy is to Mill's well-known example of a person contracting himself into slavery. In slavery, after all, the person is fully around, in full possession of his faculties. But since liberty is gone, even Mill conceded that such a choice should not be enforced in the courts.

The enforceability of contracts of slavery has some features extraneous to our present concerns, making it not a very useful analogy. For when a court enforces a contract, it lends it power to seeing that the act contracted for is done, against the present wishes of one of the contracting parties. That is a kind of state sanctioning of slavery one could well eschew. Yet that eschewal is irrelevant to the question of whether the state should punish an individual for becoming a slave. Suppose that there exists a part of the world that practices slavery and that any foreigner who goes there is automatically and inevitably made into a slave for life. Should a rightly conceived criminal code prohibit travel to such a place, punishing those who, with full awareness that they will become a slave, attempt the trip? (Like suicide, it would be impossible to punish the completed crime.)

Does it at all matter to this question that the person who decides to sacrifice her liberty will be fully in possession of her faculties after her decision? My own sense is that it does not, but if it does, then try this variation: the place traveled to does not enslave you, it only keeps you in a state of constant intoxication by drugs until you are fully addicted to them, and you fully know that when you go. May the state punish you for attempting to go? This, of course, is just the case we are dealing with.

A better way to test our sense of whether drug taking is a self-defining choice that should be protected by the basic right to liberty is to ask ourselves whether the state should criminalize and punish private citizens who prevent others from degrading their moral personalities. Suppose someone has chosen to become an addict, or has chosen to join a brainwashing cult. Suppose further that such choices are made in circumstances that make them morally wrong and not just lacking in virtue. If such choices are protected by the basic right to liberty, then it would be wrong for *anyone* to prevent them, not just wrong for the state to do so. So surely the state is justified in punishing such wrongful interference with liberty? Yet, it might be argued that there must be exceptions. One should be able to prevent their children, their spouse, or their friends form degrading themselves in these ways. And thus, they may kidnap their grandchildren out of Moonie cults or confine their friends to places where no drugs or alcohol are available in order to free them from the blight of these degradations.

My own sense is that we are not free to do these things, that we do wrong when we do them, and that such wrong is sometimes strong enough reason to overcome the presumption of liberty to justify punishment. We may of course seek to persuade, cajole, manipulate, give financial incentives, and so forth, to our grown children, spouses, and friends not to make unwise choices in these directions, and the state may do so as well. But neither we nor the state can coercively prevent them from self-destructive choices. Only when choices are made by those not fully possessed of their faculties—because they are too young or too crazy, for example—may we prevent the exercise of their choices. But once our children are grown up, and as long as our friends are sane, we must respect such life-forming choices, even if we know they are wrong.

If we turn to the presumption of liberty, even this weakest of liberty interests raises hurdles higher than can be leapt by the would-be prohibitionist of drugs. The welfare argument against prohibition has been made before, and very tellingly. In straight welfare terms the war on drugs has not had enough success to be worth the enormous costs of attempting to enforce it, including the indirect costs of the violence between dealers, the financing of organized crime, and the property crimes by addicts in search of money for drugs whose prices are artificially overinflated. The limited good obtained has not been worth the enormous cost of punishing the limited wrongs done by taking drugs.[94]

This concern with costs is probably the ground on which the political clout required to repeal the present criminalization of drugs will be found. Losing a war is a good reason to stop fighting it. In this essay, however, I have focused on more principled arguments of liberty outlining why this war was never one we were entitled to fight to start with.

CHAPTER FOUR

Liberalism, Inalienability, and Rights of Drug Use

SAMUEL FREEMAN

In recent years the criminal justice system in the United States has oriented itself toward waging a politically popular "war on drugs." It is a war that many will say is hopelessly lost, in the same way that Prohibition's war on alcohol was lost. Some argue that the war on drugs is self-defeating. No doubt, as a result of the criminalization of most psychoactive drugs (beginning with the Harrison Act of 1914), fewer people use them than would if such drugs were legalized.[1] But, as in the case of Prohibition under the 18th Amendment, this does not mean that less damage is done to individuals or to society as a whole. The criminalization of psychoactive drugs has, it is argued, grossly aggravated the incidence of violence and poverty in society and has even stimulated greater drug abuse and addiction. Having made opiates, depressants (except for alcohol), stimulants (except for nicotine), and hallucinogens illegal and attached severe penalties not only to their distribution but also to the individuals who use them, we have created a class of criminals whose size some analysts estimate to be as large as 30 to 40 million people. Less than 3 percent of those who use drugs are apprehended and punished each year, and this comes at extraordinary costs to the legal system.[2] Most of those punished are African Americans, even though as a group they consume far fewer illicit drugs than middle-class Caucasians. This can only have damaging effects on many people's attitudes toward the fairness and efficiency of the criminal justice system and only increase African Americans' sense of social alienation and injustice.

Moreover, given the severe penalties attending drug distribution, the war on drugs has caused the distribution of narcotics to be placed, not in the hands of pharmacists or ordinary business people, but rather in the hands of violent gangs who reap monopoly profits and terrorize portions of our inner cities. These gangs (with names like the Jamaican posse, the Bloods, and the Crips) would not exist, it is argued, were it not for the fact that such severe penalties are attached to the use of psychoactive drugs and that, therefore, such enormous profits can be derived from their sale. Moreover, because legislatures assign severe penalties for use of even mild drugs such as marijuana, it is claimed that the war on drugs has caused drug dealers to create and dispense far more dangerous and addictive narcotics like crack cocaine. Many people believe that crack would not exist were it not for the illegality of drug use. As a general rule, "Where drugs are illegal, more damaging drugs drive out less damaging drugs."[3] Heroin and, now, crack cocaine have come to replace marijuana as the drug of choice, since they are far more profitable and easily transportable by drug dealers.[4]

Our court system has become clogged with the prosecution of drug dealers and users. Because of the war on drugs, criminal prosecutions against the drug trade and drug use have been assigned legislative priority in the judicial system to the degree that civil actions in federal and state courts often take at least two years. (In some federal districts, 70 percent of trial time is devoted to criminal drug cases.)[5] Moreover, enormous policing efforts are devoted to the war on drugs, at immense expense, thereby draining police resources from surveillance of other illegal activities. In addition the illegality of drugs has a corrupting influence on law enforcement itself when police accept bribes from drug dealers, confiscate for themselves illegal profits, or become actively involved in the drug trade itself.[6] And even without these problems, the overzealous police methods utilized during narcotics raids often lead to violation of the rights of many innocent persons, to illegal police searches and subsequent perjured testimony in the courts by police officers, and to a casual attitude toward the rights of the innocent as well as the guilty.[7] The dignity of many people is compromised by such tactics, and serious questions are raised regarding the role of the police in a free democratic society. For these and other reasons, some argue that the war on drugs, by increasingly occupying the criminal justice system, is gradually undermining it.[8]

Given these substantially adverse social, economic, and political consequences of the war on drugs at the federal and state level, plus the fact that the demonstrable benefits are so minimal, many people argue that a rational social policy calls for the decriminalization of drug use and its replacement with a regulatory scheme only somewhat more rigid than those programs that now regulate alcohol and nicotine. This suggested policy is based in the recognition that it is practically impossible to fully eradicate the use of opiates and stimulants in the absence of autocratic power that would undermine liberal and democratic society itself. The social costs of prohibition will always far exceed whatever benefits result from interdiction, particularly when increasingly stringent methods of interdiction violate so many people's rights and come to undermine confidence in the legal system.

If these claims and arguments regarding the adverse social costs of drug interdiction are correct (I do not say that they are) then it becomes difficult to mount a good case for the system of prohibition of psychoactive drugs that we now have in place. A convincing reply would need to show that even worse consequences would attend drug legalization. In the absence of these adverse consequences, the war on drugs should go the way of Prohibition. This is the best liberal argument for the decriminalization of psychoactive drugs. It is an argument that focuses on experience of the adverse consequences of criminalization as weighed against the adverse consequences of noncriminalization.

What I primarily want to address and draw into question, however, is a different liberal argument for legalization of psychoactive drugs. It is a purely philosophical argument, one that proceeds, not from pragmatic considerations of the adverse consequences of drug interdiction, but from the contention that in a liberal society citizens have a right to indulge in drugs, whatever the adverse consequences for themselves, so long as use is voluntary and informed and does not cause harm to the rights and interests of others. My sense is that this argument is overstated. It works from the premise that liberalism excludes all prohibitions on self-destructive conduct, a premise that I seriously question. Below, I show that there are certain kinds of purely self-destructive conduct that a liberal society can legitimately prohibit, and I consider the implications of this for use of psychoactive drugs. Finally, I return to the question raised in this introduction regarding the adverse social consequences of criminalization of drugs. Here I raise certain considerations about the effects of noninterdiction for the institutions of a liberal society, considerations which are often neglected in arguments for decriminalization.

The Issue

It is commonly recognized that a liberal society can and should regulate drugs to insure that users are apprised of the consequences of drug use, that use is voluntary, and that harmful substances do not fall into the hands of minors and incompetents. These so-called soft paternalistic measures are not such a difficult issue for liberals. Many liberals, however, do not concede that the outright prohibition of narcotics or even the regulation of drug use is legitimate when it can be shown that users, without endangering others, willingly and wittingly take drugs and are aware of their likely harmful consequences for their future well-being. Such prohibitions are seen as paternalistic (in the negative sense), and liberalism, it is claimed, is incompatible with this kind of paternalism. That being the case, some people have argued that there is an unqualified right to use drugs regardless of the consequences of such use for the user.

I find the charge of paternalism in these contexts to be unhelpful at best, and for the most part misleading. It makes sense to speak of whole political systems as being paternalistic when they manage or govern individuals in the manner that a father (or parents) traditionally have governed their children. Paternalism implies systematically restricting and regulating another's conduct and, at the limit, doing this in such a way as to instill in that person not just particular values but a general morality and complete conception of the good. As applied to political systems, paternalism is a charge that individuals are treated as mere subjects, benignly perhaps, but not as free citizens who are capable of taking responsibility for their lives. Clearly no liberal democratic system of laws is paternalistic in the sense that it denies individuals the complex scheme of rights that enables them to determine their own lives within the restrictions allowed by justice. So the charge of paternalism, when it is leveled in the context of a liberal democratic regime, can be one that only applies to particular laws and not to the political system as a whole. But when applied to laws, it is an obscure claim. For the fact is that most so-called paternalistic laws (such as seatbelt and motorcycle helmet laws, laws against suicide and gambling, and many laws against drugs) in no way enforce a particular conception of the good; rather they restrict or require specific actions, while leaving open the range of conceptions of the good that one may choose from. What more is being said, then, when a law is called paternalistic, than that this law prohibits some kind of self-destructive conduct? Some claim that the law also denies individuals the rights of self-determination and autonomy upon which liberalism is based. But (assuming that this is an accurate account of liberalism's basis) the issue then becomes whether liberal autonomy and self-determination require that there be no restrictions whatsoever on self-destructive conduct. I take this to be the really interesting issue in the debate over paternalistic laws, and it is not a debate that can be won by simply stipulating that part of the true meaning of autonomy is a complete absence of laws against self-destructive conduct.

My position is that liberalism is not incompatible with certain restrictions on self-destructive conduct, even if such conduct is informed, voluntary, and rational in the ordinary sense. When the aim and effect of restrictions against self-destructive conduct is to maintain the moral and rational integrity of the person—in the sense of the capacities for rational agency and moral responsibility upon which liberalism and liberal autonomy are based—then there is nothing illiberal about imposing restrictions on conduct that is harmful only to the agent concerned. By implication, citizens in a constitutional democracy have a duty to maintain the degree of competence necessary to exercise the capacities of agency that enable them to reflect on their good and observe the moral requirements of social life.

My argument does not imply that liberalism allows for the restriction of all psychoactive drugs. Such mildly intoxicating substances as marijuana, for example, cannot be prohibitable on the grounds I set forth. It may even be that most currently available drugs are not prohibitable on these grounds, including heroin and cocaine. This is an empirical issue. But there is, at least potentially, a class of drugs so intrinsically debilitating of one's capacities, that their prohibition is justified on liberal grounds.

What, then, is the point of this exercise? The point is to locate one of the parameters of liberalism: the extent to which individuals can go in exercising their freedom. My primary aim in this paper is to challenge the common idea that liberalism in some way requires that individuals be permitted to engage in any self-regarding conduct, no matter how detrimental its consequences may be for the agent. If nothing else, this exercise should help us gain a clearer insight into the scope and limits of a right to use drugs, if indeed such a right does exist in a liberal system.

Liberal Inalienability

Joel Feinberg, David Richards, Douglas Husak, and Michael Moore, all argue that liberalism is committed to a right to recreational drug use, that this right in some way follows from the ideas of liberal autonomy (Richards, Feinberg, Husak) and personal sovereignty (Feinberg).[9] Before I address this issue, I want to focus first on a related contention of Feinberg's. It is the much discussed question whether liberalism allows for, or even requires, that individuals have an unqualified right to alienate some or even all their rights, by either destroying themselves or by selling themselves into slavery. Focusing on this issue will, I hope, provide some orientation in dealing with the more subtle and real issue of a right to drug use.

Following J. S. Mill, Feinberg contends that what is central to liberalism is the idea that government and society have the authority to restrict people's conduct only if it harms or substantially threatens harm to others (the harm principle). Developing this Millian principle, Feinberg contends it implies an underived right of self-determination, or de jure autonomy.[10] Autonomy, according to Feinberg, is a kind of personal sovereignty (p. 48). It implies the right to act on one's voluntary choices, especially with respect to critical life decisions about how to live one's life (p. 54). But voluntary choices are not necessarily rational choices. One can voluntarily (and so autonomously) choose to act irrationally, or against one's best interests. And if autonomy is a right, this means that autonomous beings have the right to make unreasonable decisions about their own lives (p. 67), even to the point of acting self-destructively. As Feinberg says:

> A person's right of self-determination, being sovereign, takes precedence even over his own good. Interference in these cases is justified only when necessary to determine whether his choice is voluntary, hence truly his, or to protect him from choices that are not truly his; but interference with his informed and genuine choices is not justified to protect him from unwisely incurred or risked harms. He has a sovereign right to choose in a manner we think, plausibly enough, to be foolish, provided only that the choices are truly voluntary. (P. 61.)

To arrive at this position, Feinberg contends that de jure autonomy, or the right of self-determination, is "entirely underivative, as morally basic as the good of self-fulfillment itself" (p. 59). In saying this right is "underivative," I take it that Feinberg means, not just (1) that a person's right of autonomy takes precedence over her good in decisions about what we (as individuals or governments) ought to do in actions affecting that person; but more importantly (2) that in the order of argument and justification the right of self-determination is not grounded in any conception of the agent's good. It is in some sense argumentatively basic, a fixed intuition. In this sense, the right and the good are completely independent concepts on Feinberg's account. We can specify what liberal rights persons have without reference to their interests or what it is rational for them to do.[11]

What seems to be underlying Feinberg's sharp separation between rights of self-determination and the good of the agent is the legitimate concern that, as Feinberg says, "There must be a right to err, to be mistaken, to decide foolishly, to take big risks, if there is to be any meaningful self-rule; without it, the whole idea of *de jure* autonomy begins to unravel" (p. 62). Now I think that any liberal position must accept Feinberg's claim here. The question is, whether accepting a political right to take risks and choose foolishly itself implies that we have a right to act in ways that either destroy or permanently undermine our capacities for agency. In what follows, I claim the contrary, focusing on what I take to be a fixed feature of the liberal tradition, the idea of inalienability of rights.

Feinberg contends that his account of "personal sovereignty," self-determination, and the right to autonomy accurately depict the "grand liberal tradition" (p. 68). He claims that his is "the only view consistent with a conception of personal sovereignty" and that "it accords with a self-conception deeply imbedded in the moral attitudes of most people and [is] apparently presupposed in many of our moral idioms" (pp. 61–62). The grand liberal tradition requires "respect for [a person's] *unfettered choice* as the sole rightful determinant of his action except where the interests of others need protection from him" (p. 68). But these claims are highly questionable. To begin with, such grand liberals as Locke, Mill, Kant, Constant, Tocqueville, and, in this century, Rawls, all explicitly reject the legitimacy of an autonomous alienation of the basic rights that define one's dignity and autonomy as a citizen. Moreover, no court in a liberal constitutional democracy would enforce any agreement whereby a person sold himself into slavery or bondage, or for that matter transferred to another person control over any of the basic constitutional rights defining him as a citizen (freedom of religion, speech, and association, the right to vote, and so forth). This is what it means to say that persons have "inalienable rights"; certain rights cannot be given up or bargained away for other advantages because they are so central to one's status as a person and a free citizen. Given the centrality of the idea of inalienable rights to the liberal tradition, it is a peculiar argument which says that liberal autonomy itself requires the rejection of inalienability. Of course, one might argue that the hoary concept of inalienability is incompatible with liberalism's deeper commitment to individual autonomy—and this is, in effect, Feinberg's argument. (Of Mill's explicit rejection of voluntary slavery contracts, Feinberg charges Mill with "occasional lapses" and inconsistency [pp. 68, 76].) Alternatively, one might try to reconcile autonomy and inalienability by conceiving of rights of self-determination as having a different basis than that given by Feinberg.

Suppose we construe de jure autonomy in some way other than as an underivative right that is intuitively given separate from any considerations about rationality or a person's good. We could construe autonomy derivatively, in the way that Mill (perhaps) did, as grounded in a prior nonmoral conception of the good (that is, individual self-fulfillment or social utility).[12] A standard objection to this kind of account is that, by making autonomy merely instrumental to realizing an independently definable conception of the good, liberal rights are made subject to the contingencies of changing circumstances; moreover their equality is never assured and is likely to be soon practically undermined. It is a contingent, and sometime doubtful, fact whether rights of autonomy will promote the well-being or self-fulfillment of at least some individuals or of society as a whole. Their freedom is then jeopardized.

A more secure basis for liberal rights of autonomy is provided by seeing them (as Kant and Kantians such as Rawls do) as derivative in a different way, not as instrumental to a prior nonmoral conception of the good, but as grounded in a normative ideal of persons. This ideal sees persons as free, equal, self-governing agents who are responsible for their actions and their ends. In saying this ideal of the person is normative, two things are intended. First, the ideal is not a metaphysical conception of the person as free from causally determining influences, but rather a moral ideal of persons as free by right and as possessing an equal moral and civic status, a status which they have even if we concede causal determinism. Second, this moral ideal is normative in that we cannot fully say what this ideal is without invoking moral principles of right and justice. Moral principles of certain kinds are required to specify just what is involved in being a free self-governing agent with equal status. To articulate these principles, Kantians ask, What must persons be like to be self-governing agents? They must have, Kantians say, certain developed capacities that are essential to reflective deliberation and agency within social contexts. The ideal of persons as self-governing suggests that persons have certain capacities for practical reasoning which enable them to reflectively determine and order their ends, effectively plan their actions and activities to realize this scheme of ends, and conform their actions accordingly. We can call these capacities "rational powers of agency" since they are essential to rational action and to having a conception of the good. In addition, certain other powers of reasoning also equip persons to understand, apply, and abide by those moral rules that are a condition of social life. Moreover, these capacities, when fully developed, enable people to comprehend and justify their actions in terms of moral principles that are publicly acceptable to reasonable moral agents. We can call these the "moral powers of agency" since they are essential to social life or to being a cooperative member within extensive social schemes.

Why are these moral and rational powers deemed essential to agency? First, it is because individuals have moral and rational capacities such as these that we hold them as free self-governing agents, capable of assuming responsibility for their actions and pursuits. People who are entirely without these powers (as, for example, the severely retarded) are judged completely incompetent as moral and legal agents; they are not subject to judgments of accountability. And those persons whose capacities are diminished or undeveloped (such as children) are not judged fully competent agents; their actions are deemed to be in need of supervision to some lesser but still significant degree, depending upon the extent of their disability. Second, we do not see our own lives as simply happenstance, thrust upon us by our situations. Rather, within the limits of the circumstances we confront, we conceive of our actions and even our lives as under our control. It is by virtue of our capacities for rational and moral agency that we do this, enabling us to give unity to our lives by fixing our final ends and structuring a plan of life compatible with principles of rational choice and justice.

The significant point is that possession of these moral and rational powers to some requisite minimum degree is necessary to our regarding ourselves and others as free. Moreover, largely because individuals have these capacities, we see them as having an equal status as moral agents, deserving of equal respect and equal justice. Our moral and rational capacities then also provide us with a basis—if not a necessary one, then at least a sufficient one—for judgments of moral and political equality.

On this understanding of the bases of liberalism, the primary function of liberal rights is to enable individuals to effectively exercise and maintain the moral and rational capacities by virtue of which they are seen as free and responsible agents deserving of equal justice. Given this role, the primary liberal rights that we have can be ascertained by inquiring into what rights are needed to exercise and maintain the powers of moral and rational agency. Another function of liberal rights is that they enable individuals to decide and realize their good, or their "individuality," as Feinberg calls it (pp. 96–97). But not just any conception of the good, or of individuality, is permissible; to be permissible a conception of the good must be compatible with the exercise of the capacities for rational and moral agency by virtue of which agents are capable of pursuing a good over a complete life. A person's "own individuality," by which Feinberg means characteristics peculiar to a person (p. 96), does not have absolute priority over his humanity (Kant's term), the capacities of reasoning and self-control that enable him to be a free moral agent deserving of equal justice.

Taking this ideal of the person as a foundation, it follows that we should see de jure autonomy, or the right of self-determination, not as an inchoate right to do with one's life simply as one pleases, but as shorthand for a class of more specific rights designed to enable individuals to pursue a good in ways that accord with the exercise of the powers of rational and moral agency. Primary among such basic rights would be freedom of thought, speech, and inquiry; freedom of conscientious judgment in matters of ethics and religion (including questions about what gives life its meaning); freedom of association; freedom of occupation and of movement; the rights needed to maintain the physical and psychological integrity of the person; the rights of political participation; and the rights to hold (personal) property. (It would require extensive discussion to indicate why each of these rights is necessary to exercise and maintain the powers of agency. So here I simply state those rights I think could be so justified.)[13]

On this way of conceiving of liberalism, we are prompted to construe such notions as autonomy, personal sovereignty, or self-determination, not simply as an abstract right, but in terms of an ideal of persons and their social relations, an ideal which is both worth realizing and which ought to be maintained. This ideal of equal self-governing agents provides impetus for rights of self-determination; it defines their role in social relations. The role of these rights is to promote and maintain the realization of this ideal of the person. Primary among the conditions necessary for realizing this ideal is that self-governing agents develop and exercise their capacities for rational and moral agency. Rights of self-determination are then defined as the class of rights that are socially necessary for this purpose. Whatever these rights are, they are conceived as basic, since they in part specify just what is involved in being a free self-governing agent with equal status.

To say these rights are basic implies at least two things. First, basic rights are *fundamental*, in the sense that they cannot be infringed upon or limited by governments or others for the sake of other rights or values. They cannot be limited, then, for the sake of promoting overall welfare, perfectionist values of culture, the aims of efficiency, or majority will. Nor can they be limited for the sake of other nonbasic rights (such as rights of property or contract). Basic rights as a class have absolute weight with respect to non-basic rights as well as other values. A basic right can be limited for the sake of protecting and maintaining other rights that are basic to the person. (So, for example, to take a standard case, freedom of speech can be limited if one's speech creates an imminent danger of bodily harm to others, thereby jeopardizing the liberty and integrity of their persons.) This means that no basic right is, by itself, absolute with respect to other basic rights, but the class as a whole is absolute with respect to other reasons.

Second, basic rights are also *inalienable*. Not only can they not be infringed on by others; they also cannot be abandoned or contracted away by agents themselves in exchange for compensating benefits. Citizens cannot, for example, sell their political rights to vote, to hold office, to present grievances, and to assemble and therewith join and form political parties. Alienation of these rights would undermine their capacities for self-government in social contexts and destroy their equal status as citizens. Some basic rights might be involuntarily forfeited, when a person commits a serious crime. Political rights and other freedoms of the person, such as freedom of movement and association (but not liberty of conscience), are forfeited when one is justly convicted of a felony, for example. But forfeiture of one's basic rights upon violating others' rights is not the same thing as their self-imposed alienation for the sake of gaining greater apparent benefits.

Now if we see de jure autonomy, not as an underivative right that is intuitively given, nor as a capacity merely instrumental to realizing a prior independent nonmoral good, but, instead, as part of an ideal of persons that is worth realizing and which ought to be maintained, then the argument for inalienability of rights of self-determination comes into focus. To begin with, whatever rights are socially necessary to exercise the capacities for agency, it is clear that an unqualified right of alienability is not among them. By such a right I mean a legally enforceable absolute right of contract or voluntary forfeiture, one which incorporates a higher-order right to bargain or give away any and all rights one has, including all of the rights that are basic and essential to agency. When he contends that complete alienability is not simply allowed but is required by personal sovereignty, Feinberg can be construed as saying that absolute rights of contract are among the basic rights that are a condition of de jure autonomy. But how can this be? What supports this position?[14] Feinberg contends that absolute control over a domain, and therewith alienability, are connected with the concept of autonomy, conceived as personal sovereignty.[15] But one can clearly be autonomous, in the sense of being a fully functioning and equal self-governing member of society, without having the right to alienate all or some of the basic rights that constitute de jure autonomy. One can intelligently formulate a wide range of systems of ends, freely pursue them, take advantage of expansive social opportunities, and fulfill one's duties as a person and a citizen, without possessing rights of complete alienability. What function could such a right serve with respect to exercising and maintaining the capacities for agency? Complete alienability is not essential to establishing or maintaining this ideal of the person.

Now, granted there may be conceptions of the good where individuals are willing to trade off basic rights for compensating benefits.[16] But so what? In deciding what basic rights individuals have to begin with, we cannot simply take existing desires and conceptions of the good formed under any circumstance as given. (The desire to dominate others is clearly not a conception of the good that is relevant to deciding what basic rights people have, no matter how essential this desire may be to a person's "individuality.") In specifying the basic rights that are part of de jure autonomy, what we seek to formulate is the very criterion for deciding whether existing conceptions of the good are permissible. So we have to look to some other criterion than people's given ends. This is one reason for focusing on the capacities for moral and rational agency. They provide an appropriate objective criterion for defining the basic rights autonomous persons have, since these powers enable persons to form, amend, and pursue a conception of the good in cooperative social contexts. The primary role of basic rights is that they are fundamental social conditions for realizing these powers.[17] Since complete alienability is not among these social conditions, it is not a basic right.

But more to the point, self-governing agents cannot *remain* equal or self-governing if they are allowed to alienate the rights that define their status as equals. Rousseau says, "Renouncing one's liberty is renouncing one's dignity as a man, the rights of humanity, and even its duties. There is no possible compensation for anyone who renounces everything."[18] Rousseau should not be taken to mean that there are no conditions under which it can be rational, given a person's conception of the good, to give up all their liberties by, say, selling themselves into slavery. (Suppose, for instance, that a person and her family were all starving in a society which cared little for its members, and the only way for her to provide for her children's survival under those conditions was by agreeing to become another's slave.) But not just any circumstance is a relevant baseline for deciding what basic rights people have. Even if there might be extreme conditions under which it is rational for a person to alienate all her liberties, still it is a separate issue whether a social order (or an individual, in this case, the slaveholder) which enforces such a private agreement is just.

Kant goes further, to argue that there is something incoherent—a "contradiction"—involved in the autonomous alienation of the rights of autonomy.[19] Here, Feinberg insists that there is nothing *logically* incoherent about autonomously alienating one's autonomy, and this may be correct. (At least on Feinberg's thin account of autonomy; one can voluntarily choose to give up one's liberties [pp. 68–70].) Kant however is not talking about a logical contradiction but about a "contradiction in the will": what we, as free rational moral agents, could will, not just for ourselves, but universally for everyone, compatible with our shared "humanity" (that is, our capacities for rational and moral agency). In terms of Kant's categorical imperative, we could not, for the sake of our particular good, individually will to abandon all our liberties—since it would conflict with our general will as moral agents, which is to provide necessary conditions for the exercise of the moral and rational powers of everyone. The details of Kant's view aside, his general point is that there is no way that the ideal of persons as self-governing, and the ideal of their relations as equals, can be realized and maintained if alienation is morally or politically allowed. A right of complete alienability, like an unqualified right of self-destruction, defeats the very ideal of the person upon which de jure autonomy is grounded.

Inalienability then preserves a kind of moral status. The liberal insistence on the inalienability of basic rights serves the role of maintaining the equal status of citizens as free self-governing agents, which is part of the political ideal of the person upon which rights of self-determination are grounded. Granted, again, there may be extreme conditions where a person's particular good makes it rational to abandon his basic rights and liberties. But what we would rationally want under the most extreme conditions should not provide the benchmark for assessing the nature and scope of the rights of self-determination under social conditions generally. Like the desire to violate the rights of others, that desire should count for nothing in establishing and interpreting basic liberal rights.

The argument for inalienability (and, therefore, against any proposed right to sell oneself into slavery) asserts that inalienability is a social condition of realizing and maintaining the ideal of persons as equal autonomous agents, a condition upon which liberal rights of self-determination are grounded. If we are to be persuaded that autonomy is the fundamental social value in a liberal order, then it must be one that is seen as worth maintaining and which ought to be maintained, even against an agent's will to dispose of it. As a fundamental value, rights of autonomy are imperatives in the sense that they cannot be dispensed with. While the autonomous alienation of autonomy is an idea that might make sense (on some readings of autonomy), it is morally at odds with the moral significance of autonomy itself. Rights of autonomy are derived from an ideal of persons that rules out conceptions of the good that require abandoning or destroying one's capacities for agency. Inalienability then provides one sense for Rousseau's adage that citizens can be "forced to be free": they can be prohibited from alienating the rights that are essential to agency and, therefore, to their dignity as persons. Without the inalienability condition, a view is not designed to establish and maintain autonomy, but some other value, such as absolute freedom of contract and the satisfaction of individual agents' unrestricted self-regarding desires. Such a view is not, I maintain, genuinely a liberal view.

Is There an Unqualified Right to Use Drugs?

Now to turn to the issue of whether there is an unqualified moral right to use psychoactive drugs in a constitutional democracy. On Feinberg's soft paternalistic view, we have a right to act for "unreasonable" (that is, imprudent) ends so long as we are competent and choice is voluntary. Since, for Feinberg, adequate information is a condition of voluntary choice, this does not give us a right to cause harm to ourselves in an uninformed way (pp. 127–134). It is legitimate then for a liberal government to enact laws that regulate recreational drug use, to insure that the choice to use drugs is informed. But as for the competent person who is informed of the dangers of addictive drug use, so long as the decision is not due to psychological impairment, he may use such drugs, even if it will certainly harm him in the future (p. 133). So, regarding the person who does not care about the physical harm of drug use, or who even wants to harm himself, Feinberg says, "If no third-party interests are directly involved . . . the state can hardly be permitted to declare his philosophical convictions unsound or 'sick' and prevent him from practicing them, without assuming powers that it will inevitably misuse disastrously" (p. 133).

Coupled with his claim that "a person's right of self-determination, being sovereign, takes precedence even over his own good,"[20] the implication of Feinberg's example is that we have a right to use drugs; and that so long as use is voluntary, informed, and does not injure others' interests, the right to use drugs is absolute, even if it entails one's self-destruction.[21]

What now are the implications for a right to use drugs on the account of liberalism I have outlined? I do not plan to argue, nor do I think it can be argued, that a liberal government has the power to prohibit any action that does not optimally tend toward the development and exercise of the capacities for moral and rational agency.[22] On such a reading of liberalism, recreational drug use would most likely be prohibitable (along with many other nonproductive leisure activities). But this is not the role of the ideal of the person presented. This ideal is a standard for specifying basic liberal rights, duties, and institutions, with their scope and limits. It is not conceived of as a good that liberal society must maximize. Indeed, it is not clear what is meant by maximizing the development of these powers. And even if it was clear, it would be a mistake to conceive of realizing the powers of agency as an incremental good that should be maximized.[23] To seek to maximize these powers would not leave space for individuals' pursuits of other final ends and so would transform the view into a kind of (teleological) perfectionism that is at odds with liberalism.[24] Most any liberal view must provide for a plurality of goods and worthwhile ways of life that are permissible for citizens to freely pursue. The capacities for moral and rational agency enable the pursuit of the wide range of opportunities and permissible conceptions of the good that a liberal society provides for and sanctions. To see exercise of these powers as a good that is to be maximized would deprive them of their point. So, rather than conceiving of development of the capacities for rational and moral agency as an incremental good (or even as intrinsic goods for each agent), they are more correctly seen as *essential conditions* for liberal citizens, allowing them to have a conception of the good and to comply with the norms of justice of a liberal society.[25]

While it is not the role of a constitutional democracy to fix any particular conception of the good for all its citizens, it is an appropriate, and indeed necessary, role of a constitutional democracy to maintain the conditions for citizens' free pursuit of their good in society. Exercising the capacities for moral and rational agency is fundamental among these conditions. One role of a liberal constitution is to specify the basic rights and duties that are required for this purpose. By so doing, it sets limits on the domain of conceptions of the good that are permissible to pursue. A conception of the good that requires violation of others' basic rights is clearly not within this domain. Nor, I have argued, is legalized voluntary slavery among the permissible liberal lifestyles that an agent may choose; so too with any plan of life that requires abandoning one's status as an equal self-governing citizen. Our question is whether recreational drug use is among the permissible activities or ways of life in a liberal society.

Unlike the case of voluntary slavery or alienation of one's basic rights, there is no straightforward easy answer here. Once again, Feinberg is surely right in saying, "There must be a right to err, to be mistaken, to decide foolishly, to take big risks, if there is to be any meaningful self-rule; without it, the whole idea of *de jure* autonomy begins to unravel" (p. 62).

We can accept this without conceding that it implies an unqualified right to act in ways that will destroy or permanently impair one's capacities for agency. A distinction can be drawn between normal risk-taking for the sake of valued activities (such as mountain climbing, motorcycle riding, parachuting, or eating fatty foods), as opposed to activities which, by their nature, destroy or permanently undermine a person's capacities for engaging in rationally chosen valued activities. Let us call this latter class "intrinsically debilitating activities." Among this class are such things as committing suicide, enlisting another to kill you, or permanently mutilating one's cognitive or conative capacities (such as through a frontal lobotomy). A liberal society can, I believe, legitimately prohibit these kinds of activities, except when there are special reasons. Special reasons might then justify assisted suicide—perhaps even active consensual euthanasia— when one is suffering from an incurable condition and death is imminent or one's capacities for agency are degenerating. Under conditions where the capacities for agency are no longer functional, the usual liberal reasons for asserting nondestructibility of one's own life no longer obtain. But one cannot voluntarily kill oneself for just any reason (on a bet, say, or because one has been jilted, or because one just likes the idea). The same is true of self-mutilation of one's cognitive and conative capacities.

On this line of reasoning, alcohol and smoking cigarettes would seem to be permissible activities. For drinking alcohol is clearly compatible with the full exercise of powers of rational and moral agency (indeed, in due proportion, an occasional drink can even help some of us along the way). There is nothing intrinsically debilitating about alcohol. Granted it can be abused, as can many other things (including exercise or dieting). But the activity itself is not such that, by its nature, it destroys one's capacities for agency. And the same is true of cigarettes. Though they may shorten one's life, they do not necessarily, if at all, debilitate one's capacities while one is living.

But alcohol is an intoxicating substance, and cigarettes are physically addictive. If these substances are permissible in a liberal society, then so too must be certain other presently illegal drugs (other things being equal). There is nothing intrinsically debilitating about marijuana or hashish, and the same may well be true about mescaline and LSD. Granted, taking these substances can temporarily suspend one's exercise of the capacities for agency, but then so too can overconsumption of alcohol and many other permitted activities. On the standard I have proposed, a substance must be such that by its nature it permanently undermines or at least indefinitely suspends ones capacities for rational and moral agency. None of these drugs meet that condition.

What about heroin and cocaine? These drugs are on most accounts physiologically addictive, but addiction by itself does not permanently undermine the exercise of one's capacities—compare them with nicotine. Many people function fairly normally while using cocaine recreationally, and perhaps the same is even true of heroin.[26] Douglas Husak has argued that, while breaking one's addiction to these substances may be painful and require strong acts of will, still it is doable and has been done by the majority of addicts.[27] On the other hand, for many addicts readdiction is a common phenomenon, largely for psychological and social reasons.[28] I am not in a position to judge whether heroin, cocaine, or crack cocaine can be classified as intrinsically debilitating drugs. It is an empirical issue, to be decided upon with advice from pharmacologists, psychologists, and other professionals.

In any case, it is highly likely that there is a large class of drugs currently prohibited which are not prohibitable on the grounds I have considered. (I assume, however, that even these drugs are legally regulable to varying degrees for other reasons, certainly to protect others from harm, and also for the reasons Feinberg mentions, namely, to insure that usage is voluntary and informed, and that minors are not allowed access.) Nonetheless, there also is a class of drugs which can be described as intrinsically debilitating of one's capacities—even if no such substance actually exists, then there is at least the potential of one.[29] Of the substances in this class, it can legitimately be claimed that a liberal government has the authority to prohibit their use for no other reason than that they permanently or indefinitely impair our capacities for rational and moral agency.

This argument does nothing to rule out activities which temporally make it difficult to exercise the powers of agency. People have the political right to be temporally intoxicated (as they have the right to mesmerize themselves before the TV). Doing that does not continuously deprive them of their faculties for practical reasoning so that they can no longer function as self-governing agents. After they sober up, they can continue their lives in a normal way. But where normalcy is permanent suspension of one's capacities, or deprivation to the degree that one is indefinitely incapacitated, a liberal system can legitimately prohibit such activities. The right to become intoxicated does not imply a right to make a zombie of oneself.

A liberal constitution has the authority to require that people develop their capacities for agency. This is one justification for mandatory education in a liberal society. Mandatory education seeks to insure that children become capable of developing their faculties, forming a conception of their good, and understanding and taking advantage of the opportunities that are open to them; moreover, liberal education aims to guarantee that individuals can understand and comply with their public duties to respect the laws and the rights of others, and that they develop an interest in maintaining the continuation of liberal institutions.[30] For many of the same reasons, a liberal constitutional democracy has the legitimate authority to proscribe self-regarding conduct that by its nature permanently impairs the exercise or development of the capacities for agency that are part of the ideal of liberal sovereignty. One is free in a liberal society to choose whether or not to take advantage of the basic rights and opportunities it affords; one is not free to engage in activities designed to permanently impair one's capacities to exercise these rights, any more than one is free to alienate them.

On this principle, admittedly, not everything will be clear cut; there are going to be many hard cases, as there will with most any principle. But even where a principle cannot resolve all ambiguities, still it helps us to understand why certain cases are hard to resolve. In so doing, it points us toward the kinds of considerations that are relevant to finally deciding the issue. If at the end of the day all of these considerations still do not suffice to resolve all ambiguities, then in a constitutional democracy the question can be left to majority decision as a means of political settlement. This may seem unsatisfactory to those who have a desire for clear lines of demarcation and systemization. But determinacy of outcome is not the first virtue of moral principles. It is more important that principles be capable of serving as a basis for public justification and fit with our most firmly considered moral convictions, including the ideal of the person that is implicit in our moral judgments of justice in a constitutional democracy.

Social Considerations

I have advanced one argument for limiting free availability of certain psychoactive drugs in response to the common contention that liberal autonomy is incompatible with restrictions on drug use no matter how self-destructive these drugs may be. My argument, however, agrees with the position of proponents of decriminalization to the extent that it implies that many (perhaps even most) currently interdicted drugs should be legalized. But there are considerations other than the nature and requirements of liberal autonomy that need be taken into account before a complete liberal drug policy can be formulated. The argument from autonomy addresses what may well be highly artificial circumstances, namely, where use of drugs does not substantially and adversely affect the interests of others. At the beginning of this essay, I recounted the social consequences of criminalization that lead many to argue for decriminalization. Here I conclude with some considerations regarding the potentially adverse social consequences of drug use, which need be considered before this complicated issue can be resolved.

Suppose that free availability of a drug left people capable of exercising their capacities for agency to the minimum requisite degree. At the same time, it deprived them of the motivation or ability to do productive work and destabilized family life.[31] Suppose, too, that legalization and unrestricted availability of the drug had the effect of promoting widespread use on a scale larger than currently obtains. Consequently, living standards and familial stability decline considerably for many people. Large numbers of children are left impoverished and neglected, and their education and socialization is impaired. Many are abandoned or abused, and consequently come to lead lives destructive not only of themselves, but also of others. These are legitimate grounds for restricting such a drug in a liberal constitutional democracy (assuming such measures effectively mitigate these adverse consequences). While it is not the function of a liberal government to inquire into the social productivity of its citizens and require them to perform work that a majority regards as useful, still it is legitimate for a liberal government to take necessary measures to maintain and reproduce liberal society so that it can insure the conditions of its continued stability.

To elaborate, one important role of a liberal government is to secure conditions for the production of adequate material resources that are needed to maintain a just society and the dignity of each of its members. This is not at all to say a liberal government's role is to encourage maximum productive output (certainly not without regard to distribution, as many classical liberals maintain). Economic efficiency is subordinate as a liberal end; it should be regulated and directed toward maintaining a society in which each person is enabled to effectively exercise basic rights and liberties, take advantage of fair opportunities, and achieve individual independence. But given this more basic distributive end, liberal society has a legitimate interest in providing and maintaining conditions under which people can be productive and self-supporting. This does not mean the able-bodied must labor to avoid sacrificing a government-sponsored basic income.[32] It means rather that government has the responsibility to maintain a setting in which they can develop their capacities and be productive. When a subculture of addiction becomes so severe and widespread that it affects individuals' opportunities to develop their abilities and engage in production, they are in effect denied fair opportunities, and liberal institutions themselves are undermined.

Another important role of a liberal government is to secure conditions necessary for the reproduction of liberal culture and the continuation of liberal society across generations. Herein lies government's interest in maintaining the integrity of family life (in some form), and seeing to it that parents and guardians protect, support, and educate children under their care. The reproduction of liberal institutions and culture also plays a significant role in justifying and defining the purposes of a mandatory educational system (discussed above). When the family and the system of education are undermined by adverse effects of free availability of drugs, liberal society's ongoing need to perpetuate itself is endangered.

So, if the consequences of free availability of a drug substantially impair the ability of a liberal society to produce adequate sustaining resources or to reproduce liberal culture and institutions from one generation to the next, then there are legitimate liberal reasons for restricting that drug, in order to protect the interests of current and future generations. As individuals cannot exercise liberal rights in a way that is calculated to destroy their capacities for agency, so they cannot exercise these rights in a way that destroys or undermines the conditions of liberal culture needed to sustain the free exercise of these capacities. Liberalism is not committed to standing by and passively witnessing the destruction of its culture and institutions to the point where society itself can only be sustained by illiberal and autocratic measures. These considerations need to be weighed in the balance, along with the arguments against drug interdiction recited at the outset of this paper, in finally coming to a decision about the permissibility of psychoactive drugs in a liberal constitutional democracy.

PART III

DEMOCRACY, POLITICS, AND DRUGS

CHAPTER FIVE

Drugs and Democracy

J. DONALD MOON

In this essay I address two broad questions. First, what policies regarding the nontherapeutic use of drugs may legitimately be pursued in a democratic, morally pluralist society? Second, what might the discourse about drugs and our experience with drug policy teach us about democratic theory and practice, particularly about the possibilities of a deliberative ideal of democracy under conditions of moral pluralism?

In keeping with much of the literature in this area, I understand drugs to be substances that alter one's state of consciousness. Sometimes people may want to use drugs because it is fun, exciting, or just pleasant. They may instead (or also) have religious reasons, or be moved by an aesthetic or philosophical rationale such as the one Aldous Huxley offered.[1] Or they may use drugs because, as Sigmund Freud argued, it is the "crudest, but also the most effective" method of avoiding the suffering that is endemic to the human condition.[2]

I will not discuss the regulation of drugs for therapeutic purposes. Typical pure food and drug regulations limit access to medicines unless they have met certain standards, usually safety and efficacy. As a consumer, I want assurance that medicines are safe and effective, and these laws serve that purpose. Libertarians might argue that they restrict my choices, but they do so only in an incidental way, by removing from the market products that I do not wish to consume. That is obviously not the case for nontherapeutic uses of drugs. While consumers have an interest in the purity of such drugs, they do not need expert judgments of the drugs' effectiveness, since they can evaluate that for themselves. And while they might benefit from knowledge of the risks the drug poses, consumers wish to decide for themselves whether the risks (at least to their own health) are "worthwhile." While there are obvious practical problems in making the separation between therapeutic and nontherapeutic uses, I hope the conceptual distinction is reasonably clear.

Drug policy in the United States (as in most countries) prohibits the production, sale, and use of most drugs, with the notable exceptions of alcohol and tobacco. I will argue that this policy is not justifiable. My argument will proceed in three steps. In the first section, I will present what I call the fundamental principle of democratic legitimacy, showing how our current drug policy violates that principle. In the second section, I will argue that our current drug policy is unjust: by punishing those who use drugs, it treats drug users as mere instruments to the well-being of others, and the costs of this policy are disproportionately borne by the least-advantaged members of our society. In the third section, I consider and reject the possibility that drug use can be prohibited on the grounds that it causes addiction, thereby undermining capacities necessary to participate in democratic processes, irrespective of the harm addiction may also cause.[3] Finally, in the concluding section I return to the ideal of democracy on which the paper is based to examine how our experience with legislation against drugs suggests possible limitations of that ideal itself.

Drugs and Harms

Much of the debate about drug policy turns on prudential considerations. Many arguments are straightforwardly utilitarian, looking at the benefits and costs of different regulatory regimes, where benefits and costs are essentially defined in terms of the satisfaction of preferences. More often, a broadly consequentialist framework is supplemented by some consideration of individual rights, particularly rights to privacy and self-determination. The key issues are the consequences of different policies: whether intended outcomes are feasible at all, and what other consequences they will produce. An increasing number of critics have come to the conclusion that the war against drugs—the policy of prohibition—is not working and cannot work. In spite of enormous efforts to suppress the supply of drugs and to reduce demand either by intimidating or treating users, drugs are still readily available, and large numbers of people continue to use and abuse them. Moreover, the critics charge, these policies are misdirected, at least if their aim is to reduce the costs of drug use, since alcohol and tobacco are far more harmful than illegal drugs, particularly when compared to marijuana. Indeed, the critics argue, most of the harms associated with drugs, such as crime, corruption, disease, and the disintegration of family and community life in certain areas, are the result not of drugs, but of the policy to prohibit their use. Steven B. Duke and Albert C. Gross, for example, advocate a "harm minimization approach" to drug regulation, one that would attempt to minimize the damage of drug use by such means as legalizing the sale of drugs through licensed suppliers to adults while prohibiting public consumption, sale to juveniles, and "the use of brand names on packaging" (to discourage advertising).[4] They would also provide generous support for treatment and thoughtful programs of education. They argue that this approach would realize vast economic savings, reduce police corruption, help restore the integrity of the legal system, and respect rights to individual privacy and autonomy, all without significantly increasing the level of drug abuse in society.

These are important arguments, and weighty considerations can be offered on both sides. Just as critics of our current policies can point to the terrible costs they involve, defenders can point to the damage that drug users do, not only to themselves, but also to others. Joel Hay, for example, argues that the damage that pregnant women cause to their babies by using crack are enormous. Believing that a movement away from the current system would lead to even higher levels of drug use and, thus, higher costs, Hay would prefer "a real drug war, with swift and certain punishment of casual drug users, to a drug-legalization surrender."[5]

Arguments such as these can never be conclusive, because they depend upon uncertain forecasts of what would happen under different regulatory regimes. In the face of such difficulty, one is tempted to short-circuit such arguments by appealing directly to overriding values. Libertarians claim an inviolable right to act in ways that do not harm others, a right that cannot be infringed by any government, not even a democratic one.[6] But this move is fraught with well-known difficulties, most prominently the absence of any plausible account of how such a right can be grounded.[7] Moreover, it is subject to obvious counter-examples. It would, for example, appear to rule out "animal welfare legislation," laws against "public nuisances that are not health risks," and regulations limiting what one can do to or on one's property which are designed to realize aesthetic values, such as the preservation of historical structures or sites.[8]

Prohibitionists, on the other hand, are tempted to skirt these issues by appealing directly to the moral wrongness of drug use itself. The real objections to drug use, Richards has argued, are probably rooted in ideals of human excellence that have wide currency in our culture. Richards suggests that at least one of the roots of America's aversion to drugs can be found in the "Radical Reformation," particularly the demand that "all members spiritually imitate Christ," which led to the condemnation of the use of drugs for nonmedical purposes.[9] Since the beginning of systematic thinking about politics most political thinkers have taken it for granted that laws should require citizens to conform to moral ideals.[10] That presumption is based on the view explicated by Robert George that, while laws cannot make people virtuous, they

> can help people to establish and preserve a virtuous character by (1) preventing the (further) self-corruption which follows from acting out a choice to indulge in immoral conduct; (2) preventing the bad example by which others are induced to emulate such behavior; (3) helping to preserve the moral ecology in which people make their morally self-constituting choices; and (4) educating people about moral right and wrong. (Robert George, *Making Men Moral* [Princeton: Princeton University Press, 1993], p. 1.)

Thinkers differ in the emphasis they place on these factors; communitarians, for example, focus on (3), while many Christian thinkers emphasize (1), but perfectionism, the view that politics should aim at the cultivation of moral excellence, or what Michael Sandel calls a "formative politics," has probably been the dominant position in the history of political thought.

Few proponents of prohibition articulate these issues clearly, but they appear to be implicit in much of what they say. James Q. Wilson, for example, argues that the reason we must prohibit drug use is out of a concern with "character," that is, with the moral virtue of citizens. Acknowledging that we "cannot coerce people into goodness," he argues that "we can and should insist that some standards must be met if society itself . . . is to persist. Drawing the line that defines those standards is difficult and contentious, but if crack and heroin use does not fall below it, what does?"[11]

The standard of moral judgment, Wilson argues, is the consistency of an action or practice with "man's social nature"; by that standard, he argues, "alcohol and cocaine addiction . . . degrade the spirit," making users "less than human."[12] Given the moral weight of these considerations, it is not surprising that prudential arguments fail to persuade many who defend prohibition.

Just as the libertarian response is inadequate, there are powerful reasons for rejecting the perfectionist position, at least in the context of a democratic society that is characterized by moral pluralism. In the rest of this section, I will set out a conception of democratic legitimacy which limits, but does not entirely rule out, the admissibility of such perfectionist appeals. The position I defend gives substantial support to critics of prohibition, but it does not necessarily support a program of full legalization, nor does it rule out public action to discourage the use of drugs.

A society is morally pluralist when different groups within it hold different and even opposed conceptions of the fundamental goods or ends of human life. Moral pluralism gives rise to disagreement, but it must be stressed that moral disagreement does not presuppose skepticism or any form of noncognitivism. Even if there is a true, coherent ordering of all genuine values, reasonable disagreement about that ordering may still be possible because of what John Rawls has called the "burdens of judgment." Reasonable disagreement, he writes, "is disagreement among reasonable persons," who "share a common human reason, similar powers of thought and judgment: they can draw inferences, weigh evidence, and balance competing considerations."[13] Disagreement among reasonable persons is possible, he argues, because the grounds on which we make judgments (both theoretical and practical) are often inadequate in various ways. The evidence may be conflicting and hard to assess, or people may disagree about the weight to be assigned to different considerations, or different normative considerations may be found on both sides of an issue. Although the public use of reason may be adequate to resolve many issues, there will be some that cannot be settled in this way.

The difficulties of settling such issues run even deeper than Rawls's account suggests. His account focuses on rather narrow differences, particularly regarding the adequacy of the empirical evidence that can be offered for particular claims. But the more profound difficulties involve deep philosophical issues, such as the defensibility of functionalist or teleological accounts of nature. Other difficulties involve the adequacy of the conceptual and theoretical framework within which a particular account is developed, such as the adequacy of Hobbes's account of rationality as instrumental reasoning. Contrary to skeptical or noncognitivist views, value judgments regarding the human good and the forms of human excellence are (or at least can be) grounded in more or less articulated and elaborate theoretical and conceptual frameworks which are subject both to philosophical criticism and to empirical testing. But because the world does not present itself to us arranged by the categories of the true conceptual scheme, our theories—both in their normative and in their explanatory-descriptive aspects—are always underdetermined relative to the evidence available to us.[14] Thus, we must always bear the burdens of judgment, at least with regard to such basic dimensions of value as the human good and forms of human excellence. Reasonable disagreement on these matters is an inescapable part of the human condition.

The fact of reasonable disagreement gives rise to obvious problems for a democratic society. If we cannot find rational grounds on which to reach agreement, it might appear that any solution to conflict would have to involve one party imposing its will upon the other. In other words, as Alasdair MacIntyre has put it, democratic politics could only be "civil war carried on by other means."[15] Happily, our situation is not so grim, for there is another approach to moral disagreement that we can employ, what Rawls calls "constructivism."

Rawls defines constructivism as the view that "principles of political justice may be represented as the outcome of a certain procedure of construction," as opposed to the view that they are "statements about an independent order of moral values" which "does not depend on, nor is it to be explained by, the activity of any actual (human) minds."[16] Broadly speaking, constructivism holds that political principles can be the objects of rationally motivated agreement among appropriately situated individuals. Their validity reflects not their correspondence, in some sense of that word, to an order of moral facts, but their being generated by, or constructed in accordance with, a certain set of procedures.

Constructivism assumes that the problem we face is to define norms governing the forms of social cooperation that can be regarded as valid or binding, so that everyone can be justified in acting in accordance with them. Perhaps the most felicitous formulation of this idea has been offered by T. M. Scanlon, who offers an explication of moral wrongness in the following terms: "An act is wrong if its performance under the circumstances would be disallowed by any system of rules for the general regulation of behavior which no one could reasonably reject as a basis for informed, unforced general agreement."[17]

Scanlon, who refers to his approach as "contractualism," argues that "the source of motivation that is directly triggered by a belief that an action is wrong is the desire to be able to justify one's actions to others on grounds they could not reasonably reject."[18] If the norms governing our relationships are ones that no one subject to them could "reasonably reject," then we can regard ourselves as justified when we follow those norms. He does not claim that this motivation is inherent in human nature; rather, his account is intended to explain what constitutes a moral motivation.

If acting morally is to act in a way that can be justified to others because one acts on the basis of principles they could not reasonably reject, then morality is closely tied to what we might call the fundamental criterion (or principle) of democratic legitimacy. In Rawls's words, "since political power is the coercive power of free and equal citizens [acting] as a corporate body, this power should be exercised, when constitutional essentials and basic questions of justice are at stake, only in ways that all citizens can reasonably be expected to endorse in the light of their common human reason."[19] When I can endorse the grounds on which power is exercised, I recognize that exercise of power as justified or legitimate. When I cannot endorse those grounds, I am a victim of superior force, and not a participant in democratic self-governance.

It follows that a pluralist society respecting the criterion of democratic legitimacy must be based on norms that people who hold different views about the ends of human life can nonetheless accept. This will be possible only if the scope of political authority is limited, allowing individuals freedom to pursue their different visions of human well-being. Public policy may not be used in order to promote a particular conception of the ends of human life, even one supported by a majority, if it is opposed to the values held by other citizens. On the contrary, the state should as much as possible be neutral or impartial among the different values held by its citizens.[20]

This ideal of impartiality, expressed by the principle of democratic legitimacy, tends to rule out perfectionist arguments in support of prohibition on nontherapeutic uses of drugs. When there is reasonable disagreement about the role of drugs in a good life, then basing public policy on a narrow or sectarian ideal is an unjust imposition on those who do not share that ideal. This is not a matter of "bracketing controversial moral questions for the sake of political agreement," as some critics have charged.[21] Rather, it is a moral obligation rooted in a deep commitment to moral action as action that can be justified to others.

It might be argued that access to drugs does not involve "constitutional essentials" for it could hardly be claimed that there is a fundamental right, say, to smoke pot. But drug prohibition raises such issues indirectly. The criteria justifying the use of the criminal law to restrict individual liberty involve fundamental questions of justice, inasmuch as basic rights to self-determination and the control of one's body are at stake. Further, the principle of democratic legitimacy should be seen as a regulative ideal that extends to all aspects of public policy. There are certainly questions that do not raise serious issues of principle and so may be decided through whatever procedures have been established, but even in these cases the ideal is, or should be, one of nonimposition. America's drug policy is accompanied by a massive use of force against its citizens; with over 300,000 people in state and federal prisons (not counting those in local jails) serving time for drug offenses, it is essential to ask whether "all citizens can reasonably be expected to endorse [these laws] in light of their common human reason."

But can people "reasonably" reject norms prohibiting the nontherapeutic use of drugs? The argument for government neutrality that I have been making does not free us from the need to address the questions perfectionists raise precisely because it does not appeal to merely prudential considerations, but makes a moral claim instead. Even if moral pluralism and the burdens of reason require us to reject the age-old conception of politics as dedicated to making people virtuous, we still have to ask whether the rejection of a proposed norm is "reasonable," which in part, at least, involves the question of whether the norm would prevent someone from living what can be seen as a good life. Since we all know of people whose lives have been shattered because they have abused drugs, it may seem easy to conclude that drug prohibition can pass the test of democratic legitimacy.

At this point we must return to the empirical observations and prudential arguments discussed above. There seems to be little doubt that the most damaging drugs by far are legal drugs. Tobacco, used by 60 million people, kills 390,000 people a year, or 650 per 100,000 users; marijuana, used by almost 10 million, is not known to have caused any deaths.[22] Alcohol is perhaps the most dangerous drug; because it appears to cause at least some users to lose their inhibitions against violence toward others and their sense of judgment regarding their own abilities, alcohol consumption can lead to assault and to mayhem on the highways.[23] The obvious conclusion to draw from these considerations is that our policy of prohibition should, in principle at least, be extended to include dangerous but not currently illegal drugs, but few people propose doing so today. At least in the case of alcohol, most people are willing to concede that it can play a valuable role in a full human life. Quite apart from its religious and culinary value, it contributes to stress reduction, sociality, and causes pleasurable sensations. Indeed, that mood-altering drugs have value is encoded in our language; the phrase "drug abuse" designates undesirable uses of drugs, as contrasted with uses that play a positive role.

It is necessary to stress that this sketch of a justification for alcohol is not intended to show that alcohol *is* of value, only that the claim that it is good is not unreasonable, so that the demand for its prohibition could not pass the Rawlsian "burdens of judgment" test. Similar arguments can be made for other mood-altering drugs, although because they lack the long traditions of alcohol use (at least in our culture), their value may seem less evident or compelling. To demonstrate this would require the kind of case-by-case analysis that Husak offers in a careful, finely balanced argument showing that, whatever the harms resulting from the use of drugs, they are either not sufficiently serious to justify criminalization, or they can be combatted more effectively in other ways.[24]

Thus, our current policy of prohibition violates the principle of democratic legitimacy, insofar as it is designed to promote a particular conception of the good. But that is not to say that a democracy must adopt a policy of full legalization, or that its policies must be neutral between those who find drug use to be immoral and those who do not. Drug use can cause harm to others, and the addictive properties of drugs may justify special measures to keep them out of the hands of juveniles, and even to discourage their use for adults. But regulation and prohibition are quite different.

Drug Prohibition and Justice

I have been arguing that prohibition cannot pass the test of democratic legitimacy in a pluralist society and is unjust for that reason. But it is also unjust for other reasons: in punishing users, it denies them the respect that we owe human beings, and it imposes heavy costs on the least advantaged members of our society. Earlier I endorsed the view that drugs, including especially alcohol and tobacco, do cause real damage, both to the people who use them and to others. If we are to live, or at least to live decently, in society with others, we cannot be indifferent to the conditions of our fellows citizens, even when their conditions are in large part the consequences of their own actions. "Friends don't let friends drive drunk," the bumper sticker reminds us.

But there is a difference between admonishing one's friends and using the criminal law to prohibit drug use. Such a policy violates the fundamental principle of democratic legitimacy because it amounts to the imposition of a particular conception of the ends or good of human life on others who do not share that conception. It is therefore inconsistent with the requirements of justice in a pluralist society of free and equal persons. But it is also unjust in a more direct and obvious way.

The war on drugs, particularly the criminalization of drug use, has led to the imprisonment of a large number of people, sometimes for long periods of time, and has forced even larger numbers to live in a way that is impoverished and often degrading because a central activity of their lives involves using illegal substances. It is hard to see how such cruel treatment can be justified in terms of the good of the drug users themselves. Wilson argues that the "compulsion" (for which we must read "violence") directed at drug users is beneficial in that it forces some of them into treatment.[25] But the emphasis in his writings, and in other prohibitionist writings, is on deterrence. By dramatically raising the costs of using drugs, prohibitionists argue, large numbers of people who would otherwise try them and become addicted are spared that fate. Wilson cites the example of the Vietnam veterans who gave up heroin when they returned from Vietnam, asking how many would have done so had the drug been legally available? It would appear that the major argument against legalizing recreational drug use is that it would lead to an increased number of people using drugs.

There is a great deal of controversy about whether legalization would lead to greater drug use, as opposed to the substitution of some drugs for others. But even granting the prohibitionists' prediction, this justification for criminalizing the use of drugs amounts to using some people as mere instruments for the well-being of others. This is, of course, a major problem with deterrence theories of punishment generally, but it is greatly exacerbated in the case of drug use. When we punish a thief in order to deter others from committing theft, the thief is the person who has committed a wrong, and the punishment does (supposedly) prevent yet other victims from being wronged—innocent third parties are spared suffering. In the case of drugs, however, the people who are benefited are, to a large extent, the same individuals who are discouraged from using drugs because of the threat of punishment. My punishment serves to stop you from doing something that would harm you. If we wish to express our concern for those whose lives have been damaged by drugs, the appropriate means is not to inflict pain on them, but to provide the resources and opportunities (insofar as they can be provided at all) that would give these individuals reasons for choosing to avoid or to control their use of psychoactive substances.

A second injustice caused by applying the criminal law against recreational drug use is the harm it inflicts upon the most vulnerable people in society. The self-defeating or at least self-limiting character of the war on drugs has often been pointed out. Efforts to suppress the sale of a commodity lead to black markets; in general, the more effective the efforts, the greater the potential profits available to compensate for the high risks involved in supplying the illegal commodity. Thus, short of truly draconian measures, law enforcement efforts can only limit, but not eliminate, the market. But the existence of such markets imposes significant costs, perhaps the most obvious being the "systemic" crime that results from the use of violence to settle disputes in production and distribution networks, as well as the corruption of police and other officials. Because of the high rewards in these markets, individuals are induced to give up the modest, if not meager, earnings they could achieve legally and become criminals. The crucial point is that these costs fall disproportionately on the most vulnerable sectors of the society, on those communities that have the least capacity to organize against and resist their penetration by criminal groups producing or supplying drugs and that have the fewest opportunities for attaining satisfying ways of life through legal means. Because poor sections of a town lack the political power and the skills to command much police support, they become the sites where drug dealing and drug wars take place.

The devastating effects these processes have had on inner city, African-American communities in the United States are obvious to virtually all observers.[26] Some contend that criminalization results in a reduction of drug use in these communities, and that these gains more than compensate for harms criminalization causes.[27] Because the analysis of this issue necessarily rests on counterfactuals (What would have happened if . . .), no definitive resolution is possible. But given the easy availability of drugs, and the high levels of drug use in these areas, the claimed reductions in drug use for inner city residents are hardly plausible; on the other hand, as Wilson points out, for "novice, middle-class users" drugs "are hard to find and are found only in unattractive and threatening surroundings."[28] This is certainly consistent with the point made earlier, that criminalization has led to a shift in the pattern of drug use from middle-class, middle-aged people to poor and young people. It is hard, then, to resist the conclusion that criminal prohibition is a means to reduce the damage drugs do in middle-class communities by shifting their costs to the poor.

Voluntariness and Addiction

To this point, my argument has focussed on considerations of harm and justice; both of these factors point strongly in the direction of legalization of recreational drug use. But there is one possible counterargument that must be considered, which holds that addiction undermines the capacity for agency, which is necessary for democratic citizenship.[29] Although in general the conception of democratic legitimacy I have presented rules out the use of the criminal law for perfectionist ends, preserving citizens' capacities for agency represents a partial exception. Democratic legitimacy presupposes that, as free and equal citizens, we have the ability to act as agents, to control and direct our activities in accordance with our beliefs and purposes. Without such capacities, the notion of our endorsing the grounds on which coercive power is used makes no sense. Therefore, the commitment to democratic legitimacy entails a commitment to providing those rights and powers necessary to exercise the capacities of agency. These include familiar negative rights, such as freedom of communication and privacy, as well as certain welfare rights.[30] But this commitment to agency also grounds certain duties, such as compulsory education, an obligation applying to both parents and children. Because of the centrality of agency, there is a kind of residual perfectionism implicit in the conception of democracy I have defended.

To the extent that drug use undermines agency by fostering addiction, it might be argued that "we" collectively are free to interfere with the choices of individuals in order to secure the conditions necessary for democratic processes. Furthermore, to the extent that addiction renders drug use nonvoluntary, the damages drugs do to the users themselves are involuntary and, thus, constitute harms that society may legitimately prevent.

Addiction, not surprisingly, has long been compared to slavery by those arguing for the prohibition of drugs. Goodin, for example, argues that for "truly addictive" products "we have no more reason to respect a person's voluntary choice (however well-informed) to abandon his future volition to an addiction than we have to respect a person's voluntary choice (however well-informed) to sell himself into slavery." Goodin does express some doubt about how far to push the argument, because we, as a society, do allow people to bind themselves in various crucial ways, thereby radically limiting their freedom. But, he concludes, "it is the size of the stakes [and] the difficulty of breaking out of the bonds that makes the crucial difference"; "acquiring a lethal and hard-to-break addiction is much more like a slavery contract than it is like an ordinary commercial commitment."[31]

But even if addiction were as overwhelming as some prohibitionists claim, the analogy would be fundamentally misplaced. First of all, the issue regarding slavery is whether a democratic society should enforce a contract of slavery when the person who entered into it changes her mind and wants to renege. To be analogous to drug prohibition, our policy on slavery would have to be to criminalize the making of a promise to become a slave, and to threaten people who do so with imprisonment—that is, with something very much like the condition we are presumably trying to prevent! In fact, there is no need to invoke a paternalist defense of the refusal of liberal regimes to enforce contracts of slavery. Part of the wrong of slavery is its incoherence in a way that is directly related to the idea of enforcing its "contracts." The very notion that the slave has obligations which we would enforce presupposes that the slave is an agent in a way that is incompatible with the status of slavery itself. Slavery is logically incoherent, insofar as it involves the notion that slaves have obligations (to follow orders, for example) while being denied the very freedom and agency that are presuppositions of having obligations in the first place. Becoming addicted to a drug may be stupid, but the concept of being a drug addict is not an incoherent one.[32] Finally, one can only imagine someone voluntarily becoming a slave because he or she faced brutally constricting options. Perhaps some people become drug users because their life conditions are equally desperate, and drug use provides the only realistic means to escape them. Our response to that, however, should be to offer additional options (insofar as that can be done through social policy). To threaten the drug user with imprisonment is only to compound the wrong.

Even if the analogy with slavery is extravagant, it might be claimed that addiction renders one's action sufficiently involuntary to justify restrictions, even when the addicts themselves suffer the costs of their addiction. On virtually any accounting of the harms resulting from the recreational use of drugs, users themselves bear the greatest share. Smokers and heavy drinkers suffer and die from disease, and heavy drug users lose a significant amount of income due to lost work days, the failure to receive promotions, and so forth.[33] In deciding whether to prevent people from using drugs, many analysts include these among the social costs of drug use, although the justification for doing so is not obvious. If users are willing to suffer illness and premature death, or to forgo income they could otherwise earn, in order to gratify their desire for drugs, that could be taken as evidence that the value they receive from using drugs is greater than the monetary and nonmonetary costs the drugs impose. Far from these costs being net losses to society, the willingness of users to pay them shows that the activity must, in this respect at least, provide even greater benefits.

But if drug use is not voluntary, then the reasoning of the last paragraph collapses: the fact that users pay these costs does not show that they do so willingly. If they have "no choice," then we can't take their behavior as revealing their preferences for drug use over other activities. And, the story goes, the fact that they are addicted means that they have no choice. In this vein, John C. Lawn, Administrator of the Drug Enforcement Administration from 1985 to 1990, insists that drugs are addictive and cites animal studies to prove his point: "Medical research with monkeys, for example, demonstrates that given unlimited access, monkeys will continue using cocaine until they die."[34] There are obviously a lot of problems in talking about "reality" or what is "true"—let alone in inferring from the behavior of caged monkeys, deprived of any activity save pushing a lever that provides them with a powerful stimulus, to human behavior in a complex social environment. But for present purposes, I beg these questions and look at the issue of addiction in a naive way. Does the preponderance of evidence support the idea that typical psychoactive substances are addictive, so that individuals cannot control their use of them?

Robert Goodin, with tobacco smoking in mind, argues that the answer to this question is yes. Although Goodin acknowledges the obvious point that many people have given up smoking and that there is a great deal of evidence that a majority of addicts are able to give up harder drugs, including heroin, entirely on their own, he insists that "the test of addictiveness is not impossibility but rather difficulty of withdrawal." Too often, Goodin argues, we assume that an action that is in any respect voluntary can be regarded as fully voluntary, but "for purposes of excusing criminal conduct, we are prepared to count forms of 'duress' that stop well short of rendering all alternative actions literally impossible," including "a credible threat of serious pain, or perhaps even very gross discomfort." The same should apply to "addiction-induced" behavior. The issue is not whether it is literally impossible, but merely whether it is unreasonably costly, for addicts to resist their compulsive desires. If a "desire is so strong that even someone with 'normal and reasonable' self-control" would succumb to it, we have little compunction in saying that the addict's free will was sufficiently impaired that his apparent consent counts for naught." Because they are addicted, Goodin argues, "present users will pay any price for cigarettes for the same reason they will pay any price for heroin: they cannot help themselves."[35]

Like Lawn and many critics of drug use, Goodin is particularly impressed by the existence of physiological evidence of dependence. There is, he claims, a physical need for nicotine on the part of those who start using it, due to the action of "receptors for the active ingredients of tobacco smoke" in the brain, which impairs the will of the smoker. The argument seems to be that when there is a physical basis for a desire, addiction exists and is manifested in involuntary behavior.

There is no denying the intuitive plausibility of this point. But on reflection it is hard to see why a physiological component to desire is so important in itself. It doesn't take much imagination to see that other desires are often as compelling as those based on physical addictions, even though there is no "physical link" of the sort we find in psychoactive drugs. Gambling and even working are among the many activities to which people are often said to be addicted. The question is not whether there is a physical link, but whether someone with "normal and reasonable self-control" can resist the desire for the activity or substance involved. Indeed, Goodin recognizes this point, arguing that it is not "literally impossible for smokers to resist the impulse to smoke," since they might be able to do so through "extraordinary acts of will." Since "nicotine addicts have to try very hard" to break their habit, and often fail to do so, we can conclude that smokers suffer from "the absence of free will."[36]

Since literally millions of people have quit smoking, and since there is no reason to suppose that those who have quit are people with extraordinary powers of self-control, it's hard to accept the conclusion that smokers' behavior is involuntary in a way that discharges us from our responsibility to respect their choices.

And what is true of nicotine appears to be true of other psychoactive substances. Davies, among others, has reviewed the studies purporting to show the explanatory and predictive power of the concept of addiction, and concludes that the "idea that addiction is a state in which the driving force for autonomous action becomes lost to the individual, and is taken over by craving, an irresistible psychological force fuelled by inevitable and excruciating withdrawal symptoms, is untenable."[37] Franklin Zimring and Gordon Hawkins, who appear to support the continued use of the criminal law against many forms of drug use, nonetheless argue that the "notion of addiction that has provided an implicit or explicit justification, or rationale, for all drug prohibition movements and legislation is the product of a remarkable degree of conceptual confusion and factual error."[38] I will not take the time to review all of the evidence and arguments bearing on this complex topic, but two sets of considerations seem to be of decisive importance: the experience of most users, including "addicts," and the evidence from various animal and other experimental studies.

There is no denying that people can become addicted to drugs, or to other things, in the sense that they can develop powerful desires for these objects and seek to pursue their satisfaction even at a high cost to other values, and in the face of considerable social disapproval. What is problematic about the concept of addiction is the suggestion "that people take drugs because some mechanism over which they have no control forces them to do so."[39] Of course, with many drugs continued use frequently leads to a condition in which the body develops a tolerance for the drug, so that higher doses are required to produce the desired effect. Users may also experience painful withdrawal symptoms when they stop using the drug. But these physiological effects do not immobilize the will of the user, making one's behavior essentially involuntary.

One of the reasons that drugs appear to be so dangerous is that much of the reporting about them is based on the experience of the minority of users who become heavy users and who persist in doing so in spite of the costs. But (with the notable exception of smokers) the majority of drug users do not become heavy users. Rather, they control their use in order to fit the drug into the rest of their life activities; for these people, drug use appears to be genuinely recreational.

There is, in fact, little evidence in the case of alcohol and other addictive substances for the existence of a distinct class of addicts. If addicts were a distinct group, and if substance use caused addiction, then one would expect that substance consumption within the population would show a bimodal distribution. The general population would use relatively small amounts of it, but there would be a distinct group of addicts whose per capita consumption would be very high; few people would be found between these two modes because as a person's consumption increased, the person would become an addict and move on to the higher level. However, as numerous studies have shown, the distribution of consumption is unimodal: there is no sharp break distinguishing addicts as a group from others.[40]

It is certainly true that a minority of the people who try a particular drug will become heavy users, and they might be called "addicts" in the sense that a significant part of their lives are organized around procuring and using the drug. Nonetheless, even for this group the image of a complete loss of control appears to be false, as heavy users show the ability to control their behavior in relationship to their other goals and to the incentives they face in the situations in which they find themselves. Heroin users, for example, tend to reduce their consumption of heroin in order to prevent the development of tolerance for the drug, so that they can achieve the "highs" they seek and avoid the need to increase the dosage too much. Alcoholics also appear to be able to control their drinking, in spite of the widespread belief that once alcoholics begin to drink, they will be unable to stop drinking until they have become inebriated. Fingarette, for example, cites numerous studies of alcoholics varying their drinking in a way that demonstrates that the consumption of alcohol does not by itself cause them to drink more; in one of the most convincing experiments, groups of alcoholics tended to vary their drinking on the basis of their *beliefs* about the alcohol content of what they were drinking, rather than the actual alcohol content.

If we suppose that addicts do exercise significant control over their consumption of a substance, it does not mean that they will be able to give it up completely, or even reduce their consumption to a much lower level without great difficulty. Because heavy users, like everyone else, usually have a number of different objectives and commitments, they will sometimes find that their use of drugs interferes with their other life goals, at which point they may try to alter their pattern of consumption but fail. We do not have to explain that failure by the power the drug has over them, however.

Fingarette offers an alternative account. He argues that heavy drinking is a central life choice, not unlike religion or occupation, around which one structures one's life and activity. As such, it is not something one can change through a simple act of will, but requires making changes in a whole range of areas, including one's typical leisure time activities, one's choice of friends and companions, and possibly one's choice of spouse or partner and the kind of job one takes. This must be even more true for the use of illegal drugs, since acquiring and consuming them will structure many aspects of one's life. Thus, giving up an addiction involves far more than altering one specific activity. Restructuring several central aspects of one's life simultaneously is very difficult and requires a great deal of motivation and persistence. Those who see real gains from doing so can carry it off, but many others are unable to do so, either because they lack the motivation to make the necessary changes, or because they don't have satisfactory alternatives in terms of relationships, jobs, or other sources of support, which would be necessary to alter a central life choice.

Evidence for Fingarette's view that addiction does not paralyze the will of the addict is the fact that most people who become heavy users of illegal drugs are able to give up their addictions after a few years. Miller notes that there was a significant change in the pattern of opiate use after the passage and amendment of the Harrison Act (1914; and 1918); although information is sketchy, prior to that time, habitual users tended to be established, middle-class, and middle-aged individuals in "mainstream" social positions. After that, users tended to be drawn from the young, the poor, and minorities—groups whose marginal status in the society made them much more able to bear the costs of using illegal substances. But as young people grow older and develop interests and commitments incompatible the heavy use of an illegal substance, they overwhelmingly tend to abandon it. Similarly, as noted above, the vast majority of Vietnam veterans who had regularly used heroin in Vietnam were able to abandon their habit upon returning home.[41]

It is also noteworthy that treatment programs for alcohol and drug abuse are of questionable effectiveness. If there were some organic basis for addiction, if addiction were a kind of disease, then one might expect that, over time, treatment programs would have been developed which could cure it. But, as is well known, treatment programs are effective only when addicts are personally committed to the treatment and to making the necessary changes in all aspects of their lives. Indeed, most people who quit using drugs do so by themselves, without the aid of any program at all.

Much of the common belief in the addictive power of certain substances comes from animal studies. I have already cited Lawn's reference to such studies, and there is no question that animals in laboratory experiments often self-administer drugs in a pathological manner. The real question, however, is, what significance is to be attached to this behavior? The experiments in question almost invariably feature an isolated animal placed in a barren environment, in which the only behavior open to it is to take a drug which provides some escape from its oppressive surroundings. As Davies argues, "the animal studies show little except that ethologically senseless environments produce ethologically ridiculous behaviours." Davies goes on to cite two animal studies in which the behavior of isolated rats was compared to that of rats living in social groups; in these studies, the latter group used significantly less morphine when permitted to self-administer than the former. An obvious hypothesis explaining this difference is that "colony rats avoided opiates because opiate consumption interfered with the performance of complex species-specific social behaviours that had no relevance when the rat was artificially isolated."[42]

I have been offering reasons to doubt that addiction makes the behavior of heavy drug users involuntary, at least in a sense that permits "us" to set aside "their" judgments, and to justify coercive measures against them to prevent them from pursuing their habits. But drug users often insist that they are addicted, that "they cannot help themselves."[43] Surely in these cases "we" are free to view them as victims, and to take steps to help them reestablish control over their lives and so, in a sense, regain their humanity. Don't we make a mockery of the value of autonomy, which we profess so strongly, when we fail to acknowledge its loss and refuse to implement policies that would enable addicts to regain it?

Without doubt, this argument raises serious issues, but it is important to see that these considerations are not sufficient to justify intervention. What the naive argument from addiction fails to recognize is the way in which the language of addiction is rooted in the culture as a whole, and how its use is functional for addicts and other critical actors alike. Given that the use of drugs is socially disapproved, drug users can deflect that disapproval by attributing their behavior to addiction, thereby discharging them from responsibility for their actions by removing them from the realm of choice. Davies cites (and has conducted) a number of studies which document this process. In one, for example, heavy drug users were interviewed by two different interviewers, one who was "straight" and one who was himself a drug user. Of the twenty users, fifteen presented themselves to the straight interviewer as more addicted and as heavier users than they did to the other interviewer, while only one user moved in the opposite direction.[44]

In an even more revealing study, a group of twenty women were interviewed regarding their smoking behavior, but the interview was designed in such as way as not to suggest the nature of the issues being studied. Among other things, the women were asked about the extent of their smoking and the extent to which they saw their behavior as controllable. The women were later reinterviewed, but only after each had been classified as a heavy or a light smoker, and the classification had been revealed to the subject. Those classified as "light smokers," however, were the women who were actually *more* likely to describe themselves as addicted during the first interview than those who were classified as "heavy smokers." The result was that on the second interview, the women's self-attributions were reversed. In their self-reports, the "light smokers" reduced their use of the language of addiction, while the "heavy smokers" increased it. The mean addiction attribution rating of the "light smokers" went from 5.7 to 2.4, while that of the "heavy smokers" went from 3.9 to 4.9. Evidently, being viewed as a light smoker freed subjects to describe their behavior in terms that suggested it was under their control, but being seen as a heavy smoker led them to search for a language that would excuse their behavior by making it something they could not control.[45]

Invoking addiction as a metaphor of illness is also functional for social service providers. By adopting the language of illness, the drug problem calls for a medical response, in which "experts" provide treatment programs designed to enable the victims of addiction to overcome their disability. But it is not just experts who need the concept of addiction. More generally, as Davies points out, "as a society we appear to have difficulty with the idea of offering help to people whom we believe do not deserve it." Seeing substance abuse as an illness (that is, as addiction), "gives us permission to help people we [would otherwise] see as bad."[46] There is an on-going struggle in our culture, and in drug policy, between the use of coercive measures against drug-users and the provision of treatment services to them, a struggle which reflects in part our ambivalence about substance abuse. To the extent that we see it as a choice, for which people can be held responsible, we condemn those who make that choice and feel justified in inflicting penalties on them. But to the extent that we see drug use as an addiction, we can see users as victims who need our help and support policies such as expanded treatment facilities and prevention efforts designed to reduce demand for psychoactive substances.

Drugs and Democratic Discourse

To this point I have been addressing recreational drug use as a policy issue confronting a pluralist, democratic society. I have argued that current drug laws violate what I have called the fundamental principle of democratic legitimacy, as they deploy "the coercive power of free and equal citizens [acting] as a corporate body" to achieve ends that are not endorsed by all citizens. Further, the use of criminal sanctions against drug users in order to raise the costs of drug use for others, particularly when the harms to be prevented are harms to potential drug users themselves, is a violation of the respect we owe each person as a human being. Moreover, the "systemic" costs of the effort to criminalize drug use fall disproportionately on the most vulnerable sections of our society, in violation of any notion of distributive justice. Finally, I have tried to show that a policy of prohibition is not justified on the grounds that nontherapeutic drug use undermines capacities for agency.

But, as many defenders of current laws hasten to point out, criminalization of drug use enjoys widespread, popular support. How can it be undemocratic when it is supported by overwhelming majorities, majorities greater than would be required to amend the constitution itself? The obvious answer is that democracy requires more than majoritarianism. And even if we believe that majorities should be the ultimate arbiters of constitutional procedures and that there is, and can be, no effective check on what they decide, their power to make such decisions is not arbitrary. Different conceptions of democracy offer different accounts of the limits on majorities necessary for democracy itself; I have been arguing from a broadly deliberative framework which presupposes the possibility of genuine agreement on norms in the face of moral pluralism. The issue of drugs, however, brings out (in yet another way) just how problematic this ideal is. Let me conclude by saying a few words about how drug policy raises serious issues for the deliberative ideal of liberal democracy.

I have already referred to the fact that patterns of drug use changed after the passage of the Harrison Act early in this century; increasingly, users came from the young and socially marginal disadvantaged groups. A number of reasons explain this shift, but one important factor is the symbolic aspect of law itself, something which critics of decriminalization have stressed over and over again. Law functions symbolically to define what behavior, and what values associated with that behavior, are acceptable. In doing so, it also defines what groups or subcultures are acceptable, establishing a relationship of dominance among groups within the society based upon their (at least outward) acceptance of these norms. Groups that are associated with norm violations are stigmatized as deviant and are regarded either as threats to legitimate values or as objects of sympathy to be subjected to programs designed to assist them in correcting their deviant practices. They become enemies or potential wards of the state. Thus, the debate over drugs is dominated by the warriors (who invoke the metaphors of war, seeking to root out users and suppliers who become the "enemy"),[47] and therapists (who invoke the metaphors of illness, seeking to provide treatment to "addicts" whose lives have been shattered by their drug habits).

In the United States, as many commentators have noted, these images have been overlaid by racialized symbols as well. After examining over one-third of the video, print, and radio public service announcements sponsored by the "Partnership for a Drug-Free America," Elwood notes that these messages "never depict white men as drug dealers and drug addicts," and that the overwhelming majority of images of drug users are of blacks and Hispanics.[48] In one spot, Elwood points out, an adolescent African-American drug dealer speaks while his face "gradually transforms into the head of a cobra, replete with a forked tongue and accompanying hiss." Even an apparent exception, in which whites males are depicted as drug users, reinforces "the idea that illegal drugs are an urban minority problem," as the two males are young, unemployed, "blue-collar Italian-Americans who speak with a distinctive Brooklyn accent."[49] These racialized images reinforce the images which originally accompanied the effort to criminalize drugs, in which opium was associated with Chinese immigrants, cocaine with African Americans, and marijuana with Hispanics.

Not only does the law symbolically express a social hierarchy, it can contribute to its reinforcement in what Carson calls a "deviation amplifying system," through which individuals who violate established norms are cut off from the community and so come to see themselves as deviant and, thus, come to behave in a more deviant fashion. This in turn leads to greater repression, reinforcing their self-images as deviant. This process can lead from what might be called primary deviation (rule-breaking) to secondary deviation (rule-breaking as a way of life).[50] All of these processes, then, transform citizens into targets of disapprobation, people to be fought or treated, rather than legitimate interlocutors in democratic discourse. Not surprisingly, the image of drugs in our society remains one that is available for politicians to exploit; they can draw on popular fears of a drug menace to mobilize support and divert attention from other, more urgent concerns.

Back in the sixties, during the struggle against de jure segregation, it was popular in some quarters to argue that laws could not change people's values and in that way justify, or at least excuse, inaction in the face of manifest injustice. Rather than defend the indefensible, the claim was that there was little that could be done through political action. But both the Civil

Rights Movement and the history of drug prohibition suggest that legal change has the capacity to affect the values and beliefs of large numbers of citizens. By defining standards of acceptable behavior, law can powerfully reinforce or even shape the attitudes both of dominant and subordinate groups. But unlike the Civil Rights Movement, the history of drug policy gives little comfort to those of us committed to a deliberative model of liberal democracy. It raises the question of how discourse can be used to test norms, when the very existence of norms contributes to the creation of radically opposed orientations, a condition which tends to undermine the possibility of discourse itself.

CHAPTER SIX

Drugs, National Sovereignty, and Democratic Legitimacy

Pablo De Greiff

In contrast to the other authors in this volume, I am interested in the question of the justice of present U.S. drug policy from an international perspective. Most of the preceding papers examine whether the current drug policy is fair to citizens within a particular liberal society, namely the United States. The focus of my paper is rather whether U.S. drug policy is fair to those beyond the nation's borders whose lives are affected by American antidrug legislation. One of the purposes of this essay is to articulate and to justify the claim that U.S. drug policy is unfair to drug-producing countries. In the first section of this essay, I take note of some of the difficulties associated with the attempt to justify this claim by means of the ordinary notion of fairness which involves examining the distribution of burdens and benefits. I therefore move to a more theoretically guided discussion in order to ground my claim. In the second section, I argue that one can make use of Habermas's account of the relationship between morality and law in order to argue in favor of a conception of democratic legitimacy that shows why U.S. drug policy is unfair. In the third section, I move from normative ideal to empirical reality by examining three positions that might be defended on the basis of Habermasian premises. First, I point out the sort of cosmopolitan democratic structures that would satisfy the moral and legal requirements spelled out by Habermas. I then consider the formation of international jurisdictions for crimes such as drug trafficking as a more immediate possibility than the construction of a democratic world order. In the end, though, I argue that in the short term, and in the absence of the sort of institutions that would guarantee the fairness of the two positions just mentioned, we ought to consider dismantling or radically transforming the legal order responsible for the creation of virtually irresistible economic incentives to participate in the drug business.

Is U.S. Drug Policy Fair?

The course of the actual debate regarding the fairness of U.S. drug policy provides few reasons to think that the question of justice can be decided by appealing only to considerations concerning the equitable distribution of burdens and benefits. For years this debate has been marked by fruitless recrimination rather than clear thinking. Representatives of different American administrations have insisted repeatedly, contrary to the elemental laws of the classical free market model which they otherwise not only defended but also tried to impose, that U.S. demand for drugs is a function of their availability, for which the members of producing countries are mainly responsible. A late (and largely insignificant) recognition of an American share of responsibility for the problem of drugs has done little to assuage Latin American reservations with regards to the U.S. position; it was only in 1991, during the Cartagena Drug summit that the United States finally signed a document in which it acknowledged that demand—not only supply—fosters the drug business. This acknowledgment, though, has been inconsequential, for it has not lead to any appreciable changes in strategies or in the composition of the U.S. antidrug budget. From 1989 until 1993, the supply-reduction part of the budget comprised between 65 and 70 percent of the growing yearly antidrug budgets. Bill Clinton, who emphasized demand-reduction during the campaign, has done little as president to change the focus of the war on drugs: the 1994 and 1995 budgets devoted 62 to 64 percent of expenditures on supply-reduction programs.[1]

The United States' insistence on claiming an exception for drugs from the general classical economics explanatory scheme, according to which it is demand that leads to supply and not the other way around, is partly responsible for the Latin American qualms about U.S. drug policy. These reservations also stem from the conviction that producing countries are being blamed for a problem which is "not theirs." Latin Americans believe this in two different senses: they did not cause the problem, and second, they do not consume its product. First, although coca and marijuana had been grown in different parts of Latin America for centuries, there was no international trade in these substances until American dealers got involved in the business. The Colombian drug trade, on which I will concentrate my attention in this chapter, started only in the late 1970s as one more instance of the "push-down-pop-up" phenomenon—namely, of the mere transfer of drug production from one country to another[2]—when American drug traders moved into the Colombian Caribbean shores led by the U.S. success in forcing the Mexican government to spray marijuana fields with the defoliant Paraquat.[3] The Colombian sense that the problem, strictly speaking, is not theirs, is based also on the fact that internal consumption levels have remained relatively low.[4] Colombian traffickers and producers are not in business for the sake of an internal market; they are in business for the sake of an international market whose craving for drugs is capable of generating profits in the billions of dollars.

More importantly, and closer to the point of this section, Colombians feel not only that the problem is not theirs primarily, but also—quite legitimately from my perspective—that they have had to pay an unfair share of the burden of fighting it. The war on drugs has generated levels of violence that are reaching intolerable levels. The violence has been directed against both official and private targets: there is no branch of the Colombian government that has not suffered the hardships of the fight against drugs. Members of the legislature, more than seventy judges, and three candidates to the presidency, including Luis Carlos Galán, who was most likely to win the 1989 elections, have been killed for reasons having to do with the drug business. Beyond the political victims, though, lie the 11,000 lives lost in drug-related violence in 1990 alone. In the first eight months of 1995, 15,000 persons were killed in the country,[5] and although not all this violence was drug related, no one doubts that the drug business has exacerbated the violence.

But those who defend the fairness of U.S. drug policy as an equitable distribution of burdens and benefits will of course have a ready response. They will cite the thousands of lives in the United States ruined by addiction,[6] the thousands of lives wasted in drug-related gang violence, and the increasing numbers of police officers killed in the line of duty.[7] Additionally, the critics will claim that whereas drug producing countries are receiving an economic benefit, the United States is suffering an economic loss not only because of the money spent on the purchase of goods with little or no value added, but also because of the money spent fighting the war—more than $80 billion spent by the Federal Government alone from 1989 until 1995[8]—and the lost productivity of workers high on drugs.

This argument, however, is deficient in several respects: first, if what the debate is about is burdens, then the sheer numbers of lives lost is obviously greater south of the border. Second, the argument assumes both that the economic impact of the drug business in the United States is clearly negative—as if the funds spent on drugs and drug enforcement disappear into a black hole—and that that impact in producing countries is clearly positive. In purely economic terms, however, the drug business has been a bad deal for producing countries.[9]

Although there are no reliable figures on the inflow of drug money to producing countries—a fact reflected in the wide differences between estimates—it is said that the Colombian economy received between $4 and $10 billion from the drug business in 1994 alone.[10] The question is whether the impact of this money is positive or negative. Because I am considering this question in part as a reaction to the claim that producing countries have enjoyed economic benefits which balance the burdens of the drug war, I will leave aside for the moment considerations about the negative social impact of this influx of money, the corruptive power of these newly and illegally acquired fortunes, their disruptive effects on traditional patterns of socialization, or their effects on the work ethic and aspirations of success.[11] The question is whether producing countries have benefited economically in such a way that their suffering as a result of the war against drugs is still fair; drug-producing countries, it is argued, have profited so much from this business that the balance between benefits and burdens remains in their favor.

But are the economic benefits so great? The $4 to $10 billion received by Colombia from the illicit drug trade in 1994 amounted to 50 to 130 percent of the country's *legal* exports! But obviously, the fact that this increase is due to illegal activity makes a difference economically. First, the influx of hard currency rather than stimulating the economy, may slow it: a large accumulation of external reserves forces the government to either reduce expenditures or expand the monetary base: the former decreases aggregate demand, the latter generates inflation. In either case the consequence is the same, a reduction of economic growth.[12] Second, the increase in external reserves forces the revaluation of the peso, making legal exports less competitive abroad.[13] Third, the unpredictability of this influx of currency makes the implementation of monetary policy particularly difficult. Fourth, illegal capital creates demand for luxury goods, most of which are not produced in the country.[14] Fifth, this capital creates speculative pressures, especially in the real estate market, worsening the country's chronic housing shortage. Finally, the drug business has given rise to a reverse land reform: land which had been distributed to peasants by the government during the 1970s has been bought back by traffickers.[15]

Consequently, it may be the case that drug proceeds should not even be counted as benefits. At the very least, one can justifiably say that the case of the alleged economic benefits is more complicated than it seems at first. The difficulties in reckoning benefits and burdens, and especially of comparing the benefits and the burdens enjoyed or endured by different countries is what makes this whole argument undecidable. This is why I think that explaining and justifying the claim that U.S. drug policy is unfair to Latin American countries can only go so far.

Procedural Fairness

It should not be surprising that a complicated question of transnational justice fails to be solved by means of an ordinary conception of fairness. In this section I would like to take a different approach to the question. Instead of tackling it from the perspective of distributive justice, I will treat it from the standpoint of democratic legitimacy. The problem of course, is that democracy has usually been applied in the context of sovereign nation-states. But the international drug problem generates an interesting question about the meaning of sovereignty and national self-determination in an increasingly interdependent world. The concepts of sovereignty and of democratic legitimacy lead to the idea that as long as a country respects democratic procedures, it can pass whatever laws its people consider appropriate for the regulation of social interactions within its own borders. Naturally, this does not authorize any country to impose its legislation beyond its territorial limits. Leaving aside the fact that in the midst of the war against drugs the United States has imposed its preferred policy, sometimes by means of an overt display of force[16] and sometimes by more subtle but equally effective methods,[17] I want to deal here with a philosophically more interesting case. After all, the case of the imposition through force of particular policies does not generate special philosophical complications; international coercion is reprehensible, and this judgment can be made by reference to the classical notion of national sovereignty.

Part of the Latin American discontent with the United States is caused by instances of overt imposition—but only part; the remainder of its discontent is deeper. Even in the absence of pressure, overt or covert, the problem of drugs raises the following question: Do legislators and policymakers stand under a moral obligation to consider, as part of the deliberation about the legitimacy of their proposals, the consequences that the measures they propose might have beyond the borders of the nation they serve? I will argue that the claim that U.S. antidrug policy is unfair to Latin American countries can be best grounded by answering this question in the affirmative. Simply stated, the notions of democratic legitimacy and of national sovereignty ("national interest") are insufficient guides to problems which are essentially international in scope. I will argue that if we want to preserve a meaningful notion of democratic legitimacy, we ought to render more flexible the notion of national sovereignty. The so-called war on drugs provides a sad, but clear case in point in support of my position.

On the face of it, this seems like a hard case to argue. The American public, as Newt Gingrich has reminded us recently, opposes the legalization of drugs.[18] The federal legislature has only followed suit by enacting a myriad of antidrug laws. Assuming that these laws have been enacted through procedurally acceptable means and after truly open discussion, these laws appear perfectly legitimate.[19]

But, from the standpoint of drug-producing countries the matter is not so simple; American legislation has a profound impact on them. It is a fact that without the American market, the international drug business would shrink sizably. How the United States manages its drug problem determines, to a large extent, what happens in drug-producing countries. Given this fact, it would be disingenuous for Americans to argue that whatever they do regarding the drug problem is their business alone.

But, isn't the United States rightfully entitled to decide what its citizens can and cannot do under the law? Certainly. But American citizens are not free to determine the fate of citizens beyond U.S. borders. And this is precisely what they are doing in passing legislation which criminalizes an activity which laws have been unable to stop, but which are the cause of tremendous consequences in other countries. U.S. legislation, in the articulation of which Latin Americans have absolutely no representation, dramatically shapes life in most producing countries, even if there were no attempts at "diplomatic" interference. From a Latin American perspective, what is unfortunate is the conjunction of, on the one hand, millions of consumers ready to pay the price necessary to bring drugs from producing countries into the United States and, on the other hand, a series of laws which create an economic incentive to produce drugs that significantly outweighs the incentive to produce other goods. The mere creation, *by means of laws*, of a huge market for narcotics in which profits are higher than those for most legal businesses distorts the range of available choices for individuals both in the United States and in foreign countries.[20]

The claim of unfairness of U.S. drug policy, then, can be framed in the following terms: even if the United States did not coerce other countries to adopt a particular drug policy, the sheer size of the market and the magnitude of the economic incentives it sends has such an enormous impact on other countries that politically, economically, and morally speaking, it cannot be that antidrug laws are simply a question of national sovereignty to be decided solely by U.S. citizens, regardless of how others may be affected by their decisions. The sense of injustice that U.S. antidrug policy awakens, I am arguing, stems from the intuition that there is a moral obligation, which legislators in particular bear, an obligation which requires them to assess the impact of their law making in terms that go beyond considerations of national expediency.

Democratic Legitimacy and Transnational Issues

The challenge, of course, consists in articulating and justifying this idea that the legitimacy of laws depends upon their consequences for all those who are substantially affected by them, not only within national borders, but wherever those affected reside. It is precisely around the concept of sovereignty, and more precisely, around the relationship between sovereignty and democratic legitimacy that I intend to construct my explanation and justification of the claim that U.S. antidrug policy is unfair. I will make use of Habermas's reconstruction of democratic legitimacy in order to argue that given the relationship that Habermas proposes between legitimacy and morality, the concept of legitimate legislation ought to include the point of view of everyone affected by the legislation.[21]

My argument does not attempt to provide a detailed presentation of Habermas's position. The following sketch will suffice. For Habermas, moral and legal norms complement each other: contemporary moral theory makes a mistake in attempting to explain normativity unilaterally, as if the only norms available to the subject who asks herself, What ought I to do now? were moral norms. In fact, we always find ourselves in contexts in which, in addition to moral rules, pragmatic and legal norms form the background against which we decide what action to take next.

Adopting a functional standpoint, the acknowledgment of our embeddedness in this complex normative context is advantageous, for it is then possible to appeal to legal norms in order to make up for three sorts of deficits which afflict moral norms:[22] (1) Morality overburdens the agent cognitively, in expecting him to come to his own judgment about what to do in concrete circumstances, while offering only indeterminate and in many cases competing moral principles. (2) Morality overburdens the individual from a motivational standpoint, for even if she attains a correct insight about the morally desirable course of action, posttraditional morality has lost the links with motivational structures present in traditional forms of life. Whereas in traditional morality a reason for action provides not only insight but motivation, after the breakdown of traditional worldviews, having insight does not amount to having a motivation to act in the appropriate manner. Worse still, universalistic morality provides insight only on the assumption of generalized compliance. Individuals, who as a rule are not foolish, understand the counterfactual character of this assumption and, therefore, are left with little motivation to comply with the dictates of morality. (3) Finally, morality is deficient from an organizational point of view as well, for while it may tell us what our duties are, morality does not necessarily tell us how we are supposed to discharge our responsibilities, especially in the case of complex duties. So, for example, the duty not to let people starve, says nothing about how to put together effective antifamine campaigns.

In sum, morality does not always tell us clearly how to act, does not always provide us with sufficiently strong motivation, and does not always help us coordinate our actions effectively. Yet society needs mechanisms of action coordination. Law makes up for these deficiencies by (a) spelling out in detail relevant norms, decision procedures, and standards of competence; (b) redrawing the calculus of losses and gains, making certain classes of actions punishable; and (c) establishing organizational criteria that lend a degree of efficiency to our attempts to carry out complex social tasks.[23]

Habermas's analysis of the functional complementarity of morality and law, interesting and timely as it may be, says nothing about the validity of moral norms, nor about the legitimacy of laws, and therefore provides little indication of how to proceed in the face of concrete cases such as the drug problem. If this theoretical reconstruction of the relationship between morality and law is to prove useful for the articulation of a moral-political point of view that might justify the claim that U.S. drug policy is unfair, the relationship between morality and law will have to be examined from a standpoint that goes beyond functional considerations. It is precisely the relationship between moral validity and legal legitimacy which will help me make my point, for as long as morality is understood in universalistic terms, and provided that legitimacy is tied to morality, this relationship introduces a universalistic requirement into law making which is clearly unfulfilled in the case of drug laws.

In essence, Habermas's position is that given a posttraditional world in which metaphysical or religious justifications of morality and law are no longer sufficient, one can still make use of the notion of justification, in a universalist sense, by reconstructing the notion of validity in terms of discursive acceptability. According to this position, we can dispense with metaphysical and religious justifications because the presuppositions which speakers inevitably make in using language to reach an understanding, especially those presuppositions having to do with the openness of dialogue and with the symmetry of participants, constitute one of the premises in the derivation of a universalist principle of validity according to which "just those action norms are valid to which all those possibly affected could agree as participants in rational discourses."[24]

This principle, which provides an abstract understanding of validity in general, does not discriminate yet between moral and legal norms of action. It can, though, be specified for both, yielding two different principles: one of moral validity and the other of democratic legitimacy. The principle of moral validity states that every valid norm of action has to fulfill the condition that "*all* affected can accept the consequences and the side effects its *general* observance can be anticipated to have for the satisfaction of *everyone's* interests (and these consequences and interests are preferred to those of known alternative possibilities for regulation)."[25] The principle of democratic legitimacy states that "only those judicial statutes may claim legitimacy that meet with the assent [*Zustimmung*] of all citizens in a discursive law-making process that is itself legally constituted."[26]

The common origin of the principles of moral validity and of legal legitimacy does not imply, however, the identity of morality and legality. In fact, there are at least three important differences between them:

(1) While both morality and law constitute systems of *knowledge* of some sort, law constitutes in addition a system of *action* which has at its disposal the coercive force of the State.[27]

(2) The kinds of reasons which decide a moral and a legal discussion are different in each case. While morality requires discourses in which rational assent depends on the acceptability of the same reasons for all participants, legal discourses are penetrated by reasons of diverse kinds, including pragmatic, ethical, and moral considerations, and therefore there need not be convergence on the same reasons as one finds at the end of a moral discussion.[28] This is precisely why laws generally do not declare why they must be obeyed. Rather, laws permit their acceptance on a variety of grounds: which of these grounds is the weightiest is left to each citizen to decide.[29]

(3) The relevant constituencies for moral and legal discussions are different: a universalistic understanding of morality makes humanity as a whole the relevant community for moral discourse. Following Kant, we can say that what makes moral norms distinctive is that they raise a universal validity claim, and so differ both from pragmatic discourses, the validity of whose conclusions (Kant's "imperatives of skill") is contingent on the commonalty of particular ends, as well as from ethical discourses, whose claims (Kant's "counsels of prudence") are valid only for members of a community which already shares a tradition and its strong evaluations.[30] To the extent that legal matters do not appeal to moral reasons alone, but involve considerations about means and ends, as well as about the collective identity of the community of citizens, the relevant constituency seems no longer to be humanity at large, but a more restricted group.[31] This relevant constituency for democratic law making has traditionally been defined territorially, in terms of state borders. Habermas follows the tradition:

> Unlike moral rules, legal rules do not normalize possible interactions between rationally competent subjects in general, but the interaction contexts of a concrete society. This follows simply from the concept of the positivity of law, i.e., from the facticity of making and enforcing law. Legal norms go back to the decisions of a historical legislator, they refer to a geographically delimited legal area and to a socially delimited collective of legal consociates, and consequently to a special sphere of validity.[32]

To be sure, acknowledging the possibility of resolving legal matters in a community that does not span across humanity as a whole is important, for it allows particular groups to embody their sense of identity in the legal structure, which could, in turn, strengthen both ethics and the law: ethics, understood in the sense of a particular *ethos*, a concrete and traditional conception of the good life shared within a particular community, may be strengthened if at least some of its features are given legal force. On the other hand, the law, insofar as it is seen as closely connected to the shared notion of the good, will by this very fact receive a measure of legitimacy.

The problem, however, is that a territorial definition of the relevant community of democratic law making is woefully inadequate. And the international drug crisis underscores this fact. Given the dearth of factual evidence supporting U.S. drug policy, one is entitled to conclude that this legislation rests more on ethical considerations having to do with the society's self-image or ideal of moderation—an ideal belied systematically in so many other ways, including by its consumerism—or with its suspicion regarding ecstatic activities and emotions—a suspicion which loses its force, it seems, when it comes to other activities and substances, such as its passion for spectacular sports and the not entirely unrelated alcohol consumption during these events.

It is of course true that law making is not carried out on the basis of moral reasons alone, that it includes pragmatic and ethical considerations. But if this is not to lead to the destruction of morality, moral considerations ought to be recognized as having priority over the others. That is to say, legislators are free to frame laws on the basis of pragmatic and ethical reasons as long as these laws do not conflict with moral norms—and these moral norms, as explained before, are derived not just from the community served by them, but also from the community affected by the proposed legislation. In the case at hand, assuming that there were consensus within the United States about the policy of criminalizing drugs, and assuming that these laws were procedurally legitimate, the United States would be entitled to this policy only on the condition that its laws did not give rise to situations which substantially violated the rights of other peoples. But, arguably, this is not the case. Drug criminalization, even if enforced benignly, without international coercion, contributes to the establishment and maintenance of an illegal market which in turn has the economic and social consequences we have come to know so well.

The acknowledgment that law making can and should include pragmatic and ethical considerations cannot subvert the priority of morality. If it is true that the principles of morality and of legitimacy are simply two articulations of the same abstract principle of discursive validity which is left standing in a posttraditional world, this introduces a universalistic impetus to legitimate law making. If the notion of the legitimacy of law is derived from an abstract understanding of validity which is universalistic in scope, a territorially based closure of the concept of legitimacy is justifiable only in those cases in which it can safely be assumed that legislation will have little or no impact on the rights of peoples beyond a nation's borders. Most law making addresses such situations.

But there are cases, and drugs is one of them, in which pragmatic, ethical, and moral considerations may conflict with one another. In such cases, siding with pragmatic or ethical considerations carries a heavy price: the claim to moral validity, and consequently, to democratic legitimacy is thereby surrendered. Habermas expresses the complex relationship between legitimacy and ethical and moral reasons thus:

> By their very structure laws are determined by the question about which norms citizens want to adopt for regulating their living together. To be sure, discourses aimed at achieving self-understanding—discourses in which participants want to get a clear understanding of themselves as members of a specific nation, as members of a locale or a state, as inhabitants of a region, etc.; in which they want to determine which traditions they will continue; . . . in short, discourses in which they want to get clear about the kind of society they want to live in—such discourses are also an important part of politics. But these questions are subordinate to moral questions and connected with pragmatic questions. Moral questions in the narrow sense of the Kantian tradition are questions of justice. The question having priority in legislative politics concerns how a matter can be regulated in the equal interest of all. The making of norms is primarily a justice issue and is gauged by principles that state what is equally good for all. And unlike ethical questions, questions of justice are not related at the outset to a specific collective and its form of life. *The politically enacted law of a concrete legal community must, if it is to be legitimate, at least be compatible with moral tenets that claim universal validity going beyond the legal community.*[33]

When countries surrender the claim to moral validity of their laws by basing them on considerations of expediency, or on ethical considerations, the sense of injustice on the part of those who have to pay the consequences of such policies is then entirely justified. This, I believe, is grounding for the claim that U.S. drug policy is unfair.

A final clarification is in order. I have not attempted to derive a particular policy with respect to drugs from an understanding of the relationship between moral validity and legal legitimacy. I do not think such quick derivation is possible. Neither an argument in favor of legalization, nor one in support of criminalization follows from such abstract premises. What does follow from these premises is some guidance for law makers: a universalistic understanding of morality, in addition to the relationship between morality and law that I have reviewed here, imposes an obligation on legislators to think about the legitimacy of their proposals in terms of the rational acceptability of their proposed laws for everyone affected by them, even if the affected parties live beyond national borders.

Three Morally Defensible Policies

Now, insofar as one of the aims of political theory is to design and to justify institutions, so that life in fair societies will not depend exclusively on the good will of their leaders, the argument above, strictly speaking, requires the formation of a cosmopolitan world order. Such a world order has been advocated by Kant, and more recently, by Thomas Pogge and David Held. The proposals made by these authors do not call for the replacement of the system of nation states by a single sovereign power, but rather, in Pogge's words, for "a multilayered scheme in which ultimate political authority is vertically dispersed."[34] David Held, who has elaborated the notion of a democratic cosmopolitan order, argues that within it, "people would come . . . to enjoy multiple citizenships—political membership in the diverse political communities which significantly affect them. They would be citizens of their immediate political communities, and of the wider regional and global networks which impact upon their lives."[35]

This cosmopolitan order would operate on the basis of the old but presently truncated idea that the validity of legislative acts depends on their acceptability to all those who are affected by them, wherever they might be. Political participation, then, would be gained not by virtue of territorial membership, but by virtue of falling under the influence of particular problems and the laws passed to cope with them. This gives rise to several kinds of political communities dealing with local, national, regional, and global issues, and calls for the formation of "issue-boundary forums or courts" to adjudicate cases concerning "where and how a 'significant interest' in a public question should be explored and resolved."[36] Since the point is to give those who are affected by laws—and not others—political representation, these forums or courts could use three tests in order to guide policy issues to the different levels of governance:

The test of *extensiveness* examines the range of peoples within and across delimited territories who are significantly affected by a collective problem and policy question. The test of *intensity* assesses the degree to which the latter impinges on a group of people(s) and therefore, the degree to which national, regional or global legislation or other types of intervention are justified. The third test, the assessment of *comparative efficiency*, is concerned to provide a means of examining whether any proposed national, regional or global initiative is necessary insofar as the objectives it seeks to meet cannot be realized in an adequate way by those operating at "lower" levels of decision-making.[37]

It is likely that under these three tests the issue of drugs would qualify for treatment at a higher organizational level than that where it receives treatment right now, that is, the level of national decision making, and occasionally, the field of force of present-day international politics. Gaining true political representation in the formulation of the policy which has the greatest impact on the destiny of producing countries would go a long way toward redeeming their claim for justice. Whether this larger constituency would choose a strategy of legalization or of criminalization is an open question, but what is almost certain is that either way, the burdens of either policy would be more equitably shared.

Given how unlikely the formation of a cosmopolitan order is, however, it would be unfortunate if this were the only consequence to be derived from the argument about the relationship between moral validity and legal legitimacy. Since this argument leads only to an understanding of the universalistic requirements of legitimate law making, one could attempt to construct on this basis an argument in favor of the continued criminalization of drugs, except that now this would require a kind of international cooperation that goes well beyond the arm-twisting which has characterized drug-policy relations between the United States and Latin America. Probably, this cooperation would entail both the creation of an international jurisdiction for drug-related crimes and massive economic transfers (as compensation for producing countries for being placed in a position in which they are both given immense economic incentives to participate in the business and yet required to fight those involved in it).[38]

Compared to present strategies, an international jursidiction seems to offer several advantages. First, the application of the mandated sanctions would be greatly simplified. Under present arrangements, bilateral extradition treaties are liable to be seen as the result of pressure on the part of powerful countries, as illustrated by recent U.S. attempts to make Colombia reinstate the extradition of drug criminals.[39]

Second, the internationalization of the problem would make it easier, in theory, to broaden the scope of the fight, enabling us to take a look, say, at the behavior not just of individuals, but of industries; we should keep in mind that, for example, most of the chemical compounds used in processing coca paste are not produced in the so-called cocaine exporting countries. Under the present legal status quo, it is close to impossible for Latin American countries to pursue legal action against companies that knowingly provide chemicals for the drug trade. It is conceivable that an international court could examine matters such as this.

Third, the existence of an international jurisdiction would make it harder for governments to get involved in drug activities themselves, because they would be unable to make deals with their own judiciaries leading to the release or lenient treatment of those involved with the business. This would be true both of those governments that willingly partake of these activities and of those that are pressured by circumstances to be soft with persons or groups guilty of these crimes.

Fourth, an international jurisdiction would remove the drug issue as a factor in international trade and aid policy negotiations, the presence of which can always lead to abuses.[40]

Fifth, it is possible that an international court would be more immune to biases in the prosecution and conviction of suspects than the present courts in each country. When, as now, countries engage in heated recriminations against one another, blaming the other for the scourge of drugs, the public bitterness expressed by politicians risks infecting public institutions, including the courts. One's citizenship may determine the aggressiveness with which a prosecutor charges the suspect, the care with which a court reviews the amount, quality, and legality of evidence against the suspect when entertaining a motion to dismiss charges, and the degree of bias against a defendant that a judge or jury brings to the courtroom (notwithstanding the sworn oath to be impartial and to regard the defendant innocent until proven guilty beyond reasonable doubt). An international tribunal could mitigate these harmful effects of state-sponsored prejudice.[41]

Of course, the creation of an international court presents tremendous difficulties. The history of the international fight against drugs provides almost no grounds for optimism. In the absence of an international democratic cosmopolitan order such a court could become a threat to justice if it is not a part of a broader international democratic order. First, the fact that an international court would simplify the application of sanctions does not mean that their fairness would be guaranteed. This highlights the importance of cosmopolitan democracy not only at the level of the integration of the court itself, but perhaps more importantly, at the prior stage of international law making. Second, whether the powers of the court become a constructive force or not depends on how they are used. Presently existing international institutions can be faulted more for their unwillingness to treat like cases alike than for lacking either the required legal framework to be effective or the actual means of enforcing the law. The same problem may obtain once the problem of drugs is internationalized in the manner under discussion. Without the required democratic institutions, the international community may also make a selective use of the court. In summary, if the composition of the court and especially of the background legislation does nothing more than reflect the existing balance of power, it is not clear why this proposal would be any more defensible from a moral standpoint than the status quo.[42] In short I have grave misgivings about this proposal. Insofar as drug-producing countries are kept under the threat of seeing their trade preferences suspended and their access to credit interrupted if they do not comply with U.S. drug policy demands, there is no reason to believe that they would be in a position to participate as equals in the constitution of an international drug tribunal.

Given the difficulties associated with the two proposals mentioned above, and considering the questionable basis of the case for criminalization, perhaps the United States might start considering the regulation of the drug business. There are ample pragmatic reasons in support of such change, not the least of which is the probable increase in public health that would follow the adoption of a sound "medicalization" strategy such as that practiced in Holland.[43] But there are moral reasons to consider this policy change as well. I have been arguing that it is manifestly unfair to place drug-producing countries in a situation in which U.S. demand for drugs conjoined with antidrug legislation provides those countries with economic incentives that are without parallel in other industries and, then, not only blames those countries for producing drugs, but requires them to spend their resources, both human and material, to fight the production of these very drugs. Under present circumstances, the satisfaction of international moral demands may be easier to accomplish by applying to drugs the same rules which are applied to the production and trade of other goods. The day when the profits associated with production of drugs fall in line with the profits associated with the other goods that developing countries produce, some, but not all, of the claims to justice raised by these countries will be met. On that day, we might resume the other conversations about international justice.

Drugs, the Nation, and Freelancing: Decoding the Moral Universe of William Bennett

WILLIAM E. CONNOLLY

> As I sometimes did, I was freelancing. I hadn't received White House clearance for
> my remarks. . . . But I would also try to throw out an idea with the intent of sparking
> a debate, to get the national conversation going in a new direction.
>
> William J. Bennett, *De-Valuing the Nation*

The Drug Confessional

If you are a liberal politician, journalist, or academic in contemporary
America, there is a definite expectation that you confess before discussing
drugs and drug policy. This demand reflects the sense that we know where
the drug problem in America started, what dangers drugs pose, how to
respond to those dangers, and who ought to preside over the responses.
More pointedly, it conveys the judgment that the generation of Americans
now called upon to wage war on drugs is the same one that initiated a
decade of drug fantasies in the middle sixties. Those over fifty are guilty.
Confession might cleanse our souls, clear our minds, and allow us to become born again. We can regain a measure of moral legitimacy by placing
ourselves squarely within the culture that makes morality possible.

Perhaps you once found that cocaine was an aphrodisiac. Or that LSD
disclosed profound truths otherwise unavailable to rationalists and tech-
nocrats. Or that marijuana enhanced your sensitivity, enabling you to experiment with new thoughts and ways of life in a corrupt culture. Whatever discoveries you made about drugs as a youth, now in middle age, you

must confess your sins. The typical confessional begins like this: "I was a Liberal (secularist, New Leftist, recreational drug user, countercultural radical) in the Sixties. . . ." Here is my version:

"I am an amateur when it comes to drugs. I inhaled a little pot in the good old days. I take aspirin to relieve pain. I drink white wine when the social occasion allows it. I still love the runner's high, and I claim to have risen to 'the zone' in basketball a few times (though many of my former playing partners doubt it). I have yet to become addicted to the drugs I take to be most dangerous, such as cocaine, religious fervor, tobacco, heroin, or nationalism. Even academic drugs of choice such as alcohol, rationalism, Prozac, empiricism, and deconstruction remain under pretty decent control, though some of my colleagues may argue with me about this—there is always the danger of denial in this domain."

After the typical confession, drug warriors go on to offer suggestions on the drug problem. So now with my confession out of the way, let me offer a few proposals. As this amateur sees it, there are a few modest things that might be done to reduce the self-destruction and social violence accompanying the most addictive drugs:

First, if fundamentalist religion and powerful street drugs are often found in the same or adjoining neighborhoods, we might conclude that both often involve protective, defensive responses to extreme suffering, demoralization, and hopelessness. So, federal, state, and local action to promote jobs, housing, education, and safety in the poorest communities is the most crucial action to take.

Second, several now illegal drugs might be decriminalized and either sold by the state or sold privately and taxed. Drug policy in the Netherlands might provide a model to emulate and adapt to the American setting. State proceeds from decriminalized drugs would go entirely to information, prevention, and volunteer treatment programs. Advertisements and places of use for these drugs would be restricted about as much as they now are for tobacco. (Indeed, I favor further restrictions in tobacco advertisements aimed at teenagers.) Every attempt would be made to gear the expenditures for prevention and treatment to the level of drug income received from specific communities. One side effect of decriminalization would be to reduce pressures to corruption within local police departments, for no illegal drug trade (or prostitution or gambling) flourishes anywhere unless the police are involved. And police corruption is a great danger facing a democratic culture.[1]

Third, drugs that are the most highly addictive, are the most damaging to the mind, and/or contribute most to violence should be illegal. It remains very debatable which drugs cross this threshold, but suppose we treat alcohol as a benchmark. If it remains legal—and my taste for wine makes me hope it does—then other drugs with similar pleasures and dangers should be legal, too. Furthermore, both legal and illegal drugs should be accompanied by extensive educational programs about their addictive levels and dangers. And how should we deal with illegal drug use? Should users of illegal drugs receive criminal penalties? I don't think so, but perhaps they should be fined. Violence or other illegal activity following from drug use should be penalized according to the established standard for that specific illegality. Voluntary treatment programs should be expanded. In addition, I don't think there should be drug testing in the work place; in fact, every attempt should be made to reduce state and corporate practices of surveillance, for they constitute serious threats to the ethos of a democratic society. *Performance* tests, on the other hand, in high risk jobs are reasonable.

That's about as far as my amateurish thinking has proceeded to date. There are, of course, dangers in my approach. For instance, if the last two parts were adopted while the first was ignored, the whole project might fail. The approach would then suffer the fate that has already befallen the welfare state in America: conservatives would charge that the program had failed after a real try, conveniently forgetting that its essential connection to decent jobs and good education had never been established. Moreover, treatment programs and performance tests could easily become corrupted or misused. There is a strong case to made against the proliferation of state and corporate surveillance and testing programs. There is also a risk that the state could become dependent on the funding provided by drug revenues, even though the proposal tries to guard against such a problem. Finally, judgments about which drugs are the most dangerous could easily become controlled by narrow partisan considerations. Each of these issues would need extensive exploration and debate.

The most devastating objection to such an amateurish proposal by far, however, is that it is culturally unrealistic and politically utopian in the current context. Proposals of this type are discussed just widely enough to provide campaign fodder for conservative elites who seek to intensify a now familiar set of cultural divisions. The proposal, in short, would be seen by many people as the abstract scheme of an amoral academic, one who has lost touch with the standards of individual responsibility, religious belief, national identity, and antistate sentiment of the political culture in which it is set.

I am not suggesting that we go back to Prohibition. Alcohol has a long and complicated history in this country, and unlike drugs, the American people accept alcohol.

William J. Bennett, *De-Valuing the Nation*

Bill Bennett knows people like me. He may even be obsessed with us. He
certainly talks about us a lot. He and I are of the same generation, and
we have spent large parts of our adult lives in the university. Most of us,
like him, drink spirits freely. Each of us belongs to a constituency that is
energized, even sometimes intoxicated, by the appearance of the other.
Bennett, however, has been far more effective at identifying, marking, and
demonizing my type than my type has been at responding to him. We
don't seem to understand how he feeds off us, how he uses us to engender,
enlarge, and energize the "cultural war" he wages. Maybe we can learn
a thing or two from this former philosophy teacher, Secretary of Education, Drug Czar, Republican publicist, and contemporary intellectual of the
American nation.

In the *De-Valuing of America: The Fight for Our Culture and Our Children*,
Bennett defines the American condition as one of war between the traditional culture of working, religious, responsible individuals and a variety
of elites in the media, the academy, and a few churches who have corrupted
the culture:

> The battle for culture refers to the struggle over the principles, sentiments,
> ideas, and political attitudes that define the permissible and impermissible,
> the acceptable and the unacceptable, the preferred and the disdained, in
> speech, expression, attitude, conduct and politics. This battle is about music,
> art, poetry, literature, television programming and movies; the modes of ex-
> pression and conversation, official and unofficial, that express who and what
> we are, what we believe in, and how we act. (William Bennett, *De-Valuing of
> America: The Fight for Our Culture and Our Children* [New York: Touchstone,
> 1992], p. 25.)

An "open declaration of war over the culture" is necessary, according to
Bennett, because over the last few decades "significant portions of American society have been culturally deconstructed" by liberal and radical
elites, imposing "particularly devastating effects" on "our schools, colleges

and universities, mainline churches, the legal profession, the Congress and others."[2] Liberal artists, intellectuals and journalists are indispensable foils in the cultural war. Most things Bennett opposes, for instance, are first put into the mouths of liberal intellectuals and then brought back to "the American people" as alien, amoral, abstract products. Liberal academic and media intellectuals inhabit a "preconceived reality," "walled off" from traditional values and realities. Bennett recognizes "typical academic myopia" because he participated in it before he was born again. "The old saw that a neoconservative is a liberal who has been mugged by reality applies to me" (p. 36). He gives his confessional quite succinctly: "though I never used drugs, I spent almost all of 1965 through 1975 on or around a college campus" (p. 99).

Bennett forges two links between academics and drug users. First, the university of the late 1960s was the place where "America lost its moral bearing regarding drugs" (p. 94). Other candidates for this ambiguous honor—such as the end of Prohibition, the formation of subcultures of hopelessness, the withdrawal of the state from programs of development for the inner city, or the organization of commercial advertisement—Bennett simply ignores. Second, the loss of character and demoralization he associates with drug use in the inner city and in the elite art communities today corresponds to the "radical nihilism" and "cultural deconstruction" that governs universities.

Once those two links are forged, Bennett can render suspect everything the academic says about drugs because of the suspicious source from which it emanates. He accents the difference between him and us by saying that academics interpret the world through abstract theories while his postacademic conservatism emerges from "what I have seen with my own eyes, traveling up and down and back and forth across America and visiting hundreds of cities and schools over nine years" (p. 36). Once the liberal media and academic elites have been rendered alien, those same elites can provide the reference point through which to devalue the ideas of anyone else who sees things differently than Bennett does with his own two eyes. Even if they serve on the front lines in that war. Listen to how Bennett devalues cops who dissent from his war on drugs:

During the tour of downtown [Detroit], one of the police officers accompanying me asked, "Why should a kid earn four bucks an hour at McDonald's when he can make two or three hundred dollars a night working drugs?"

"For a lot of reasons," I said on that first tour, as I was to say a hundred times after. The police officer had picked up this line of reasoning from the media. (P. 105.)

Or again in a somewhat different situation:

I expected that some of our biggest allies in our law enforcement efforts would be the police and national leaders in law enforcement. And most street level police and many police chiefs did support our strategy from the very beginning. But . . . increasingly I found that talking to some chiefs was like talking to some of the school superintendents I had encountered while Secretary of Education. . . . They spoke of deep social problems, alienation and illiteracy. They sounded as they wished to sound, like contemporary social scientists. . . . They, too, had become theoreticians of society's woes. (P. 133.)

So media and academic elites provide a filter through which miscellaneous misfits formally within the constituency Bennett courts are screened out. They now become defectors to the enemy in a culture at war. To erase the negative marks scrawled upon them, they must repudiate the preconceived, abstract, amoral world view of journalists and social scientists. A confession would help. Bennett's strategy is to draw members of the white working and middle classes, street cops, suburban dwellers, veterans, the military, conservative politicians, conservative religious believers, and working African American urban dwellers plagued by street drugs and violence into a bellicose cultural coalition. That coalition is mobilized and animated through hostilities to university intellectuals, liberal journalists and politicians, moderate school administrators, disaffected residents of the inner city, illicit drug users, drug dealers, welfare recipients, philosophical police chiefs, and convicted felons. Each constituency on that latter list is marked by its association with others on the same list and by its absence on the former list; and the most negatively marked constituencies (for example, prisoners and drug dealers) place stains of suspicion upon everything said and done by those associated with them. The battle lines are clean: the "American people" value America; the losers and amoral elements devalue it. Artistic, media and academic elites provide the cultural insignia enabling anyone to judge who belongs on which side of that divide.

That is why Bennett himself must be so selective (so abstract) in his invocations of moral principle, the will of God, clean decisions, individual responsibility, and the American people. His principled invocations must not disrupt the lines of cultural division he contrives. Take alcohol. It must be dissociated from other drugs—it must, in fact, not be called a drug—so that the war against drug users does not spill into constituencies at the epicenter of the cultural coalition Bennett constructs.

One of the clear lessons of Prohibition is that when we had laws against alcohol, there *was* less consumption of alcohol, less alcohol related disease, fewer drunken brawls and a lot less public drunkenness. . . . I am not suggesting that we go back to Prohibition. Alcohol has a long, complicated history in this country, and unlike drugs, the American people accept alcohol. They have no interest in going back to Prohibition. But at least advocates of legalization should admit that legalized alcohol, which is responsible for some 100,000 deaths a year, is hardly a model for drug policy. . . . The question is, should we accept both legalized alcohol *and* legalized drugs? The answer is no. (P. 118.)

Bennett makes some slick moves here. Alcohol is bracketed from drugs, even though alcohol is implicated in issues of addiction, violence, and loss of self-reliance offered as the paradigmatic reasons for a war on drugs. What political subtext governs this moral text? Well, this legal nondrug is popularly associated with working white males and unmarked minorities, while illegal drugs are associated with cultural elites, heterodox sexualities, and black ghetto dwellers. The political/legal demarcation between drugs and alcohol enables the "American people" to become that moral majority which would use ghetto police sweeps, harsh prison sentences, new prison construction, and military interventions abroad to wage war on drugs and the target populations identified with them. Assorted minorities who initially fit into neither formation, those who, say, would decriminalize some drugs and relax many drug penalties, or curtail commercial advertisement of alcohol and tobacco, or build housing, public transportation, and incentives to create jobs in the inner cities, are ushered out of the "American people" and into the disparate populace it targets for action. In Bennett's world, no attention can be given to the case for treating, say, alcohol, marijuana, and tobacco in the same way, perhaps legalizing all three, regulating or curtailing their commercial advertisement, and using receipts or taxes from the sale of each for programs of education and voluntary treatment. To exclude marijuana from the list of drugs would make the target population too small to wage cultural war against; to include alcohol would require the American people to wage war against itself.[3] Alcohol and crack are distinguished first and foremost by the position of each in the cultural war; so are tobacco and marijuana.

Bennett is a two star general in this war. He is distinguished from the other generals through his role as chief of war games. He tests potential strategies of cultural engagement. Thus, the most revealing moments in *The De-Valuing of America* occur when Bennett brags about "free-lancing" in public. While still Secretary of Education and before the "war on drugs" had become refined, Bennett first reiterated his usual litany of "heightened inspections of international cargo . . . , more prisons, higher fines, and, for parolees, longer probationary periods and regular drug tests" (p. 103). Things got hotter when Bennett, without prior authorization, called upon the American military to eradicate drugs in Latin American countries. "It is to be hoped we can do this in collaboration with foreign governments," he said, "but if need be we must consider doing this by ourselves. And we should consider broader use of military force against both the production and shipment of drugs." Here is Bennett on his own pronouncement:

> As I sometimes did, I was free-lancing. I hadn't received White House clearance for my remarks, and I heard through back channels that my remarks caused heartburn among some members of the Domestic Policy Council, and especially at the Pentagon. But I was not troubled. . . . This episode revealed a tactic I frequently used. I believed in what I said. But I would also try to throw out an idea with the intent of sparking a debate, to get the national conversation going in a new direction. . . . Sometimes this approach worked. This time it did. (Pp. 103–104.)

In what terms did it work? Well, the constituencies that Reagan, Meese, and Bennett sought to mobilize were aroused by this approach. The introduction of the military into the equation allowed the drug war to take on real meaning. Equally pertinent, the proposal flushed out liberal journalists who had reservations about this conflation between the drug war and military action against foreign countries. The political effect was to fix the potent masculine symbols of strength, will, and military power on one side of the culture war and traditional feminine signs of weakness, ineptness, and lack of will on the other. Bennett's freelancing bound the war against restless minorities at home to that against rebellious populations abroad by drawing the American military into both sides of the equation: it would fight abroad to stop the import of drugs into the ghettoes at home. Reagan loved the symbolic effect engendered, but took no direct action. George Bush, after winning the presidency and selecting Bennett to be drug czar, eventually enacted it.

On another occasion, during an interview with Larry King, Bennett agreed with the sentiments of a caller who advocated beheading drug dealers.

I could see King's eyes light up. He asked for a clarification. "Behead?"

"Yeah. Morally, I don't have any problem with it."

"You would behead . . . " King began again.

"Somebody selling drugs to a kid?" I said. "Morally, I don't have any problem with that at all. I mean, ask most Americans if they saw somebody out on the streets selling drugs to their kid what they would feel morally justified in doing—tear them from limb to limb.

"What we need to do is find some constitutional and legally permissible way to do what this caller suggests, not literally to behead, but to make the punishment fit the crime. . . ." During the program I called for capital punishment for major drug sellers. (P. 116.)

Bill Bennett freelances again. The same dynamic was set in motion. Liberals were stunned and outraged. Public opinion—among troops in the cultural war—was drawn to Bennett and his moral toughness. Soon, other conservatives joined in. A new line was drawn in the mud. Every leader was now newly marked by where they stood on the death penalty for drug dealers.

The Reagan/Bennett/Gingrich political formula was, first, to block or underfund "welfare state" approaches to the drug issue, second, to blame liberals for inaction and weakness in this domain, third, to use this failure as a pretext for further dismantling the welfare state, fourth, to call for a violent state response as the only alternative to public inaction, and finally, to brand those who protest the unconstitutionality, cruelty, or immorality of these proposals as paradigmatic agents of inaction and moral uncertainty.[4] The favorite targets for Bennett are inner-city African Americans and white intellectuals; but the former constituency does not need to be named explicitly because the cultural coding of terms like "drug dealers" and "drug war" is already available to Bennett's troops. And the intellectuals? We keep naming ourselves through our reactions to Bennett's freelancing.

Because the objective is to mobilize an implacable constituency out of a diverse, opaque section of the populace, Bennett serves as war games simulator, experimenting loudly and brashly with words to see what it takes to shape and hold the appropriate friend/enemy constellation. You can be confident, for instance, that Bennett uses a different vocabulary when it comes to the question of what punishment Edward Meese deserves for breaking laws he was sworn to uphold. Nor is Bennett likely to demand a thorough investigation of charges that the CIA either supported or condoned drug trafficking by those involved in the war of the Contras against the Sandinistas in Nicaragua in the 1980s. If the morality of drugs were the issue, Bennett would draw upon all the rhetorical powers available to him to demand such an investigation; he would want to uncover and purge any connection between American intelligence and drug traffic to American cities. But if the moral war against drugs is shaped above all by a political agenda to create a set of cultural divisions, then this issue must be obfuscated. For it threatens to compromise the moral posturing indispensable to prosecution of the cultural war.

Prosecuting the War

The accomplishment of *Jaws* consists in an act of purely formal conversion which provides a "container" for all these free-floating, inconsistent fears by way of anchoring them . . . in the figure of the shark.

Slavoj Žižek, *Tarrying with the Negative*

The Bennett war on drugs is not most effectively addressed, then, as a series of attempts to solve the problem of drug use. If that were the issue, it would suffice to show how expensive, ineffective, and intrusive the war has been. But if the real objective is elsewhere, failure on the policy front might even contribute for a time to success of the political agenda. If the objective is to identify an available target population of urban drug users, drug dealers, media representatives, and liberal academics, then Bennett's tactics are very successful. They have, for example, changed the terms of discussion within each major political party as well as between the two parties. Bennett's command of the drug war resembles the relation of a blockbuster film maker to the film audience more than that of a policy-maker to a discrete problem. Take, for example, the killer shark in Spielberg's *Jaws* as discussed by Slovoj Žižek:[5]

> A direct search for the shark's ideological meaning evokes nothing but misguided questions: does it symbolize the threat of the Third World to America epitomized by the archetypal small town? is it the symbol of the exploitative nature of capitalism itself (Fidel Castro's interpretation)? does it stand for the untamed nature which threatens to disrupt the routine of our daily lives? In order to avoid this lure, we have to shift perspective radically: the daily life of the common man is dominated by an inconsistent multitude of fears (he can become the victim of big business manipulations; Third World immigrants seem to intrude into his small orderly universe; unruly nature can destroy his home; etc.), and the accomplishment of *Jaws* consists in an act of purely formal conversion which provides a common "container" for all these free-floating, inconsistent fears by way of anchoring them, "reifying" them, in the figure of the shark. (P. 149.)

The war on drugs, in turn, clarifies and concentrates a series of vague, shifting anxieties and resentments in everyday life. It brings within the apparent reach of political agency threats that otherwise seem beyond reach. What are these threats? They might involve, for some, the threat of black violence in the city; or the loss of good working-class jobs, projected onto women and minorities said to have stolen them; or the shifting ethnic and racial composition of the country; or the globalization of corporations which disempowers American workers; or the reduced capacity of the state to control its fate in a globalized economy; or the unsettling diversification of religious and irreligious creeds; or the porosity of territorial boundaries; or the feeling that taxes are high while their positive effects on the quality of life are low; or the vague sense that the tempo of cultural change is whirling out of control. Which anxieties and impulses to revenge become most salient for whom shifts and moves in unexpected ways; which symbolic-operational programs are most pertinent change with cultural variations in the experience of danger. Freelancing is necessary. Bennett knows who his key constituencies are. He knows which agents of responsibility are most available to him and which must remain above reproach. But within those two boundary-setting conditions, he must experiment to locate the most productive fears, mark the most vulnerable enemies, recruit the most available constituencies, identify the most potent strategies of mobilization and isolation.

What remains constant in the cultural war is the symbol of the American *nation*, an abstract entity Bennett sees with his own eyes. This container speaks to the common sense of the core constituencies he courts. That is, it binds diffuse feelings of uncertainty, anxiety, and resentment to the national memory of a nation lost. When liberals and deconstructionists misread the spirituality through which the Bennett troops are mobilized, their protests often operate to invigorate it. To the extent they themselves implicitly participate in this spirituality, their calls for restraint and caution in its pursuit fuel charges of moral weakness and uncertainty against them.

It may be important, therefore, to take the measure of this spirituality. Let us call it the abstract common sense of a nation of regular individuals. Whenever Bennett invokes "the American people," "our culture," "our children," "the Judeo-Christian tradition," "family values," "real people," and "common sense," he summons a spiritual image of the nation in which each regular individual is a microcosm of the nation and the nation is a macrocosm of the regular individual. And the church, the nuclear family, the elementary school, the media, and the university are the institutions that must maintain each primal unit as a reflection of the other. If and when the "nation" begins to fall apart, these are the institutions to hold responsible. The endlessly reiterated phrase "the American people" captures this combination precisely: it at once speaks to a general yearning for identity between individual and nation and conveys the sense of a diverse host of individuals, perhaps even a majority, falling below this spirituality. It sustains the image of an ethnic, religious, linguistic center under duress, rather than of a pluralistic culture with multiple lines of connection between diverse constituencies.[6]

What drug users, drug dealers, inner-city residents, non-European immigrants, state bureaucrats, deconstructionists, homosexuals, liberal church leaders, secularists, atheists, liberal arts academics, and liberal journalists share is that each constituency contains a large number of people who deviate in various ways *as individuals* from the individualistic spirituality of the nation. Every defection from the nation is a product of individual will: this is the fundamental faith of the nation and the fundament that marks you as deviant if you defect from it. While it may feel strange to some to be lumped with these others despite their great diversity, what they all share is the fact of deviation from the individualistic norm of the nation and the national standard of the regular individual. As a corollary, any individual initially marked by one or more of these ascriptive liabilities can become a full-fledged member by aggressively reasserting the conventional code of the nation: individual responsibility for your own fate, faith in the capitalist market, belief in a moral god, commitment to the opportunity society, opposition to the welfare state, support for family values, identification with the military, and commitment to normal sexuality. The formula is to be generically skeptical toward the state, fervently committed to a nation of regular individuals, and selectively disposed to the state whenever it wages cultural war against deviants from this enigmatic nation.

Most fundamentally, since the *empirical average* in America today splits and diversifies in response to a series of endemic pressures, such as changing patterns of immigration, the acceleration of speed in cultural communications, the globalization of capitalist economic relations, and the effects of these forces in magnifying the experience of contingency in those racial, sexual, religious, and ethnic identities that inhabit us, the spirituality of a nation of regular individuals is maintained by the repetitive exhibition of contemporary policies, ethical codes, and styles of living that *deviate* from the spiritual norm. The fictive ideal of a nation of regular individuals catalogs much of the actual populace into a nation of diverse deviants in need of coercive correction. And the promise to realize this ideal of the nation requires extensive programs of social engineering, programs that are doomed to fail in producing their putative end. The drug war is merely a major campaign in the larger culture war.

The common sense of "the American people," then, is held together by the political designation and cultural segregation of constituencies that negate it; the promise of return to a nation lost is kept alive by militant campaigns against those groups and dispositions said to be responsible for the loss. Some potential scapegoats are politically unavailable, however, given the projected dissonance between the spirit of the nation and the clumsiness of the state. Agents of capital must not become primary targets, for instance, even though they are implicated more than any other constituency in those forces that scramble the common sense of the American nation. Capitalists remain exempt because national faith in the market as the primordial mechanism of individual freedom is the one key that enables the *nation* to be turned against the social activism of the *state*. Otherwise, the state itself might be called upon to tame the corrosive effects of the capitalist market. The politically available targets of the renationalization campaign, then, are liberals, drug users, state bureaucrats, drug dealers, deconstructionists, the nonreligious, the media, and universities.

If you resist the ugly drive to renationalization, it is important not to misidentify the adversary. When liberals or deconstructionists, for instance, accuse American nationalists of racism they set themselves up for effective refutation. The American nationalist is not a racist, if by racism you mean (as the nationalist does) the view that some "races" are congenitally inferior to others. Individuals and families from any racial or ethnic group are deemed capable of assimilation to the American nation, if they work hard and assert the right identifications actively enough. The accusation of racism opens the door to the counteraccusation that the academic accusers themselves lack the capacity to distinguish between the sin of racism and the simple virtue of national patriotism. What *is* the relation between race and the nation of regular individuals, then? Critics are on more solid ground when they say that assimilating all constituencies to the individualistic nation through private effort and formal opportunity is an impossible goal and that its pursuit produces a negative effect on race relations in contemporary America.

Similar traps for critical theorists are waiting in other domains, such as welfare policy and the public expression of religious faith. Bennett acknowledges, for example, that "the American people" do not support one faith within Christianity, nor does this authoritative abstraction decertify separation of church and state as that principle is interpreted within Tocquevillian-American discourse. Rather, it sets faith in a less sectarian, monotheistic, moral God as the consummate sign of moral virtue and the defining condition of legitimate participation in public debates over cultural issues and policy options. "Do you pray?" A yes or no answer will suffice. In this way the atheist, the secularist, the Unitarian, the postmodernist, and a few others are rendered morally suspect without committing "the American people" to public enforcement of any particular sect within the Judeo-Christian tradition.

The war on drugs organized around military intervention, long prison terms, capital punishment, morality as crusade, and intellectuals as morally bankrupt provided an effective configuration of national symbols and modes of state action for a while. This potent signifier of antinationals mobilized floating anger and anxiety among white working- and middle-class males; identified minority constituencies marked by urban location, race, and class for punitive action; relieved pressures on the state to support education, job training, and welfare; placed a thin veil of deniability over the site and racial composition of the primary targets; and opened dissenting media and academic elites to charges of moral laxity. The New Right's inversion of the New Left view of the drug experience contributes to the cultural potency of its war on drugs. While the cultural left in the sixties claimed that some drugs disclose deep truths hidden by the routines of mundane experience, the nationalist commanders of the drug war insist that these same drugs pull people away from verities of the nation that otherwise shine through the experience of every individual. The deepest cultural connection between users of street drugs and academic deconstructionists, then, is that both types are too drugged to endorse the unity of the nation. Forrest Gump is the counterexample here: his uncomplicated character opens him to the simple virtues of the nation; and his example implicitly recalls a (putative) time when the issues of ethics and politics were not so complicated.

The war on drugs has played a critical role in the campaign to renationalize America. But freelancers like Bennett may soon find it losing its cultural potency. Too many police chiefs may defect. Or continued drug use may belie the effectiveness of the war. Or the very familiarity of this evil may fail to mobilize the appropriate cultural energies. Or exciting new signifiers of negations of the nation may displace it. Prayer in the schools to secure the religiosity of the nation, or the deportation of illegal aliens to restore the ethnic composition of the nation, or the renormalization of sexuality to reinstate the normal family unit, or state reculturation of schools and universities to protect our children may emerge to push the drug war into a modest, supporting role.

Freelancing, then, remains crucial to signification of the nation. For powerful institutional forces—such as the globalization of the market economy fervently endorsed by many of the nationalizers themselves—function to denationalize the contemporary democratic state. But even as the organizing symbols of negation shift, the targets of attack and the strategies of demonization pursued remain fairly stable. The abstract spirit of the individualistic nation provides the vacant center around which cultural war is organized; and secular, liberal intellectuals provide the medium through which it is processed.

Dis-nationalizing the Democratic State

And yet . . . the fifty-one year old Bennett is genuine in the passion of his preaching. He cares about real things that matter—the destruction wrought by the drug epidemic, the crisis of black America, the failure of the education system . . . , the character of the nation.

Michael Kelly, "The Man of the Minute," *The New Yorker*, July 17, 1995, p. 27.

Contrary to Kelly, I find that the fundamental problem with Bennett is that he draws upon the widely held fiction of "a nation lost" to demonize difference in America. How can liberal journalists, media critics, and academic deconstructionists respond to these strategies? (I lump this disparate group together partly because Bennett is so eager to do so and partly because I think lines of connection must be established between them if the Bennett strategy is to be resisted.) The first temptation may be to lapse into silence, since so many avenues are so full of traps. But one salient response may be to rework the roles of social scientist, political theorist, reporter, editorialist, philosopher, and policy analyst that many now accept. Neither secular liberalism as agreement on a few values of public life, nor deconstruction as the decoding of contemporary codes of violence, nor journalism as detached reporting of the events of the day is sufficient. Each of these role definitions has been rendered defensive, neutralized, effectively negated, or all three by the cultural politics of the day. The irony is that today journalists and academics on the right form powerful networks of mutual support while a deep split has opened up between the academic and journalistic left. The latter fear that academic critiques of old models of objectivity threaten their very standing as responsible journalists. And the former encounter hostility from journalists whenever they advance critical perspectives disconnected from a positive agenda. It may be that critical journalists need to fashion a new model of responsibility, one less governed by the old standard of detached objectivity, one shaped more by the demand to build civility and forbearance into public debates between multiple perspectives. And academics, influenced in one way or another by the deconstructive project, must today augment that project by taking more explicit and positive positions on public issues of the day. In particular, we must explore positive alternatives to the imagination of the unified nation that governs so much of public discourse today. For as long as the image of "a nation lost" haunts public discourse the cultural drive to identify and demonize those held responsible for its absence will also be powerful.

The need, first, is to cultivate ourselves as critical intellectuals who can learn some tricks from the political style of William Bennett. We seek to expose the impossible dream energizing Bennett's cultural war while we also become more closely attuned to troubles, anxieties, and hopes that grip people in a variety of contexts. We experiment with themes that tap into those concerns while moving people in more noble and generous directions. We try out new proposals to respond to the issue of drugs, for example, seeking to show how our proposals curtail the drive to cultural war even while they help to reduce the worst effects of drug traffic and use. We become, thereby, freelancers ourselves, exposing the experiments of those who seek to divide the culture against itself and articulating as best we can the assumptions, risks, and stakes governing our cultural experiments.

As we proceed, it may be imperative to identify just how our adversaries seek to define us and what might turn upon these war games for other constituencies targeted by them. Is it timely to participate in talk shows? To put ourselves on the line more often, without taking refuge behind those fading veneers of expertise, neutrality, objectivity, or critical detachment? The initial objective is to decline to play the role scripted for us in the cultural war of William Bennett. In the process, we strive to learn from a variety of constituencies what troubles them even as we seek to show some of them how the circumstances of their lives deteriorate when they get sucked into a cultural war on behalf of restoring nationhood.

As we proceed it may be necessary to reconfigure the common sense of a nation of regular individuals. For Bennett is both right and wrong. He is right that a series of deeply divisive cultural wars is inevitable as long as the sense of "a nation lost" remains common and intense. He is wrong in his promise that a sustained cultural war could win a positive victory for this vision. The very conditions that create nostalgia for the nineteenth-century vision of the nation ensure that it can function today only as a clarion of cultural war. It can mobilize antistatism. It might even foster a punitive, corrupt police state. But it cannot nourish a positive, democratic state capable of acting in support of the institutional, ethical, and spiritual conditions of a pluralistic democracy. The nation and the state will remain at war as long as the call to national restoration prevails: the renationalizers will enlist the state to secure the nation by attacking itself. Citizen militia groups embody an extreme example of this tendency, praising violence in the name of restoring a nation of regular individuals.

One task of critical intellectuals today is to show how the project to assimilate numerous constituencies into a nation of regular individuals multiplies the cultural enemies to be defeated and perpetuates the troubles inspiring the nationalist drive. Another task is to show how a democratic culture flourishes best when it transcends the sense of a nation lost. The positive alternative is to support a pluralistic culture without a national center. Action in concert through the state does not require common identification with one spiritual source, such as, say, the Judeo-Christian tradition (or, more accurately, one version of it). It requires forging numerous lines of connection and forbearance between multiple constituencies inspired by diverse sources of morality. This is the cultural spirituality to be placed in competition with the abstract sense of a lost nation.[7] To refute the charge that we are either amoral ("secular devotees of the neutral state") or agents of cultural fragmentation ("deconstructionists and postmodernists") we must show how the effective performance of a pluralist, democratic state involves moving past the schemes of social engineering and cultural war upon which pursuit of renationalization is predicated. We must show how democratic action in concert through the state is a product of creative coalitions of multiple constituencies coming together from diverse places, animated by numerous moral sources, and united by the paradoxical presumption that no single constituency by itself embodies the lost spirit of the nation.[8]

As I noted at the outset, I am an amateur in this territory. Perhaps we all are. The largest agenda remains: to show how a democratic civilization flourishes best when a large variety of constituencies overcomes nostalgia for the innocence of a nation lost.

Notes

Introduction: Liberal Commitments and the Problem of Drugs

1. In the same tenor, see the essays in *Liberalism and the Moral Life*, ed. Nancy Rosenblum (Cambridge: Harvard University Press, 1989), and most of the essays in *Liberalism and the Good*, ed. Bruce Douglass, Gerald Mara, and Henry S. Richardson (New York: Routledge, 1990).

2. According to Elster's thin conception of rationality, an agent is rational if her conduct, desires, beliefs, and evidence cohere with one another. This thin conception does not, by itself, impose constraints on the agent's beliefs and desires: an act is rational if it is conducive to the realization of the desires the agent happens to have and if it is compatible with the agent's own beliefs and with the relevant evidence she might have about facts of the world.

3. This is not to say that defenders of the current prohibitionist regime in the United States will be comforted by the authors' conclusions about where that line ought to be drawn.

4. This is in contrast, for instance, to David Richards, who defends drug consumption on the basis of enhanced "self-control." According to Richards, drugs allow users to "regulate the quality and versatility of their experiences in life to include greater control of mood." See David Richards, *Sex, Drugs, Death, and the Law* (Totowa, N.J.: Rowman and Littlefield, 1982), p. 170.

5. Compare Douglas Husak's attempt to clarify the notion of addiction in his *Drugs and Rights* (New York: Cambridge University Press, 1992), pp. 100–130. See also my review of Husak, "Right Talk about Drugs," *Criminal Law Forum* 6 (1995): 525–537.

6. See John Stuart Mill, *On Liberty* (Indianapolis: Hackett, 1978).

7. As Charles Larmore puts it, "If we were only consequentialists, we constantly would have to set aside our own projects and friendships, since each of us has countless opportunities for increasing preference-satisfaction within a wider sphere" (Charles Larmore, *Patterns of Moral Complexity* [Cambridge: Cambridge University

Press, 1987], p. 132). Of course, Bernard Williams criticizes utilitarianism on similar grounds in Bernard Williams and J. J. C. Smart, *Utilitarianism, For and Against* (Cambridge: Cambridge University Press, 1973) and in some of the essays in his *Moral Luck* (Cambridge: Cambridge University Press, 1981). The tension between Mill's interest in protecting freedom in *On Liberty* and the consequentialist stringency of his utilitarianism has been the subject of many studies. See Fred Berger, *Happiness, Justice and Freedom: The Moral and Political Philosophy of John Stuart Mill* (Berkeley: University of California Press, 1984).

8. Joel Feinberg, *Harm to Self*, vol. 3, *The Moral Limits of the Criminal Law* (Oxford: Oxford University Press, 1986).

9. John Rawls, *Political Liberalism* (New York: Columbia University Press, 1993); T. M. Scanlon "Contractualism and Utilitarianism," in *Utilitarianism and Beyond*, ed. Bernard Williams and Amartya Sen (Cambridge: Cambridge University Press, 1982).

10. A pragmatic "strategy of avoidance" has been defended by Bruce Ackerman ("Why Dialogue?" *Journal of Philosophy* 86 [1989]: 5–23). This strategy is criticized by Michael Sandel (*Democracy's Discontent* [Cambridge: Harvard University Press], p. 21).

11. Here Moon is quoting John Booth Davies, *The Myth of Addiction* (Chur, Switzerland: Harwood, 1992), p. 110.

12. By way of a comparison, reliable studies estimate the number of violent deaths in Colombia in the seven-year period between 1988 to 1994 at 165,000. Not all these deaths were drug related, but no one doubts that the drug business is one of the two leading factors behind the violence. In the eight-year period between 1986 to 1993, there were 9,314 "murders related to narcotic drug laws" in the United States. See *National Drug Control Strategy Executive Summary* (1995). For the Colombian figures see Juan Gabriel Tokatlián, *Drogas, Dilemas, y Dogmas* (Bogotá: TM Editores/CEI, 1995), p. 130. One more comparison may help put the Colombian numbers in context: the Pinochet military regime in Chile has been blamed for the loss of 1,600 to 3,000 lives in a period that lasted more than ten years!

13. See the essays in *Beyond Westphalia? State Sovereignty and International Intervention*, ed. Gene M. Lyons and Michael Mastanduno (Baltimore: Johns Hopkins University, 1995).

14. See Jürgen Habermas, *Between Facts and Norms*, trans. William Rehg (Cambridge: MIT Press, 1996). See also Habermas, *The Inclusion of the Other: Studies in Political Theory*, ed. Ciaran Cronin and Pablo De Greiff (Cambridge: MIT Press, 1998).

15. See Michel Foucault, *Discipline and Punish: The Birth of Prison*, trans. Alan Sheridan (New York: Pantheon, 1977). See also Connolly's *The Ethos of Pluralization* (Minneapolis: University of Minnesota Press, 1995) and his *Identity/Difference* (Ithaca: Cornell University Press, 1991).

16. Connolly refers in his essay to William B. Bennett, *The De-Valuing of America: The Fight for Our Culture and Our Children* (New York: Simon and Schuster, 1992).

17. Similarly, to assume that preventing the state from using the penal system in order to curb drug use demonstrates the willingness on the part of reformers to leave drug abusers completely on their own suggests that social groups have no power of their own that can be exercised independently of a guardian state. Thus, Connolly correctly points out that, for instance, despite Bennett's general antistatism, "Bennett is a statist, when it comes to action on behalf of the political morality of punishment he endorses." Ultimately, the authors of the essays collected in this volume see liberalism as a political (but nevertheless moral) doctrine. As such, it does not try to *replace* communal bonds, especially not by coercive ties.

18. Jonathan Simon (in "Governing through Crime" [paper presented at the Baldy Law and Society Center, November 20, 1996, pp. 5–6]) tracks the increased use of criminal law across a wide variety of sites of governing. He makes the significant but oft-repeated observation concerning staggering incarceration rates in the United States: "Imprisonment rates in the United States fluctuated between 75 and 130 per 100,000 from the beginning of reliable statistics in the 1920's through the late 1970's. Between 1980 and 1990 the figure rose from 138 to 292. In 1995 it reached 409" (p. 6). But moreover, Simon's aim is to point out the fact that "wherever we govern, through the family, through work, through education, there is a tendency toward a more penal approach" (pp. 5–6).

Chapter 1. Rationality and Addiction

1. Donald Davidson, "How Is Weakness of the Will Possible," in *Essays on Actions and Events* (Oxford: Oxford University Press, 1980); David Pears, *Motivated Irrationality* (Oxford: Oxford University Press, 1984).

2. Gary Becker and Kevin Murphy, "A Theory of Rational Addiction," *Journal of Political Economy* 96 (1988): 675–700; Gary Becker, "Habits, Addictions, and Traditions," *Kyklos* 45 (1992): 327–346; Gary Becker, Michael Grossman, and Kevin Murphy, "An Empirical Analysis of Cigarette Addiction," *American Economic Review* 84 (1994): 396–418.

3. Richard J. Herrnstein and Drazen Prelec, "Melioration," in *Choice over Time*, ed. Richard Loewenstein and Jon Elster (New York: Russell Sage Foundation, 1992), p. 333.

4. Roy A. Wise and Michael Bozarth, "A Psychomotor Stimulant Theory of Addiction," *Psychological Review* 94 (1987): 469–492.

5. Richard J. Rosenthal and Loreen J. Rugle, "A Psychodynamic Approach to the Treatment of Pathological Gambling: Part I. Achieving Abstinence," *Journal of Gambling Studies* 10 (1994): 33–34.

6. Henry R. Lesieur, *The Chase: The Compulsive Gambler* (Rochester, Vt.: Schenkman, 1984), p. 16.

7. See Avram Goldstein, *Addiction* (New York: Freeman, 1994); E. Gardner and J. David, "The Neurobiology of Chemical Addiction," in *Getting Hooked: Rationality and the Addictions*, ed. Jon Elster and Ole-Jørgen Skog (Cambridge: Cambridge University Press, forthcoming).

8. Lesieur, *The Chase*, p. 44.

9. Amos Tversky and Dale Griffin, "Endowment and Contrast in Judgments of Well-being," in *Strategy and Choice*, ed. Richard J. Zeckhauser (Cambridge: MIT Press, 1991), pp. 297–318.

10. See Richard L. Solomon and John D. Corbit, "An Opponent-Process Theory of Motivation," *Psychological Review* 81 (1974): 119–145.

11. Personal communication.

12. See Tibor Scitovsky, *The Joyless Economy*, rev. ed. (Oxford: Oxford University Press, 1992), p. 130.

13. Tversky and Griffin, "Endowment and Contrast in Judgments."

14. Stanton Peele, *The Meaning of Addiction* (Lexington, Mass.: Lexington, 1985), p. 64.

15. For a related discussion, see Richard Klein, *Cigarettes Are Sublime* (Durham: Duke University Press, 1993).

16. Elvin M. Jellinek, *The Disease Concept of Alcoholism* (New Haven: Hillhouse, 1960), p. 38.

17. Peele, *The Meaning of Addiction*, p. 24.

18. For a fuller discussion, together with comments on nonstandard versions, see Jon Elster, *Sour Grapes* (Cambridge: Cambridge University Press, 1983); Jon Elster, "The Nature and Scope of Rational-Choice Explanation," in *Actions and Events: Perspectives on the Philosophy of Donald Davidson*, ed. Ernest LePore and Brian McLaughlin (Oxford: Blackwell, 1986), pp. 60–72; Jon Elster, *The Cement of Society* (Cambridge: Cambridge University Press, 1989).

19. David Hume, *A Treatise of Human Nature*, ed. L. A. Selby-Bigge (Oxford: Oxford University Press, 1960), p. 415.

20. O. Gjelsvik, "Addiction, Weakness of the Will, and Relapse," in *Getting Hooked: Rationality and the Addictions*, ed. Elster and Skog.

21. See Davidson, "How Is Weakness of the Will Possible."

22. George Loewenstein, "A Visceral Theory of Addiction," in *Getting Hooked: Rationality and the Addictions*, ed. Elster and Skog.

23. Aristotle, *Nicomachean Ethics*, 1146b.

24. George Ainslie, *Picoeconomics* (Cambridge: Cambridge University Press, 1992).

25. See Jon Elster, *Ulysses and the Sirens*, rev. ed. (Cambridge: Cambridge University Press, 1984).

26. Baruch Fischhoff, "Risk Taking: A Developmental Approach," in *Risk-Taking Behavior*, ed. Jacques F. Yates (New York: Wiley, 1992), p. 137.

27. W. Kip Viscusi, *Smoking* (Oxford: Oxford University Press, 1992), p. 132.

28. George Akerlof, *An Economic Theorist's Book of Tales* (Cambridge: Cambridge University Press, 1984). See chap. 7.

29. Mark G. Dickerson, *Compulsive Gamblers* (London: Longman, 1984), p. 134.

30. See notably, Willem A. Wagenaar, *Paradoxes of Gambling Behaviour* (Hove and London: Lawrence Erlbaum, 1988).

31. Lesieur, *The Chase*, p. 49.

32. Athanasios Orphanides and David Zervos, "Rational Addiction with Learning and Regret" (unpublished manuscript, 1992).

33. Viscusi, *Smoking*.

34. Robyn Dawes, *Rational Choice in an Uncertain World* (New York: Harcourt Brace Jovanovich, 1988), pp. 71–72.

35. Derek B. Cornish, *Gambling: A Review of the Literature and its Implications for Policy and Research* (London: Her Majesty's Stationery Office, 1978), p. 108.

36. Mark G. Dickerson, *Compulsive Gamblers* (London: Longman, 1984), pp. 66–67.

37. Becker and Murphy, "A Theory of Rational Addiction," p. 683.

38. Becker, Grossman, and Murphy, "An Empirical Analysis of Cigarette Addiction."

39. Thomas C. Schelling, "Self-command: A New Discipline," in *Choice over Time*, ed. Loewenstein and Elster, p. 167.

40. On strategic behavior, see Finn E. Kydland and Edward C. Prescott, "Rules rather than Discretion: The Inconsistency of Optimal Plans," *Journal of Political Economy* 85 (1977): 43–92.

41. Griffith Edwards et al., *Alcohol Policy and the Public Good* (Oxford: Oxford University Press, 1994), p. 137.

42. Becker, "Habits, Addictions, and Traditions," p. 329.

43. Loewenstein, "A Visceral Theory of Addiction."

1. Gary Becker and Kevin Murphy, "A Theory of Rational Addiction," *Journal of Political Economy* 96 (1988): 675–700; Gary Becker, "Habits, Addictions, and Tradition," *Kyklos* 45 (1992): 327–346; Gary Becker, Michael Grossman, and Kevin Murphy, "An Empirical Analysis of Cigarette Addiction," *American Economic Review* 84 (1994): 396–418.

2. Elster argues that being subject to withdrawal is a "(more or less) objective" factor and that being liable to experience cravings is a subjective factor. Seeing that he defines withdrawal not in terms of physical symptoms but in terms of welfare comparisons, I am not sure what the subjective/objective distinction is supposed to be here.

3. Kant presents the categorical imperative as a command issued by our reason. See Immanuel Kant, *Groundwork of the Metaphysics of Morals*, trans. H. J. Paton (New York: Harper and Row, 1964).

4. David Hume, *An Enquiry concerning the Principles of Morals* (1751), ed. Jerome B. Schneewind (Indianapolis: Hackett, 1983), sec. 9, pt. 2.

5. Elster argues explicitly that time preferences cannot be irrational by the thin conception, and I agree that it is not irrational to care very much more about one's present happiness than about one's happiness tomorrow or a year from now. (Note the fairness of Elster's conception of rationality here. It would be much easier for him to show that addiction is irrational if he invoked a notion of rationality on which it is irrational to care much more about the present than about the future.) But I am less sure about more bizarre time preferences such as the one entertained by Parfit, who gives the example of a person with a strong desire for his own future happiness who, nevertheless, cares nothing about his happiness on future Tuesdays (though he does care in quite the normal way about his present happiness when it is Tuesday). See Derek Parfit, *Reasons and Persons* (Oxford: Oxford University Press, 1984), p. 124. The whole of section 46 is pertinent.

6. I say "evidence" rather than "information" to make clear that no truth claim is implied. We are, after all, working with a conception of rationality that is "subjective through and through."

7. Jon Elster, *Ulysses and the Sirens* (Cambridge: Cambridge University Press, 1969).

8. Let me make a brief remark about time discounting, the tendency to desire a given welfare gain less strongly the further in the future that that gain will be realized. Elster holds that it is irrational to become addicted if one knows that this will reshape oneself into a heavier discounter who will act suboptimally with regard to his present discount rate. This argument may work as a reductio against Becker, but it does not fit well with Elster's own definition of rationality. He writes, "To be rational . . . means only that one has no reason, after the fact, to think that one should have acted differently." The new addict, with the new, heavy discount rate, has no reason to think he should have acted differently, because, modulo his new, present discount rate, his conduct is superior to conduct motivated by the old, preaddiction discount rate. Here Elster may need to modify his definition.

9. Elster also makes the point that false beliefs about what in fact are games of pure chance are more common among gamblers than in the population at large. But this does not show that gambling makes persons prone to false beliefs. It may show instead that having false beliefs makes persons prone to gamble (a possibility Elster rejects without evidence). Moreover, it is by no means clear that it is irrational to engage

in activities that make one prone to false beliefs. For one thing, the agent may lack evidence that the activity has this effect. And, furthermore, even if the agent has such evidence, he may rationally decide that the activity in question offers an advantage in terms of desire fulfillment that outweighs the negative effect it will have on the accuracy of his beliefs. So, the charge that gambling makes one prone to false beliefs really belongs under the heading of conduct irrationality, not under that of belief irrationality.

10. I assume here that a diagnosis of belief (ir)rationality requires some knowledge of the agent's desires in order to determine whether the agent's beliefs are unduly influenced by his desires (wishful thinking).

Chapter 3. Liberty and Drugs

1. Three of the leading books on the topic of drug policy devote but little attention to the general idea of limited state power or of citizen liberty. See Douglas N. Husak, *Drugs and Rights* (Cambridge: Cambridge University Press, 1992), pp. 61–68; David A. J. Richards, *Sex, Drugs, Death, and the Law* (Totowa, N.J.: Rowman and Littlefield, 1982), pp. 1–25; John Kaplan, *The Hardest Drug* (Chicago: University of Chicago Press, 1983), pp. 102–109.

2. For my theory of constitutional interpretation, see Michael Moore, "Do We Have an Unwritten Constitution?" *Southern California Law Review* 63 (1989): 107–139; Moore, "A Natural Law Theory of Interpretation," *Southern California Law Review* 58 (1985): 277–398. A version of this chapter has been revised to illustrate the application of my theory of constitutional interpretation to the meaning of liberty in the Fifth and Fourteenth Amendments. See Moore, "Discovering Liberty," in *Objectivity in Constitutional Law*, ed. Lawrence Alexander (Cambridge: Cambridge University Press, 1997).

3. The position that the very idea of a right involves the idea of liberty is an idea of Locke's that the "choice theory" of rights embraces and elaborates. The choice theory of rights is so named because it emphasizes that the holder of a right has the choice as to whether to waive it or exercise it. For discussion and citations, see Michael Moore, *Law and Psychiatry: Rethinking the Relationship* (Cambridge: Cambridge University Press, 1984), pp. 92–93.

4. The view of John Rawls, *A Theory of Justice* (Cambridge: Harvard University Press, 1971), and of Ronald Dworkin, *Taking Rights Seriously* (Cambridge: Harvard University Press, 1978), pp. 270–271.

5. As in, for example, Wilhelm von Humboldt, *The Limits of State Action* (1854), trans. J. W. Burrow (Cambridge: Cambridge University Press, 1969); Herbert Packer, *The Limits of the Criminal Sanction* (Stanford: Stanford University Press, 1968); Michael Moore, "The Limits of Legislation" (Asia Foundation Lectures on Legislation, Seoul, Korea, 1984), published in *USC Cites* [Fall 1984], pp. 23–32.

6. See Moore, *Law and Psychiatry*, p. 91.

7. Olmstead v. United States, 277 U.S. 438, 478 (1928).

8. Robert Bork, *The Tempting of America* (New York: MacMillan, 1990).

9. See, e.g., Rawls, *A Theory of Justice*, p. 244; John Hospers, "What Libertarianism Is," in *The Libertarian Alternative*, ed. Tibor Machan (Chicago: Nelson-Hall, 1974).

10. Compare Martin Heidegger's analysis of death: "Death is the possibility of the absolute Impossibility of Dasein." *Being and Time*, trans. J. Macquarrie and E. Robinson (New York: Harper and Row, 1962).

11. Samuel Freeman, "Criminal Liability and Duty to Aid the Distressed," *University of Pennsylvania Law Review* 142 (1994): 1486.

12. Dworkin, *Taking Rights Seriously*, pp. 268–269.

13. Joseph Raz, *The Morality of Freedom* (Oxford: Clarendon, 1986), p. 13.

14. Rawls, *A Theory of Justice*, p. 396.

15. For an explication of Kant's evaluation of good motives, see Barbara Herman, "On the Value of Acting from the Motive of Duty," in *The Practice of Moral Judgment* (Cambridge: Harvard University Press, 1993).

16. The exception is to be found with some of the costs of enforcing criminal laws; some of these costs are concentrated in the passage of laws aimed at certain kinds of behaviors.

17. This terminology can be found in Joel Feinberg, *Harm to Others* (Oxford: Oxford University Press, 1984), pp. 9, 207.

18. Douglas Husak, "The Presumption of Freedom," *Nous* 17 (1983): 345–362. Raz, *The Morality of Freedom*, pp. 8–12.

19. For an encapsulated critique of this kind of Burkean conservatism, see Michael Moore, "The Dead Hand of Constitutional Tradition," *Harvard Journal of Law and Public Policy* 19 (1995): 263–273.

20. See Raz, p. 12.

21. John Stuart Mill, *On Liberty* (1859), in *J. S. Mill's "On Liberty" in Focus*, ed. John Gray and G. W. Smith (London: Routledge, 1991).

22. Joel Feinberg has been the most careful taxonomist of Mill's excluded legislative aims. See his magisterial *Harm to Others*; see also Feinberg, *Harm to Self* (Oxford: Oxford University, 1985); Feinberg, *Offense to Others* (Oxford: Oxford University, 1986); and Feinberg, *Harmless Wrongdoing* (Oxford: Oxford University, 1988).

23. James Fitzjames Stephens, *Liberty, Equality, Fraternity* (1873), ed. Stuart Warner, (Indianapolis: Liberty Fund,1993), p. 17.

24. Ibid., p. 231.

25. See Michael Davis, "Harm and Retribution," *Philosophy and Public Affairs* 15 (1986): 236–266.

26. Mill, *On Liberty*, p. 32.

27. These are some of Feinberg's examples in *Harmless Wrongdoing*.

28. A criticism of Mill voiced, for example, by Gerry Dworkin in his "Paternalism," in *Law and Morality*, ed. Richard Wasserstrom (Belmont, Cal.: Wadsworth, 1971).

29. Samuel Scheffler, *The Rejection of Consequentialism* (Berkeley: University of California Press, 1982).

30. For other examples of what is sometimes called "perfectionist" liberalism, see Raz, *Morality of Freedom*, and Robert George, *Making Men Moral* (Oxford: Oxford University Press, 1993). Given the discussion to be had shortly, "perfectionist" is not the right label of my brand of moralistic liberalism.

31. Herbert Morris, "A Paternalistic Theory of Punishment," *American Philosophical Quarterly* 18 (1981): 263–271; Jean Hampton, "The Moral Education Theory of Punishment," *Philosophy and Public Affairs* 13 (1984): 208–238.

32. Albert Camus, *The Fall*, trans. Justin O'Brien (New York: Vintage, 1956).

33. Herbert Hart made this observation in his qualified defense of Mill; see Herbert Hart, *Law, Liberty, and Morality* (Stanford: Stanford University Press, 1963).

34. Notice that this retributivist argument for a derived right to liberty does not go beyond restrictions in the use of the criminal sanction. Sin taxes and other forms of nonpunitive discouragements to smoking are not ruled out. Compare to Mill's state-

ment: "To tax stimulants for the sole purpose of making them more difficult to be obtained, is a measure differing only in degree from their entire prohibition, and would be justifiable only if that were justifiable" (*On Liberty*, p. 114).

35. This is the apparent view of Lord Devlin in his *The Enforcement of Morality* (Oxford: Oxford University Press, 1965).

36. As Simon Blackburn points out, one does not have to be a moral realist to regard this distinction as fundamental to everyone's moral experience. Noncognitivists like Blackburn also find it so. See Blackburn, "Rule-Following and Moral Realism," in *Wittgenstein: To Follow a Rule*, ed. S. Holtzman and C. Leich (London: Routledge and Kegan Paul, 1981), p. 171. See also Michael Moore, "Moral Reality Revisited," *Michigan Law Review* 90 (1992): 2467–2468.

37. Feinberg is very persuasive on this point. See his *Offense to Others*, pp. 10–22.

38. Griswold v. Connecticut, 381 U.S. 479 (1965).

39. Roe v. Wade, 410 U.S. 113 (1973).

40. Judith Thomson, "A Defense of Abortion," *Philosophy and Public Affairs* 1 (1971): 47–66.

41. Suggested by the facts of Briscoe v. Readers Digest, 4 Cal. 3d 529, 93 Cal. Rptr. 866, 483 P. 2d 34 (1971).

42. Cf. Keeler v. Superior Court, 2 Cal. 3d 619, 470 P. 2d 617 (1970).

43. The late Judith Shklar catalogues our many daily immoralities in *Ordinary Vices* (Cambridge: Harvard University Press, 1984).

44. In one sense, there would be some liberty, namely, the liberty to act where morality is silent and the liberty to act in a nonvirtuous way, where the lack of virtue was a failure of supererogation and not a failure of obligation.

45. Heidi M. Hurd, "Justifiably Punishing the Justified," *Michigan Law Review* 90 (1992): 2203–2324.

46. Mill, *On Liberty*, pp. 32–33.

47. Ibid., p. 96.

48. Ibid., pp. 73, 90.

49. John C. Rees, *John Stuart Mill's "On Liberty"* (Oxford: Clarendon Press, 1985), pp. 137–155.

50. Feinberg, *Harm to Others*.

51. Mill, *On Liberty*, p. 90.

52. Louis Schwartz, "Moral Offenses and the Model Penal Code," *Columbia Law Review* 63 (1963): 669–686; Sanford Kadish, "The Crisis of Overcriminalization," *Annals* 374 (1967): 157–170; Gordon Hawkins and Norval Morris, *The Honest Politician's Guide to Crime Control* (Chicago: University of Chicago Press, 1970), pp. 1–28; Herbert Packer, "The Crime Tariff," *American Scholar* 33 (1964): 551–557.

53. E.g., Richard Epstein, "A Theory of Strict Liability," *Journal of Legal Studies* 2 (1973): 151–204.

54. Thornburgh v. American College of Obstetricians and Gynecologists, 476 U.S. 747, 772 (1986) (Stevens, J., concurring).

55. Griswold v. Connecticut, 381 U.S. 479, 486 (1965).

56. Eisenstadt v. Baird, 405 U.S. 438, 453 (1972).

57. Bowers v. Hardwick, 478 U.S. 186, 217 (1986) (Stevens, J., dissenting) quoting Fitzgerald v. Porter Mem. Hosp., 523 F2d 716, 719 (7th. Cir. 1975) (Stevens, J.).

58. Bowers, 478 U.S., pp. 204, 205 (Blackmun, J. dissenting).

59. Ibid. (quoting Roberts v. United States Jaycees, 468 U.S. 609, 619 [1984]).

60. Ibid. (quoting Paris Adult Theatre I v. Slaton, 413 U.S. 49, 63 [1973]).

61. Mill, *On Liberty*, p. 76.

62. Ibid., p. 75.

63. This roughly corresponds to Harry Frankfurt's notion of "second-order" mental states. See Frankfurt, "Freedom of the Will and the Concept of the Person," *Journal of Philosophy* 78 (1971): 5–20.

64. See Michael Moore, "Authority, Law, and Razian Reasons," *Southern California Law Review* 62 (1989): 878–882.

65. T. H. Huxley, "On Descartes' *Discourse on Method*," in *Methods and Results* (New York: Macmillan, 1893).

66. For other explications of the value of self-definition, see Stanley I. Benn, *A Theory of Freedom* (Cambridge: Cambridge University Press, 1988), pp. 155–156, 170–183; John Gray, "Mill's Conception of Happiness and the Theory of Individuality," in *J. S. Mill's "On Liberty" in Focus*, ed. Gray and Smith; Thomas E. Hill, Jr., *Autonomy and Self-Respect* (Cambridge: Cambridge University Press, 1991), pp. 29–37, 43–51.

67. I come back to the finer-grained analysis in the succeeding subsection where the surviving candidates can be assessed.

68. Raz, *The Morality of Freedom*, chap. 13.

69. It is not enough to show that morality is objective, even in the strong sense of the moral realist. One must also connect realism in ethics to bivalence, the thesis that every meaningful proposition about morals is either true or false. I argue that the first meta-ethical position makes the second more plausible. Michael Moore, "Moral Reality Revisited," *Michigan Law Review* 90 (1992): 2437–2438.

70. Nietzsche may well be right, however, that asceticism is one way to develop that kind of self-control and transformative power we value as Millian autonomy.

71. As David Richards points out (*Sex, Drugs*, pp. 165–166), many of the bad things drug use is said to cause can plausibly be laid at the doorstep of criminalizing drug use. Stealing to get money to buy drugs, for example, is a function of the high price of drugs, itself a function of the artificial restriction of supply caused by criminalization. Likewise, the violence of drug dealers is due to criminalization. Unlike Richards, I assume that use of some drugs "releases inhibitions or criminal tendencies" and thus does result in other crimes, even without the effects of criminalization of drug use.

72. See Michael Moore, "Prima Facie Moral Culpability," *Boston University Law Review* 76 (1996): 319–334.

73. See Stephen Morse, "Undiminished Confusion about Diminished Capacity," *Journal of Criminal Law and Criminology* 75 (1984): 1–55.

74. I argue this point in Michael Moore, "Causation and the Excuses," *California Law Review* 73 (1985): 1091–1149.

75. I argue for the illegitimacy of "proxy crimes" in Michael Moore, *Act and Crime* (Oxford: Oxford University Press, 1993), pp. 21–22. Compare this with Husak (*Drugs and Rights*, pp. 178–195), who does not disapprove of such crimes per se but limits the use of proxy crimes so as to make drug prohibitions unjustifiable on any analogy to such crimes.

76. Benjamin Rush, *An Inquiry into the Effects of Ardent Spirits on the Human Body and Mind* (1814), quoted and discussed in Richards, *Sex, Drugs*, pp. 171–172.

77. John Kaplan (*The Hardest Drug*, p. 132) gives another example in the prohibition of bowling during the time of Edward III on the ground that it distracted men from archery practice.

78. I follow Doug Husak here, regarding what he calls an "inchoate principle" according to which no act should be prohibited on the ground that it causes another act unless the latter act is itself criminal. Husak, *Drugs and Rights*, p. 184.

79. See Richards, *Sex, Drugs*, p. 170, where Richards finds that some drug use can help "to express self-respect by regulating the quality and versatility of [people's] experiences in life," "promote the rational self-control of those ingredients fundamental to the design of a fulfilled life," and function as "one means by which the already existing interests of the person may be explored or realized."

80. R. D. Laing, *The Divided Self* (London: Tavistock Publications, 1960); Laing, *The Politics of Experience* (New York: Ballantine Books, 1967).

81. I explore the concepts of rationality as it relates to mental illness in Moore, *Law and Psychiatry*, chap. 2. I explore autonomy and the rationality of intention in Moore, *Act and Crime*, chap. 6.

82. See Morse, "Undiminished Confusion."

83. Kant, *The Metaphysical Principles of Virtue*, trans. J. Ellington (Indianapolis: Bobbs-Merrill, 1964), p. 88.

84. For discussion of the "wild beast" test of legal insanity, see A. Platt and B. Diamond, "The Origin and Development of the 'Wild Beast' Concept of Mental Illness and Its Relation to Theories of Criminal Responsibility," *Journal of the History of the Behavioral Sciences* 1 (1965): 355–367.

85. On alcoholism as an addiction, for example, compare Herbert Fingarette's conclusions with the literature he critically discusses in his *Heavy Drinking* (Berkeley: University of California Press, 1987).

86. Two famous examples of this are the lady who rang for her maid constantly in order to show her a spot on a table cloth (Sigmund Freud, *Introductory Lectures on Psycho-analysis* [London: G. Allen and Unwin, 1922], lecture 17) and the young officer who found himself on trains to repay a debt he did not owe (Freud, "Notes upon a Case of Obsessional Neurosis," in *Three Case Histories*, ed. P. Rieff [New York: MacMillan, 1963]).

87. For the reasons outlined in Michael Moore, "Mind, Brain, and Unconscious," in *Science, Philosophy, and Psychoanalysis*, ed. P. Clark and C. Wright (Oxford: Basil Blackwell, 1988). When we correlate brain structure with mental functioning we are likely discovering more about what the mental states in question actually are, not showing that such states are really just fictions.

88. See Justice Marshall's wry observation that Leroy Powell, an alcoholic said to be unable to control his drinking, managed to stay sober on the day of his trial because he wanted to stay out of jail. Powell v. Texas, 392 U.S. 514, 525 (1968) (plurality opinion).

89. Explored in Moore, *Law and Psychiatry*, chap. 10.

90. A legislator might handle this problem by qualifying a blanket prohibition on drug use with a general justificatory section on the balance of evils, like that in the *Model Penal Code and Commentaries (Official Draft and Revised Comments)*, ed. R. Kent Greenwalt (Philadelphia: American Law Institute—American Bar Association, 1991), sec. 3.02.

91. Fingarette, *Heavy Drinking*.

92. We should also look at such a right because some people, no doubt, disagree with my characterization that most of the moral failings of drug takers are failures of virtue, not failures of obligation. Nothing, incidentally, that was said in that regard deals with the interesting question of whether those who help drug users to use drugs

are wrongdoers or are simply lacking in virtue. Even if we think that we should not criminalize lack of virtue, it may be that those who enable or help someone else to abandon virtue do wrong and deserve punishment. We might criminalize the aiding of suicide, for example, on this ground, even if we were convinced that suicide was not wrong but only lacking in virtue by the person committing it.

93. I have glossed over the difficult question of when the state has compelling enough reasons to violate its citizens' rights, including the basic right to liberty. For some suggestions, see Michael Moore, "Torture and the Balance of Evils," *Israel Law Review* 23 (1989): 280–344.

94. I also think Kantian autonomy weighs heavily here, since refraining from temptations on one's own (i.e., without legal coercion) has much higher value than merely coerced sobriety.

Chapter 4. Liberalism, Inalienability, and Rights of Drug Use

I am grateful to the participants of the Conference on Morality, Legality, and Drugs at the State University of New York, Buffalo, September 1995, for their many helpful comments, especially to Douglas Husak, Michael Moore, Donald Moon, Anita Allen, and Pablo De Greiff. I am also indebted to Jay Wallace for his advice on a draft of this essay.

1. The difference is 30% fewer on some accounts. See Daniel Benjamin and Roger L. Miller, *Undoing Drugs* (New York: Basic Books, 1991). Others contend that there is no reliable way of predicting such figures. See John Kaplan, *The Hardest Drug: Heroin and Public Policy* (Chicago: University of Chicago Press, 1983), pp. 111ff.

2. Benjamin and Miller, *Undoing Drugs*, p. 85.

3. Ibid., p. 129.

4. Ibid. See also Kaplan, *The Hardest Drug*, pp. 64–65.

5. Benjamin and Miller, *Undoing Drugs*, p. 82.

6. Kaplan, *The Hardest Drug*, pp. 90, 97–98.

7. Ibid., pp. 95–96.

8. In addition, Pablo De Greiff's essay in this volume addresses some of the international effects of the war on drugs.

9. See Joel Feinberg, *Harm to Self*, vol. 3, *The Moral Limits of the Criminal Law* (Oxford: Oxford University Press, 1986); David A. J. Richards, *Sex, Drugs, Death, and the Law* (Totowa, N.J.: Rowman and Littlefield, 1982); Douglas Husak, *Drugs and Rights* (Cambridge: Cambridge University Press, 1992). In this volume Michael Moore argues that recreational drug use can be justified from the triple standpoint of what he calls, respectively, a presumption of liberty, a derived right to liberty, and a basic right to liberty.

10. Joel Feinberg, *Harm to Self*, p. 61. Hereafter, page numbers to this work will be cited parenthetically in the text.

11. This explains why, in his discussion of the four different ways in which the right of autonomy relates to a person's good, Feinberg makes no claim, and does not even consider the possibility, that autonomy is in some way essential to a person's good or is part of a person's "true interests" (pp. 57–62). If we do take that idea as another serious possibility, then it is not so easy to contend that autonomy implies a right to act contrary to one's good, to the point of destroying autonomy itself.

12. I am not so concerned here with the question of whether this is a correct interpretation of Mill's utilitarianism. The point is rather that this is one way to conceive of the source of basic rights. Consistent with this reading, Mill does say of his argument for the Principle of Liberty, "I forgo any advantage which could be derived to my argument from the idea of abstract right as a thing independent of utility" (*On Liberty* [Indianapolis: Hackett, 1978], p. 10). Still, "it must be utility in the largest sense, as grounded in the permanent interest of mankind as a progressive being" (p. 10). Later he makes clear that the kind of self-determination he calls "the free development of Individuality is one of the essentials of well-being" (p. 54). It may be that, in the end, Mill himself incorporates certain prior moral notions, especially sentiments of justice, into his account of individuality. See p. 60.

13. Here I follow John Rawls's account of the basic liberties that are social conditions for realizing the moral powers of free and equal persons. Rawls, "The Basic Liberties and Their Priority," in *Political Liberalism* (New York: Columbia University Press, 1993).

14. There is nothing about possessing rights or being a subject of rights that implies having the separate and distinct right to alienate all one's rights. Arguably, having rights implies that one may choose not to exercise those rights, but this permission is very different from the right of complete alienation. (And even here there are exceptions. For example, parents are often said [in political debate and rhetoric] to have a right to protect, support and educate their children. But parents cannot refuse to exercise these rights, since they have the duty to do these things. Talk of rights in this context may just signal the degree of discretion that parents have in deciding the appropriate means for fulfilling their parental duties.)

15. Feinberg identifies "autonomy" with "personal sovereignty" (p. 48) and develops the idea of personal sovereignty by analogy with the idea of national sovereignty. See pp. 47–51 and chap. 19. "If we take the model of national sovereignty seriously, we cannot make certain kinds of compromises with paternalism . . . for sovereignty is an all or nothing concept; one is entitled to absolute control of whatever is within one's domain however trivial it may be" (p. 55). The most sustained argument Feinberg makes for complete alienability of rights comes by analogy with the concept of national sovereignty:

> The idea of sovereign renunciation of sovereignty is a coherent one in the political arena, where the concept of sovereignty has its original home. It is neither unstable, contradictory, nor paradoxical. If we transfer the whole concept of sovereignty from the nation to the person, then we should expect the same implications for the personal forfeiture of autonomy. Of course, it is open to one to deny that the idea of sovereignty applies to persons in the first place, but if one is friendly to that notion, one must face up to its implications. (P. 70)

There are problems with the analogy of individual with national sovereignty. The liberal position generally maintains that nations morally derive whatever sovereignty they have from the individual sovereignty of their members. (Locke and other proponents of social contract doctrine argue as much.) If so, it would seem that individual sovereignty is the primary notion, and is needed to clarify the nature of national sovereignty, not vice versa. These problems aside, the fact remains that there are moral limits to a nation's renunciation of its sovereignty. A nation cannot renounce sovereignty if the result of that act is the enslavement of its people, or for that matter any unjust impairment of their individual sovereignty. The same holds true for individuals.

16. Feinberg cites this as one reason for complete alienability. "A rational adult could have very good reasons for giving away all his worldly goods, or even terminating his own life, or in the most extreme hypothetical case, even for selling himself into slavery" (p. 69).

17. Basic rights, it must be granted, also have the role of enabling individuals to freely pursue their admissible conceptions of the good. But, as I've argued, conceptions of the good are admissible only if compatible with the exercise and development of the capacities for agency.

18. *On the Social Contract*, bk. 1, *Jean-Jacques Rousseau: The Basic Political Writings* (Indianapolis: Hackett, 1987), p. 144.

19. See, for example, Immanuel Kant, *Metaphysical Elements of Justice*, trans. John Ladd (Indianapolis: Bobbs-Merrill, 1965), p. 98.

20. Feinberg rejects the idea that "we must balance the person's right against his good and weigh them" (p. 61).

21. Building in part on Feinberg's examples and his account of liberalism, Douglas Husak has argued that individuals in a liberal society have a right to use drugs. A free society implies, Husak says, two fundamental rights that are relevant to the right to use drugs: (1) a right to determine what happens in and to one's body and (2) a right to regulate the ways the mind processes the sensory data it receives from the world (Husak, *Drugs and Rights*, pp. 39–40). It is, Husak contends, the nature of moral rights that they outweigh considerations of welfare. "Ordinary utilitarian reasons are insufficient to justify prohibiting a person from performing an action he has a right to perform. An almost catastrophic extent of disutility is required to override the exercise of a moral right" (p. 88). On the other hand, and apparently unlike Feinberg, Husak does not contend that the right to use drugs self-destructively is absolute. "Adults do not have an absolute moral right to use any imaginable recreational drug, whatever its effects on them may be" (p. 73). If a drug creates significant harms to a great many persons who use it, if few of these people regard the use of this drug as especially significant to their lives, and if attempts to minimize the health hazards of this drug below a tolerable threshold are unsuccessful, then the state "would have good reason to prohibit [it] on paternalistic grounds" (p. 100). Husak is skeptical that any existing drug satisfies all these criteria; only the synthetic drug Angel Dust, might do so, but he contends that heroin, cocaine, and crack cocaine do not.

22. See the parallel discussion of this point in Michael Moore's essay, "Liberty and Drugs," in this volume.

23. On the idea of an incremental value, see Ronald Dworkin, *Life's Dominion* (Cambridge: Harvard University Press, 1993), pp. 70, 73–74, 87.

24. I do not mean to imply here that all versions of perfectionism are incompatible with liberalism, just those teleological versions which say that our sole duty is to maximize the good, defined as the perfection of certain aspects of character or culture. Michael Moore's perfectionist liberalism, presented in this volume, along with that of Joseph Raz (in *The Morality of Freedom* [Oxford: Oxford University Press, 1985]), are not teleological in this sense. Moore and Raz both specify autonomy as the characteristic of individuals that is to be promoted by liberal institutions; neither author contends that it is the sole relevant moral or political consideration to which all other principles and ends are subordinate.

25. According to Rawls's political liberalism, Kantian liberalism of the kind here argued for need not make the working assumption that autonomy is an intrinsic good for each person, in other words, that autonomy is among the final ends about which

it is rational for all people to structure their lives and which, therefore, provides a fundamental basis for laws and political institutions. This is one respect in which a Kantian politically liberal view differs from the perfectionist liberalism argued for by Michael Moore in this volume. I make a weaker claim: that autonomy, in the sense of the exercise and development of the powers of moral and rational agency, is essential to each person's good within the confines of a liberal and democratic society. This leaves open the more controversial claim that autonomy is an intrinsic good for each person. This may be true, but it is not necessary for the argument over what basic rights individuals have.

26. See Kaplan, *The Hardest Drug*, p. 33, on "chippers," long-term occasional users of heroin who do not become addicted.

27. As is evidenced by the majority of servicemen who gave up heroin, without subsequent readdiction, upon return from the Vietnam War. See Kaplan, *The Hardest Drug*, p. 37. Kaplan says, "heroin withdrawal is not *that* serious. Pharmacologists compare it to a bad case of the one-week flu—a considerable degree of pain and discomfort, but not so serious that it cannot be borne by someone with considerable determination" (p. 35). For a different but similarly skeptical approach to the notion of addiction, see J. Donald Moon's essay in this volume.

28. See Kaplan, *The Hardest Drug*, pp. 45–46.

29. Angel Dust may be in this category. There also exists a form of heroin called China White that matches the description of intrinsically debilitating drugs.

30. For a thorough account of the ends of education in a constitutional democracy, see Amy Gutmann, *Democratic Education* (Princeton: Princeton University Press, 1987).

31. Heroin may be such a drug. See Kaplan, *The Hardest Drug*, pp. 133–136.

32. Still it remains the case that those who are unable to work because of drug addiction have assumed ways of life that require other people's labor to support them. This is likely to cause resentment among those who labor on their behalf, and a diminished sense of self-respect among those who are unable to labor because of addiction. I do not mean to take a position here in the complicated debate on whether those who choose a life of leisure without labor should be entitled to do so without affecting their share of government benefits or an insured basic income. See the criticisms of Rawls in Phillippe Van Parijs, "Why Surfers Should be Fed: The Liberal Case for an Unconditional Basic Income," *Philosophy and Public Affairs* 20 (1991): 101–131, and his *Real Freedom for All* (Oxford: Oxford University Press, 1995), chap. 4.

Chapter 5. Drugs and Democracy

1. Aldous Huxley, *The Doors of Perception and Heaven and Hell* (New York: Harper and Row, 1963).

2. Sigmund Freud, *Civilization and Its Discontents* (New York: Norton, 1961), pp. 26–27.

3. This, along with my discussion of the notion of addiction in the fourth section, may be read as my response to Samuel Freeman's argument in his essay in this volume.

4. Steven B. Duke and Albert C. Gross, *The Longest War* (New York: G. P. Putnam, 1993).

5. Joel W. Hay, "The Harm They Do to Others," in *Searching for Alternatives*, ed. Melvyn Krauss and Edward Lazear (Stanford, Cal.: Hoover Institution Press, 1991), p. 219.

6. Since drug use can cause harm to others, there would still be grounds for enforcing some regulations.

7. Compare this with Michael Moore's criticisms of libertarianism in his essay in this volume, criticisms he makes despite his obvious attraction to this position.

8. Brian Barry, *Justice as Impartiality* (Oxford: Oxford University Press, 1995), p. 86.

9. David A. J. Richards, *Sex, Drugs, and the Law* (Totowa, N.J.: Rowman and Littlefield, 1982), p. 171.

10. It must be emphasized that this is only a presumption. Even if we agreed that any use of mind-altering substances was morally wrong and should be therefore be stopped, prudential arguments may lead us to decide that using state coercion to achieve that goal is inadvisable.

11. James Q. Wilson, *On Character* (Washington: AEI Press, 1991), p. 155.

12. James Q. Wilson, *The Moral Sense* (New York: Basic Books, 1993), p. 94.

13. John Rawls, *Political Liberalism* (New York: Columbia University Press, 1993), p. 55.

14. See my "Values and Political Theory," *Journal of Politics* 39 (1977): 877–903, for further development of these points.

15. Alasdair MacIntyre, *After Virtue*, 2d ed. (Notre Dame: University of Notre Dame Press, 1984), p. 253.

16. Rawls, *Political Liberalism*, pp. 89–90, 91.

17. T. M. Scanlon, "Contractualism and Utilitarianism," in *Utilitarianism and Beyond*, ed. Amartya Sen and Bernard Williams (Cambridge: Cambridge University Press, 1982), p. 110.

18. Ibid., p. 116.

19. Rawls, *Political Liberalism*, pp. 140–141.

20. For a fuller discussion of this issue, and qualification of the statement in the text, see my *Constructing Community* (Princeton: Princeton University Press, 1993).

21. Michael Sandel, *Democracy's Discontent* (Cambridge: Harvard University Press, 1996), p. 21.

22. See the table in Kenneth J. Meier, *The Politics of Sin* (Armonk, N.Y.: M. E. Sharpe, 1994), p. xiii.

23. See Duke and Gross, *The Longest War*, pp. 37–42, and chap. 4 (on the comparison with the criminogenic aspects of illegal drugs).

24. Douglas Husak, *Drugs and Rights* (Cambridge: Cambridge University Press, 1992).

25. Wilson, *On Character*, p. 159.

26. Part of the devastation is reflected in the dramatic increase in the number of African-American men in prison (although drugs are only one factor); on present trends, according to a recent report, in fifteen years "we will have the absolute majority of all African-American males between age 18 and 40 in prisons and camps" (*New York Times*, August 10, 1995, p. A14). The only fortunate thing to be said about this is that geometric rates of growth do not tend to persist for long.

27. James Inciardi and Duane McBride, for example, assert (without any analysis) that "legalization would increase the levels of drug dependence in the ghetto" and, so, "would serve to legitimate the chemical destruction of an urban generation and cul-

ture." James Inciardi and Duane McBride, "Legalization: A High-Risk Alternative in the War on Drugs," *American Behavioral Scientist* 32 (1989): 279.

28. James Q. Wilson, "Drugs and Crime," in *Drugs and Crime*, ed. Michael Tonry and James Q. Wilson (Chicago: University of Chicago Press, 1990), pp. 525–526.

29. This argument is forcefully presented in Samuel Freeman's essay in this collection.

30. For a fuller discussion of these issues, see my *Constructing Community*, chaps. 5 and 6.

31. Robert Goodin, *No Smoking* (Chicago: University of Chicago Press, 1989), p. 28.

32. See Jon Elster's argument for the irrationality of addiction in his essay in this volume.

33. Some of these costs are borne in part by others as well, through increased medical insurance premiums or tax payments and lower profits due to decreased labor productivity.

34. John C. Lawn, "The Issue of Legalizing Illicit Drugs," *Hofstra Law Review* 18 (1990): 710.

35. Goodin, *No Smoking*, pp. 25–26, 35. Goodin quotes the phrase "normal and reasonable self-control" from Gary Watson, "Skepticism about Weakness of Will," *Philosophical Review* 86 (1977): 331.

36. Ibid., pp. 26, 28.

37. John Booth Davies, *The Myth of Addiction* (Chur, Switzerland: Harwood, 1992), p. 55.

38. Franklin Zimring and Gordon Hawkins, *The Search for Rational Drug Control* (Cambridge: Cambridge University Press, 1992), p. 27.

39. Davies, *The Myth of Addiction*, p. 36.

40. See the studies cited in Herbert Fingarette, *Heavy Drinking* (Berkeley: University of California Press, 1988). Davies notes that in the case of illegal drugs we lack good data on "normal use," but the general pattern that we find with alcohol appears to hold with them as well (pp. 41–55). Interestingly, the only drug that appears to fit the bimodal distribution is tobacco, which of course is legal.

41. See Richard L. Miller, *The Case for Legalizing Drugs* (New York: Praeger, 1991).

42. Davies, *The Myth of Addiction*, pp. 60–61.

43. Goodin, *No Smoking*, p. 35.

44. Davies, *The Myth of Addiction*, pp. 132–133.

45. There is a cost to addicts, of course, in making this move from the language of control to the language of addiction: they escape the stigma of norm violation (to the extent that they do) only by accepting the stigma of "illness."

46. Ibid., p. 110.

47. See William Connolly's illuminating analysis of William Bennett's rhetoric in this volume.

48. William N. Elwood, *Rhetoric in the War on Drugs* (Westport, Conn.: Praeger, 1994), p. 83, and chap. 4. Elwood notes that the Partnership refused to provide copies of their materials; his sample was gathered from two state affiliates of the Partnership and a Florida television station.

49. Ibid., pp. 89, 98.

50. See W. G. Carson, "Criminal Law and Self-Destructive Action," in *The State, Society, and Self-Destruction*, ed. Elizabeth Vallance (London: George Allen and Unwin, 1975), pp. 41–45.

Chapter 6. Drugs, National Sovereignty, and Democratic Legitimacy

My gratitude to my colleagues at the Department of Philosophy at SUNY Buffalo, Newton Garver, Jorge Gracia, Carolyn Korsmayer, and Barry Smith. Andreas Føllesdal, Thomas McCarthy, Thomas Pogge, and Jason Adsit also read the paper and offered valuable suggestions. I am also grateful to the participants in the conference, especially William Connolly, Donald Moon, and Thomas Pogge, for important comments and challenges.

1. The distribution of the antidrug budgets varied from year to year as follows (the first percentage refers to the supply-reduction budget and the second to the demand-reduction budget): 1989: 71.2% and 25.2%; 1990: 69.9% and 26.6%; 1991: 67.9% and 28%; 1992: 68.6% and 27.2%. The research component has fluctuated between 3.6% of the 1989 antidrug budget to 4.2% of the 1992 budget. See *Clear and Present Dangers: The U.S. Military and the War on Drugs in the Andes* (Washington, D.C.: Washington Office on Latin America, 1991). For a thorough analysis of U.S. drug policy, see Juan Gabriel Tokatlián, "Colombia–Estados Unidos y el Tema de las Drogas: Evolución y Perspectivas" (paper presented at the University of Miami's North-South Center's Drug Task Force meeting, June 20–21, 1994) (hereafter cited as Tokatlián, "Col.-E.U."). President Clinton's budgets look very similar to those of Bush: in 1994, 64% of the budget was aimed at reductions in supply, and 36% at reductions in demand. For 1995 the balance was 65% and 35%, for 1996, 67% and 33%, and the estimate for 1998 is 66% for supply-reduction and 34% for demand-reduction. See *National Drug Control Strategy: Executive Summary* (Washington, D.C.: Office of National Drug Control Policy, 1996, 1997, 1998).

Even at the rhetorical level, the few concessions about "joint responsibility" that followed the Cartagena meeting of February of 1991 were buried by the insistence that supply continued to be the main problem, a position that the United States reiterated at the San Antonio summit in February of 1992, a meeting that brought together the presidents of the United States, Colombia, Peru, Bolivia, Ecuador, and Mexico, and the Minister of Foreign Relations of Venezuela. See Tokatlián, "Col.-E.U.," p. 12.

2. For an extensive study of this phenomenon, see Ethan Nadelmann, *Cops across Borders: The Internationalization of U.S. Criminal Law Enforcement* (State College: Penn State Press, 1993).

3. See Paul B. Stares, *Global Habit: The Drug Problem in a Borderless World* (Washington, D.C.: Brookings Institution, 1996), chap. 2, for a brief history of how area-specific supply-reduction plans have failed not only in the sense that they normally lead simply to a transfer of production to different countries, but worse, of how these plans may also have contributed to the growing sophistication of successor operations.

4. Most studies of cocaine consumption in Colombia show that although there have been increases in use, the problem does not have nearly the same proportions as it does in the United States. See Francisco Thoumi, *Economía Política y Narcotráfico* (Bogotá: TM Editores, 1994), chap. 9 (hereafter cited as Thoumi, *Narcotráfico*).

5. *El Tiempo* (Bogotá, Colombia), September 3, 1995. Tokatlián estimates the number of violent deaths in Colombia in the period 1988 to 1994 at 165,000. (To put these numbers in context, the Pinochet military regime in Chile has been blamed for the loss of 1,600 to 3,000 lives in a period that lasted more than ten years!) Juan Gabriel Tokatlián, *Drogas, Dilemas, y Dogmas* (Bogotá: TM Editores/CEI, 1995), p. 130.

6. After a significant decrease in the number of drug consumers during the latter

half of the eighties, the number of users seems to be on the rise again: In 1988 the number of monthly users of cocaine was 2.9 million. In 1990, it was 1.6 million. In 1991, though, monthly users had risen to 1.9 million. The number of weekly consumers of cocaine declined from 862,000 in 1988, to 662,000 in 1990, but rose to 855,000 in 1991. See Tokatlián, "Col.-E.U.," p. 13, citing the National Drug Control Policy Report for 1991. The 1995 report states flatly: "No significant changes in illicit drug use, up or down, were reported in 1993, compared with 1992. The net effect is that drug use appears to have stabilized in the general population during 1993, with the exception of illicit drug use by adolescents, which is on the increase" (*National Drug Control Strategy: Executive Summary* [1995], p. 7).

7. In the period between 1986 to 1993, there were 9,314 "murders related to narcotic drug laws" in the United States. These numbers, according to the *National Drug Control Strategy: Executive Summary* for 1995, have risen steadily "since the mid-1980s, peaking at 7.4 percent of all murders in 1989. Since then, the rate has declined to 5.2 percent of all murders, but this level of drug-related violence is still unacceptable" (ibid., p. 11).

8. Despite the antidrug rhetoric of the Reagan administration, it was President Bush who committed important U.S. resources to this fight. The federal government spent $6.6 billion in 1989 on antidrug efforts, $9.7 billion in 1990, $10.9 billion in 1991, $11.9 billion in 1992, $12.2 billion in 1993, and more than $12.2 billion in 1994. It will spend close to $14 billion in 1995, and the Clinton administration is requesting $14.6 billion for 1996. See *National Drug Control Strategy: Executive Summary* (1995), p. 40. According to some studies, state and local governments spend even more than the federal government in antidrug efforts. Peter Reuter, for instance, argues that in 1990, while the federal antidrug budget was $9.3 billion, state and local expenditures amounted to $18 billion. See Peter Reuter, "Hawks Ascendant: The Punitive Trend of American Drug Policy," *Daedalus* 121 (1992).

9. Most political discussions about drugs elide the fact that the bulk of the proceeds of this business remains in consuming countries. The highest realistic estimates indicate that Colombian cartels repatriate less than 25 percent of their income. (See, for example, Francisco Thoumi "El País Trabado," *Dinero* [Bogotá, Colombia], March 1995, p. 28. See also Stares, *Global Habit*, p. 84.) This should surprise no one. Latin American economies are not as stable, nor their banking systems as reliable or discreet, as those of the alternative havens of money laundering, which include Aruba, the Cayman Islands, Liechtenstein, Cyprus, Hong Kong, Luxembourg, and the United States. During the early eighties, while battered by the debt crisis in Latin America, the banking system in Florida resisted federal antilaundering regulations. Needless to say, the United States continues to be important in the laundering business, despite the regulations. See Stares, *Global Habit*, pp. 57–60.

10. In a personal note to then Prosecutor General Gustavo De Greiff, President Cesar Gaviria estimated the inflow of drug money to be around $7 billion in 1992. This is by far the highest estimate, and it does not seem supported by other studies. Thoumi refers to $2 billion in 1994 (*Narcotráfico*, p. 208). Andrés O'Byrne and Mauricio Reina put the figure between $3.8 and $4.4 billion for 1991, while Miguel Urrutia and Adriana Pontón calculate $951 million for the same year. See O'Byrne and Reina, "Flujos de Capital y Diferencial de Intereses en Colombia"; and Urrutia and Pontón, "Entrada de Capitales, Diferenciales de Interés y Narcotráfico"; both in *Macroeconomía de los Flujos de Capital en Colombia y América Latina*, ed. Mauricio Cárdenas and Luis Jorge Garay (Bogotá: Tercer Mundo Editores/Fedesarrollo/Fescol, 1993). See also Tokatlián, "Col.-E.U."

11. For a study of the devastating impact of the drug business on the social fabric of economically deprived neighborhoods in Medellín and on the character structure of young people in those areas, see Alonso Salazar J., *No Nacimos Pa' Semilla* (Bogotá: CINEP, 1990).

12. In fact, the Colombian economy grew at a significantly higher pace in the period *preceding* the boom of the cocaine business (Thoumi, *Narcotráfico*, pp. 54–58, 257, 260, 255). The other way of dealing with growing external reserves is to increase imports. But this does not help economic growth directly either.

13. "La Economía Después del Cartel," *Portofolio* (Bogotá, Colombia), December 18, 1996, p. 21.

14. Thoumi, *Narcotráfico*, p. 250.

15. See *Colombia's Commitment concerning the World Drug Problem: National Plan* (Bogotá: National Narcotics Council, 1995), pp. 38–42 (hereafter cited as *National Plan*). See also Thoumi, *Narcotráfico*, p. 248; and for a more detailed study of the effects of drug money on land holding in Colombia, see Alejandro Reyes Posada, "Compra de Tierras por Narcotraficantes," in *Drogas Ilícitas en Colombia: Su impacto económico, político y social*, ed. Francisco Thoumi et al. (Bogotá: Ariel, 1997).

16. Drug-related military intervention took place in Panamá, has taken place in Bolivia, and in a smaller scale in both Peru and Colombia—in other words, in virtually all the Latin producing countries. The U.S. invasion of Panama in 1989 was justified in part as an antidrug operation. After the invasion, U.S. ships began a "patrolling" operation in Colombian waters, an operation that threatened to become a blockade at the beginning of 1990. The crisis was defused only after strenuous protests by the Colombian government. This was not the end of U.S. military participation in Colombia, though; U.S. marines participated in "civic" maneuvers in Colombia in 1992 in the state of Valle, whose capital is Cali. The U.S. military has participated in antidrug operations in Bolivia at least since 1986. See Jaime Malamud-Goti, *Smoke and Mirrors: The Paradox of the Drug Wars* (Boulder: Westview Press, 1992). The U.S. military staffs and advises the largest antidrug operations base in the Upper Huallaga region of Peru to the present day.

17. Every year, the United States evaluates the performance of other countries in the war against drugs and proceeds to "certify" or "decertify" them as reliable partners in this fight. The latest report reviews the performance of 144 countries (U.S. performance is not evaluated). The yearly report, published by the Bureau for International Narcotics and Law Enforcement Affairs of the State Department is entitled *International Narcotics Control Strategy Report*. This review mechanism serves more than informational purposes; the law allows U.S. administrations to take action against decertified countries: these measures may include suspending aid, eliminating trade benefits, imposing trade barriers, and, most importantly, hampering access to international credit by guaranteeing a negative U.S. vote at multinational credit agencies where the U.S. vote carries almost overriding importance. With respect to the last point, the law reads:

> The Secretary of the Treasury shall instruct the United States Executive Director of each multilateral development bank to vote, on and after March 1 of each year, against any loan or other utilization of the funds of their respective institution to or for any major illicit drug-producing country or major drug-transit country, except as provided in subsection (b) of this section. For purposes of this paragraph, the term "multilateral development bank" means the International Bank for Reconstruction and Development [a.k.a., the World Bank], the International Development Association, the Inter-

American Development Bank, the Asian Development Bank, and the European Bank for Reconstruction and Development. (22 U.S.C., sec. 2291K [a] [2])

18. Indeed, Gingrich is so sure about American opposition to legalization, that he proposed a national vote on this issue, assuring reporters that the vote would be "80 percent to 20 percent against legalization." See, for example, "Gingrich Wants Referendum on Drug Legalization Issue," *Buffalo News*, July 15, 1995, p. 4A.

19. This assumption can be questioned given the distortions that have usually accompanied debates about the nature and consequences of drug consumption. See Erich Goode, "The American Drug Panic of the 1980's: Social Construction, or Objective Threat?" *International Journal of the Addictions* 25 (1990). Dickinson McGaw, "Governing Metaphors: The War on Drugs," *American Journal of Semiotics* 8 (1991): 53–74. See also Steven Wisotsky, "Not Thinking Like a Lawyer: The Case of Drugs in the Courts," *Notre Dame Journal of Law, Ethics, and Public Policy* 5 (1991): 651–692, for an account of the images (caricatures) of drug consumption that have influenced judicial decisions.

20. This is an important part of my argument: by generating these extraordinarily high profits, the role of antidrug legislation can help us to locate responsibility. The U.S. government cannot be held responsible for the consumption preferences of its citizens. But it can be held responsible for the acts of its legislature. In this case, legislative acts are the cause of gross market distortions which send virtually irresistible economic incentives: based on 1994 prices, "a kilo of Cocaine leaves Peru at US$250, goes through Colombia at US$2,000 and arrives in Miami at US$19,000, in Chicago at US$31,000 and is sold on a retail basis in that city at US$198,000" (*National Plan*, p. 40). I will come back to this point later.

21. Having said as much, it must be noted that Habermas himself is not always clear about the fact that this relevant community sometimes cuts across national borders. In this essay I rely mostly on Jürgen Habermas, *Between Facts and Norms*, trans. William Rehg (Cambridge: MIT Press, 1996) (hereafter cited as *Facts and Norms*).

22. Habermas, *Facts and Norms*, pp. 104–118.

23. Ibid., pp. 114ff.

24. Ibid., p. 107.

25. Jürgen Habermas, "Discourse Ethics: Notes on a Program of Philosophical Justification," in *Moral Consciousness and Communicative Action*, trans. Christian Lenhardt and Shierry Weber Nicholsen (Cambridge: MIT Press, 1990), p. 65.

26. Habermas, *Facts and Norms*, p. 110.

27. Ibid., pp. 106ff., and 114ff.

28. Habermas distinguishes between ethics and morality by arguing that whereas ethics moves us to answer the question, What ought I/we to do? on the basis of considerations of personal or collective identity, morality interprets that question as one that should be answered on the basis of considerations of justice or rights. I write more on this distinction below. Cf. Jürgen Habermas, "On the Pragmatic, the Ethical, and the Moral Employments of Practical Reason," in *Justification and Application*, trans. C. Cronin (Cambridge: MIT Press, 1993).

29. Habermas, *Facts and Norms*, pp. 112, 117.

30. Ibid., pp. 153ff., 160ff. [See Immanuel Kant, *Groundwork for the Metaphysics of Morals*, AK VI: 415, 416.]

31. For instance, traffic regulations do not invoke considerations of morality, but rather expediency. Laws concerning education, especially those concerning the use of particular languages invoke not only considerations of expediency, but also of community identity (although they may also invoke matters of rights).

32. Habermas, *Facts and Norms*, p. 124.

33. Jürgen Habermas, "Citizenship and National Identity: Some Reflections on the Future of Europe," *Praxis International* 12 (1992): 7–8. My emphases.

34. Thomas Pogge, "Kant's Vision, Europe, and a Global Perspective" (unpublished manuscript, 1995), p. 6. (Spanish version published as "Europa y una Federación Global: La Visión de Kant," in *Kant: La Paz Perpetua Doscientos Años Después*, ed. Vincent Martínez Guzmán [Valencia: NAU Llibres, 1997], pp. 161–171.) See also Pogge's "Cosmopolitanism and Sovereignty," *Ethics* 103 (1992): 48–75.

35. David Held, *Democracy and the Global Order* (Stanford: Stanford University Press, 1995), p. 233.

36. Ibid., p. 237 n. 6.

37. Ibid., p. 236. My emphases.

38. The United States gave Colombia approximately $100 million in 1994 and 1995 as antidrug aid. In the same period, the Colombian government spent more than $1.75 billion fighting drugs (*National Plan*, p. 58). Luis J. Orjuela argues that the costs of fighting the war on drugs forced the Colombian government to cut social investment by 17 percent from 1984 to 1989. See his "Narcotráfico y Política en la Década de los Ochentas: Entre represión y diálogo" in *Narcotráfico en Colombia*, ed. Carlos G. Arrieta, Luis J. Orjuela, Eduardo Sarmiento, and Juan Gabriel Tokatlián (Bogotá: Ediciones Uniandes/Tercer Mundo Editores, 1990).

39. The Colombian Constitution of 1991 bans the extradition of Colombian nationals. The United States, though, is engaged in an intense campaign to have the Constitution amended. See "E.U. Aprieta las Tuercas," *Semana* (Bogotá, Colombia), no. 739, July 2–9, 1996, a news report detailing the conditions the United States is imposing on Colombia under the threat of economic sanctions. The list of conditions includes extradition. It is ironic that just when Colombia's law enforcement apparatus has something to show for its efforts, having imprisoned or eliminated the leaders of the Medellín and Cali cartels—which incidentally will have little impact on the outflow of drugs—voices both in Colombia and the Unites States call for the reestablishment of extradition.

40. Recall the scope of 22 U.S.C., sect. 2291K. See note 17 above.

41. Discussions with Dan Abrahamson helped me clarify this point.

42. See De Greiff, "International Courts and Transitions to Democracy," *Public Affairs Quarterly* 12 (1998): 79–99.

43. See, for example, Russell Fox and Ian Mathews, *Drugs Policy* (Sydney: Federation Press, 1992), esp. pp. 196–205; Eddy L. Engelsman, "The Pragmatic Strategies of the Dutch 'Drug Czar,'" in *Drug Prohibition and the Conscience of Nations*, ed. Arnold Trebach and Kevin Zeese (Washington, D.C.: Drug Policy Foundation, 1990). See also *Harm Reduction*, ed. Patricia Erikson, Diane M. Riley, Yuet W. Cheung, and Pat A. O'Hare (Toronto: University of Toronto Press, 1997).

Chapter 7. Drugs, the Nation, and Freelancing: Decoding the Moral Universe of William Bennett

1. Such a program might also reduce the number of murders in large cities. If drug-related murders come most often from drug dealers rather than drug users, as the *New York Times* thinks ("Homicide Rate Drops . . . in Nation's Cities," August 13, 1995), then the reduction of drug dealers by decriminalizing the supply of some drugs might have such an effect.

2. The phrase, "open declaration of war over the culture" originated with Midge Decter but was quoted and endorsed by Bennett (*De-Valuing of America*, p. 258).

3. Dan Baum, a freelance journalist, alerted me to the indispensable role of illegal marijuana after reading a first draft of this essay in 1995. In a personal communication, he says, "Marijuana will be the last drug legalized. With it there are 70 million users of illegal drugs. Without it, there are perhaps 1.5 million with a drug problem, with a state budget of about $465,000 per head spent on the war." For a fascinating history of drug wars in the United States, see Dan Baum, *Smoke and Mirrors: The War on Drugs and the Politics of Failure* (Boston: Little, Brown, 1996).

4. Here is how Bennett puts it in *De-Valuing of America*: "The reaction was illustrative. Many of the elites ridiculed my opinion. But it resonated with the American people because they knew what drugs were doing and they wanted a morally proportional response" (p. 116). Note how Bennett first reduces the drug problem to a problem of individuals, then translates the degree of individual responsibility into a proportionate state punitive response. Bennett is a statist, when it comes to action on behalf of the political morality of punishment he endorses.

5. Slovoj Žižek, *Tarrying with the Negative* (Durham: Duke University Press, 1993).

6. The portrait of American nationalism I am attempting to draw has debts and affinities to the discussion of Australian nationalism in Bruce Kapferer, *Legends of People/Myths of State* (Washington, D.C.: Smithsonian Institution, 1988). Kapferer calls the Australian type "egalitarian nationalism," to capture the sense that all individuals are equal as members of the nation while they are unequal in the degree to which they live up, as individuals, to the spirit of the nation.

7. The pluralistic culture I admire could be called a nation. If enough constituencies endorse the ethos that enables that nation, then they could be said together to form a *pluralistic nation*. The term "nation" can be stretched that far, but such stretching is misleading; it encourages those who endorse it momentarily to contract the image of the nation right back into its narrow compass. The American arboreal model of *national pluralism*, emanating from Tocqueville, is too violent. In its early version it treats Christianity as the trunk of the tree with diversity as a series of limbs branching out from this trunk. Most contemporary models of pluralism maintain or secularize such a formula. I endorse a more "rhizomatic" pluralism, in which numerous affinities and connections emerge between a variety of constituencies, because none claims to occupy the center by itself and because a variety of constituencies cultivate critical responsiveness to new drives to pluralization—a state of minorities inhabited by a general ethos flowing from multiple cultural sources. This ideal is no further from the classical ideal of pluralism than the arboreal ideal of pluralism is, say, from the Rousseauian ideal of democracy. The key to it is that most constituencies recognize the contestable character of the beliefs most fundamental to their identities, using such reciprocal recognition to bridge multiple lines of difference.

8. In *The Ethos of Pluralization* (Minneapolis: University of Minnesota Press, 1995), I argue that democratic action in concert through the state becomes more feasible when a variety of constituencies shed fundamentalist assumptions about themselves and those they resist. Social fragmentation is not the effect of pluralism. It is most often the result of contending drives to occupy the authoritative center of the nation. That thesis, of course, sets the backdrop for my engagement here with the cultural war of William Bennett.

Notes on Contributors

WILLIAM CONNOLLY is Professor of Political Science at Johns Hopkins University. He is the author of, among other books, *Appearance and Reality in Politics* (1981); *The Terms of Political Discourse* (1974, 1983, 1993); *Political Theory and Modernity* (1988, 1993); *Identity/Difference: Democratic Negotiations* (1991); *The Augustinian Imperative: A Reflection on the Politics of Morality* (1993); and *The Ethos of Pluralization* (1995). He is also the editor of *Legitimacy and the State* (1984).

PABLO DE GREIFF, a native of Colombia, has been an Assistant Professor of Philosophy at the State University of New York at Buffalo since 1992. He is the coeditor (with Ciaran Cronin) of Jürgen Habermas's *The Inclusion of Others* and of *Deliberative Democracy and Transnational Politics*.

JON ELSTER is Robert K. Merton Professor of Social Science at Columbia University. He has written extensively on rational and irrational behavior and on the history of social thought. He is the author of several books, including *Ulysses and the Sirens* (1979), *Sour Grapes* (1983), *The Cement of Society* (1989), and *Political Psychology* (1993). His most recent books are *Alchemies of the Mind: Rationality and the Emotions* (1998) and *Strong Feelings: Emotion, Addiction, and Human Behavior* (1999).

SAMUEL FREEMAN is Associate Professor of Philosophy and Law at the University of Pennsylvania. His main publications include articles on contractualism (in the *Journal of Philosophy*); on democracy and the legitimacy of judicial review (in *Law and Philosophy*); on the social contract tradition, constitutional interpretation, and Rawls and the priority of rights (all in *Philosophy and Public Affairs*).

J. DONALD MOON is Professor of Government at Wesleyan University. He coedited *Dissent and Affirmation* (1983), edited *Responsibility, Rights, and Welfare* (1988), and is the author of *Constructing Community: Moral Pluralism and Tragic Conflicts* (1993).

MICHAEL S. MOORE is the Leon Meltzer Professor of Law and Philosophy and the co-director of the Institute of Law and Philosophy at the University of Pennsylvania. He is the author of *Law and Psychiatry* (1984), *Act and Crime* (1993), and *Placing Blame: A General Theory of the Criminal Law* (1998). A collection of his papers is forthcoming.

THOMAS POGGE is Professor of Philosophy at Columbia University. His most recent publications include *Realizing Rawls* (1989). In addition to several articles on Kant, he has written groundbreaking essays on nationalism and international politics (in *Ethics, the Journal of Philosophy, Philosophy and Public Affairs*, and other leading journals). His latest book, on international justice, *Real World Justice*, will be published in 1999.

Index